I'VE BEEN EVERYWHERE
A Johnny Cash Chronicle

Peter Lewry

Helter
Skelter
Publishing

First published in 2001 by Helter Skelter Publishing
4 Denmark Street, London WC2H 8LL
First edition
Text copyright Peter Lewry © 2001
The moral right of the author has been asserted
Photographs copyright see picture credits page

Design by Bold; Typesetting by Peter Lewry and Caroline Walker
Printed by The Bath Press

Every effort has been made to contact the copyright holders of the photographs in this book, but one or two were unreachable. The publishers would be grateful if those concerned would contact Helter Skelter Publishing.

A CIP record for this book is available from the British Library

ISBN 1-900924-22-6

All lyrics are quoted for review, study or critical purposes.

This book is dedicated to the memory of
Luther Perkins

"Now didn't Luther play the boogie strange"
(Luther Played The Boogie – Johnny Cash, 1955)

CONTENTS

ACKNOWLEDGEMENTS

A book like this cannot be written without the help and support of many individuals who assisted me during the twelve months I spent researching and writing this project. Thanks go to: Barry and Diane Rowden who ran the excellent *Strictly Cash* magazine from May 1966 to July 1985 and Colin Searle, Alex Sangster, Lilian Larsson, Val Crossley, Bob Balser for supplying me with an endless stream of press cuttings and magazines from their own private collections and putting up with the endless requests and questions. I am indebted to you all.

Thanks also to: John L. Smith, Trevor Cajiao, Bob and Monika Leal, Jeanne Witherall, Jan Flederus, Phil Davis, Shaun Mather and Ian Calford and the Brakemen (Chris Cummings and Andy Sykes), Burl Boykin, Hugh Wadell.

Very special thanks to my wife Carole for her constant support and for putting up with the hours I spent in the office and on the telephone!

Additional thanks go to, the staff at the National Sound Archive at the British Library.

I consulted many magazines and periodicals during my research: *Now Dig This*, *Record Collector*, *Billboard*, *Cashbox*, *New Musical Express*, *Strictly Cash*, *Johnny Cash & June Carter Cash International Fan Club*, *Our Kinda Cash*, *Johnny Cash Friends*.

Thanks also to the following magazines for their coverage of Johnny Cash over the years: *Country Music People*, *Country Music International*, *Country Music Round-Up* and *Country Music* magazine.

Reference was made to the following books: *Cash The Autobiography* - Johnny Cash & Patrick Carr (Harper SanFransisco, 1997); *Man In Black* - Johnny Cash (Zondervan, 1975); *The Elvis Atlas* - Michael Gray & Roger Osborne (Henry Holt, 1996); *Guinness Book Of British Hit Singles* - Paul Gambaccini, Jonathan Rice & Tim Rice (Guinness Publishing, 1995); *Guinness Book Of British Hit Albums* - Paul Gambaccini, Jonathan Rice & Tim Rice (Guinness Publishing, 1996); *The Billboard Book Of Top 40 Hits* - Joel Whitburn (Billboard Books, 1996); *The Billboard Book Of Top 40 Albums* - Joel Whitburn (Billboard Books, 1995) and *Johnny Cash: Winners Got Scars Too* - Christopher Wren (W.H.Allen, 1971).

As mentioned in the Author's Notes, I am indebted to and highly recommend the following series of discographies written by John L. Smith: *The Johnny Cash Discography* (Greenwood Press, 1985); *The Johnny Cash Discography 1984-1993* (Greenwood Press, 1994); *The Johnny Cash Record Catalog* (Greenwood Press, 1994) and *Another Song To Sing* (Scarecrow Press, 1999).

Thanks to all those who maintain the following internet sites for their often unsung efforts:
Official Johnny Cash Site (www.johnnycash.com)
themaninblack.net
Unofficial Site (www.eloine.com/JohnnyCash)
Rockabilly Hall Of Fame (www.rockabillyhall.com/PhilShaun.html)

Thanks to my editor Sean Body at Helter Skelter Publishing for believing in this book.

Last, but by no means least, very special thanks go to: Lou Robin and Johnny Cash.

PHOTO CREDITS

Every effort has been made to correctly acknowledge the source and/or copyright holder of every illustration, and the publisher apologies for any unintentional errors or omissions which will be corrected in future editions of this book.

7, 142 (Peter Lewry); 11 (Ian Calford); 19 (Burl Boykin); 17, 35, 81, 190, 193, 208 (all) (Brian Smith); 198 (Jeanne Witherall); 221 (Hugh Waddell); 238 (Harper Collins); 240, 241 (Turner Network Television); 242 (Val Crossley).

All memorabilia and paperwork (Peter Lewry collection).

All album sleeves courtesy of Sony Music except pages 143 (A&M Records); 178, 181, 187, 249A (Mercury Records); 219, 233 (American Recordings); 246 (American Recordings/Columbia); 249C (Renaissance Records).

AUTHOR'S NOTES

I've Been Everywhere: A Johnny Cash Chronicle is my attempt to list chronologically all the facts relating to the career of the legendary Man in Black – Johnny Cash. I believe a chronicle like this has never been attempted before, and despite my best efforts I cannot hope to have listed every event in what has been a remarkable career covering over forty-five years. I apologise in advance for any omissions, which I hope can be rectified in future editions. The book aims to deal only with Johnny Cash's professional life and I have endeavoured to include details on every concert date, TV appearance, filming schedule, record release and on magazine articles and interviews. I have also covered many of the important recording sessions, but for a more comprehensive look at his recording sessions I would point you in the direction of the excellent series of discographies compiled and written by John L. Smith, and listed in the acknowledgements. For the sake of space only the US releases are listed, although there are a few exceptions when releases were specific to a certain territory. Chart positions relate to the US Billboard Country Charts although, once again, there are a few exceptions when the US Billboard Pop Charts and the UK charts are listed. Where this applies it is noted accordingly. A discography is also included at the back of the book listing single and album releases. For various reasons, throughout Cash's career certain concert dates were cancelled and/or re-scheduled. Johnny Cash spent many months a year on the road and it was not always possible to find out which, if any, shows in a particular year were cancelled, but if the information was available it is included. My inspiration for writing this book has been my respect and admiration for Johnny Cash and his music, which started back in 1970 when I was given a copy of *Johnny Cash At San Quentin*. Since 1994 I have edited the fanzine *Johnny Cash – The Man in Black* and was fortunate enough to meet John backstage at the Royal Albert Hall in London in April 1997.

Peter Lewry
August 2001

FOREWORD BY LOU ROBIN

I began working with Johnny Cash and June Carter in 1969 as a concert promoter and in 1972 I became their personal manager and remain so to date. My career in the music business started in 1957 and I have worked with such stars as The Beatles, Judy Garland, The Rolling Stones, Bill Cosby and many more. In all these years I have never shared any relationship with an artist as emotionally rewarding as the one I share with Johnny and June. The Cash Family, musicians, the road crew and office staff have all worked together to help make life on the road, over 100 days each year, as comfortable as it could be.

It is said that artists are unique and different because of their talent. I believe that the real superstars in music, theatre and art have maximized their God-given talents to accomplish true greatness. Johnny Cash is certainly one of those people.

Johnny rose from humble beginnings to become an internationally acclaimed songwriter, singer, poet, actor and author. In so doing he became a role model to those who have slipped and fallen and even to those who did not slip in their travels through life. Johnny's example has enabled so many people to pick themselves up and keep heading toward their life's goals.

This book is the only published chronicle of Johnny's quest to bring his words and music to the world and to hopefully create happiness and encourage social awareness for millions of people for decades past and future.

My associate Allen Tinkley and I remember being on the road with Johnny in some unusual places. We were once in the middle of Finland playing in a warehouse to thousands of fans who had come by special train from Helsinki.

Then there was the first of four concerts in Prague, Czechoslovakia where 44,000 tickets had been sold. Just before he was about to walk on stage, Johnny turned to me and wondered aloud if the audience would understand the lyrics to his songs. Johnny was very touched when thousands who knew and understood every word began to sing along.

Another time we were in Gdansk, Poland at a folk festival while the country was still under communist control. Freedom supporters had arranged a secret meeting between Johnny and Lech Walesa at a church on the Sunday we were scheduled to leave the country. When the government learned of the meeting, it was cancelled due to "security problems."

I remember the day that Johnny and Mohammed Ali exchanged poetry they composed off the top of their heads while sitting in Ali's hotel room prior to a championship fight in New Orleans.

Another fun evening was at a private party in Hong Kong held at a deserted British military base a couple of miles from the Chinese border. The guest of honor had hired Johnny, Kris Kristofferson, Willie Nelson and Waylon Jennings, better known together as the "Highwaymen" to perform for his special evening. Johnny, Willie, Kris and Waylon stood on stage and performed requests shouted at them by the 180 or so guests in attendance.

One cold winter night we played a concert in Belfast, Northern Ireland at a church. The political factions were heavy into the fighting. Somehow the promoter quietly got a truce declared until noon the following day when we would be gone. This way the people would not be going to the sold-out, double shows dodging explosions! We also gave tickets on opposite sides of the Church to each faction. So they were all in the same room together for the first time enjoying an event of common interest. The next morning we went to the currency exchange to make a bank transfer to the U. S. before we left for Dublin on our tour bus. Later that same day we heard that the currency exchange had been blown up that afternoon!

These stories could go on forever but in summary I want to say that Johnny Cash has been able to go anywhere in the world to entertain. His music has cleared all language barriers and I believe his remarkable talent will prevail forever.

Enjoy the journey that Peter Lewry has so painstakingly recreated for you.

Lou Robin
Westlake Village, California
August 30, 2001

1920-1954

"When we finally got to Dyess, the truck couldn't get up the dirt road to our house, so Daddy had to carry me on his back the last hundred yards through the thick black Arkansas mud–gumbo, we called it. And that's where I was when I saw the Promised Land: a brand new house with two big bedrooms, a living room, a dining room, a kitchen, a front porch and a back porch, an outside toilet, a barn, a chicken house, and a smokehouse. To me, luxuries untold. There was no running water, of course, and no electricity; none of us even dreamed of miracles like that."

from *CASH The Autobiography* by Johnny Cash with Patrick Carr 1997

1920

18 August
Ray Cash, the son of a baptist minister, marries Carrie Rivers.

1932

26 February
Johnny Cash is born in Kingsland, Arkansas, situated between Pine Bluff and Little Rock. His given name is J. R. Cash and all through his career he would be asked what the R. stood for. His reply has alway been the same - "it doesn't stand for anything." Ray Cash laboured hard through the depression refusing to accept handouts and by the time J.R. came along, Ray and Carrie already had two sons, Roy and Jack, and a daughter, Louise.

1935

February-March
When JR was just three-years old, the family, which now included another daughter, Reba Ann, packed up and moved to Dyess, Arkansas and the rich cotton land of the delta region parallel to the Mississippi River. This move was prompted by President Roosevelt's 'New Deal' – the promise of a better life in a Government assisted/sponsored farming community. Dyess was situated approximately 30 miles north-west of Memphis and the 250 mile journey took two days. Ray, Carrie and the rest of the family spent their first night under a tarpaulin in the back of their flat-bed truck while Carrie Cash sang "What Would You Give In Exchange For Your Soul". Their new abode was Homestead No. 266 on Road Number Three and it was here that Ray carved his family a home out of 20 acres of flat-land. He worked hard to build a future for his family, working long hours into the night.

1936

The Cash family buy a battery radio; electricity supply to Dyess was still a few years away. Young JR listened to the gospel and country music broadcast from stations including WLW (New Orleans), KOMA (Oklahoma), WCKY (Cincinnati), WJJD (Chicago), XEG (Fort Worth) and XERF (Del Rio, Texas). It was on station XERF broadcasting out of Del Rio that he first heard the music of The Carter Family, who made regular broadcasts from the area. He absorbed all the local sounds, country, gospel and the delta blues, that emanated from the small radio. One of his favourite shows was *High Noon Round-Up*. Broadcast from WMPS in Memphis daily between 12:30 and 1:00pm, the show starred Ira and Charlie Louvin. This show was followed by a fifteen minute programme of gospel music.

1937-38

Heavy rains for several days had resulted in the Mississippi River passing the flood level. In a later interview Cash would recall "It was the winter of 1937-1938 and it had been raining for days and days and we'd heard the news reports every night. My daddy would turn on that battery radio to get the 8 o'clock news, so we knew that the Mississippi River which was only six miles from us had passed flood stage which meant it was up to the levees. Well, one day the levee did break and we heard about the flood waters before we saw them". In his song "Five Feet High And Rising", released in 1959, Johnny Cash told the story of his family's experiences during the Mississippi River flood. Talking about the song, Cash said "I got to remembering all these things, and the song just came out, you know. Just exactly as it happened."

1938

9 March
Carrie gives birth to Joanne Cash, their third daughter.

1940

5 April
Tommy Cash, the seventh and last child, is born.

1942

His mother buys JR a guitar on his 10th birthday.

1944

12 May
JR was close to his older brother Jack, who hoped to become a preacher one day. Jack was working after school cutting fence posts and on 12 May 1944 he was injured in a terrible accident when he fell on the saw. He held on for eight days but his injuries were so serious that he passed away at the age of fourteen. His funeral was held on 21 May. JR was devastated and this tragic event at such an early age was to have a profound effect on him in later life.

1947

JR worked in the fields pickin' cotton and became close to his sister Reba, they would spend hours singing together. In 1947 he heard that the *High Noon Round-Up* gang were playing at the High School in Dyess and JR went to the show and met with Ira Louvin at the end of the evening. By now JR knew he wanted to sing and be on the radio.

1948

At the age of 16, his high tenor voice changed to a deep, low pitched rumble which would be instantly recognisable for years to come.

1950-51

JR graduated from high school and his curiosity about life outside of Dyess led him to travel to Pontiac, Michigan, but he returned after three weeks. He enlisted in the United States Air Force when he turned 18 and began six months of training at Keesler Air Force Base in Mississippi. At the end of his training he was a skilled radio intercept operator. Basic training continued at Lackland Air Force Base and Brooks Air Force Base. It was during his basic training that Cash literally bumped into Vivian Liberto at a roller skating rink in San Antonio. They dated until he was sent to Landsberg in Germany where he would be stationed for nearly three years. He kept in contact via mail and even proposed to Vivian while he was still in Germany. In Germany he bought a guitar for 20 marks and focused on his music. With his friends he would often jam on the country hits of the day; material from Hank Williams and The Carter Family as well as gospel and the delta blues. The purchase of a cheap reel-to-reel tape recorder gave him the opportunity to record some of his own compositions and he soon formed an acoustic band - The Landsberg Barbarians. They would play local bars until they either shut or a fight broke out. It was during his four years in the service that he saw a film titled *Inside The Walls Of Folsom* and this inspired him to write "Folsom Prison Blues". It was also during this period that he wrote a poem called "Hey Porter" which was published in the *Stars And Stripes*, a newspaper for servicemen.

1954

July

Staff Sergeant John R. Cash is given an honourable discharge at Camp Kilmer in New Jersey.

August-September

Vivian had accepted his marriage proposal and, despite the fact that she was a Catholic and he a Baptist, they married at St. Ann's Catholic Church on 7 August 1954. They settled down and made a home on Tutweiler Avenue in Memphis where John enrolled in a DJ course and studied radio announcing at the Keegan School of Broadcasting. Married and with a baby on the way, his studying had to give way to paid employment. He found a job selling electrical appliances for the Home Equipment Company, while continuing to study part-time.

Late-1954

His brother Roy was working at Automotive Sales Garage in Union Avenue and had just been promoted to Night Service Manager. There were two mechanics also working at the garage – Luther Perkins and Marshall Grant. In their spare time and during quiet spells at the garage they would play music together. Knowing his brother's love of music and desire to make it in the music business, Roy introduced them to JR.

Luther was born in Memphis in 1928 and Marshall in Flatts, North Carolina. The first time they worked with JR was at Luther's home on Nathan Street in Memphis. One of the songs they would try was Hank Snow's "Moving On". They all played acoustic guitars and hit it off resulting in more informal sessions, although at this point neither Luther nor Marshall were interested in pursuing a musical career. Unhappy with his job as an appliance salesman and determined to make it in the music business, JR suggested they try different instruments. Luther borrowed an electric guitar and Marshall a stand-up bass, although nobody was sure how to tune it. They were all self-taught musicians and started to play more seriously. They were sponsored by JR's boss to play a 15 minute spot on country station KWEM on Saturdays. They had played together for many hours and were progressing well and the next logical step was to make a record. In Memphis at that time there was only one place to go – Sun Records and producer Sam Phillips. Johnny, Luther and Marshall along with an additional member, steel guitar player A. W. 'Red' Kernoddle, had a formal audition with Sam. At the audition Cash sang "I Was There When It Happened", "Belshazzar" and "It Don't Hurt Anymore", mainly gospel material, but Sam was not interested stating that there was no demand for that kind of music. At an early session Kernoddle was so nervous that he couldn't play and his career in the music business ended there and then. Sam was still looking for something different so Cash went away and reworked a poem he had written during his time in the air force and went back to Sun records with "Hey Porter". Sam was impressed and all he needed now was a track for the b-side. Cash wrote "Cry, Cry, Cry" after hearing DJ Eddie Hill announce "stay tuned, we're gonna bawl, squall and run up the wall" and he adapted the lyrics to *"You're gonna bawl, bawl, bawl"* but reconsidered and came up with "You're gonna Cry, Cry, Cry." And so it was that "Hey Porter" backed with "Cry, Cry, Cry" became Johnny Cash and the Tennessee Two's debut single.

And the rest, as they say, is history…

1955-63

"The 1960's were probably my most productive time, creatively speaking. I ventured out, testing different waters and I really enjoyed that."

from *CASH The Autobiography* by Johnny Cash with Patrick Carr 1997

1955

May

Johnny Cash and The Tennessee Two (Luther Perkins and Marshall Grant) record "Cry, Cry, Cry" and "Hey Porter" at the tiny Sun Studios in Memphis. This was not the first time they had recorded together, having already laid down a version of "Folsom Prison Blues" and other tracks in late 1954-early 1955. During a 1980 radio special Cash spoke about the recording: "Actually the first thing we recorded at Sun records was 'Folsom Prison Blues'. Sam Phillips liked it very much, but he wanted to hear something else so I did a song I wrote called 'Hey Porter' that I had written on the way home from Germany when I was discharged from the Air Force. And it was kind of a daydreamin' kind of thing. I used a train as a vehicle in my mind to take me back home and counting off the miles and the hours and minutes till I would get back home. It wasn't to Tennessee though, it was to Arkansas, Dyess, Arkansas where my parents were still living at the time. Hey Porter was recorded and Sam said, 'What else have you written?' I said, 'Well, like I've told you before a lot of gospel songs you know.' I had called him initially saying I'm Johnny Cash—I'm a gospel singer and I want to record gospel. And he said, 'I can't sell enough gospel to stay in business.' He said, 'We got to have something commercial and call me back when you have something commercial.' Well I kept calling back. He was always out or busy and I finally got the appointment and went in with Marshall Grant and Luther Perkins—The Tennessee Two. We had a steel guitar player working with us, but he was afraid to go in the recording studio and I guess maybe it was lucky for us that he didn't because The Tennessee Two came up with a sound that was kinda unique. I think a steel guitar would've taken us more toward Nashville than what was happening up there, so we recorded 'Hey Porter'."

24 May

John and Vivian's first child, Rosanne is born.

June

"Hey Porter" and "Cry, Cry, Cry", the two tracks recorded back in May are released and become Johnny Cash and The Tennessee Two's debut single on Sun Records (Sun 221).

August

Cash continues to make regular 15 minute appearances on Radio Station KWEM broadcasting out of Memphis.

1 August

Johnny Cash is part of the short 5-day Webb Pierce Package Tour with Elvis Presley and Wanda Jackson. Webb Pierce was the headline act but Elvis closed the show in Muscle Shoals and probably other dates on the tour. Opening date is at the Mississippi-Alabama Fairgrounds, Tupelo, Mississippi.

2 August

Sheffield Community Center, Muscle Shoals, Alabama.

3 August

Robinson Auditorium, Little Rock, Arkansas.

4 August

Municipal Auditorium, Camden, Arkansas.

5 August

Overton Park, Memphis, Tennessee.

2 September

Following an appearance with Elvis Presley, Charlene Arthur and Floyd Cramer in Texarkana, Cash joins Elvis, Bud Deckleman and Eddie Bond for another short 5-day package tour. The tour opens with a show at the Municipal Auditorium, Texarkana, Arkansas.

5 September
St. Francis County Fair And Livestock Show Jamboree, Smith Stadium, Forrest City, Arkansas.

6 September
High School Gym, Bono, Arkansas.

7 September
National Guard Armory, Sikeston, Missouri.

8 September
City Auditorium, Clarksdale, Mississippi.

9 September
McComb High School Auditorium, McComb, Mississippi.

9 October
First date of the week-long Elvis Presley Jamboree tour of West Texas opens at the Cherry Springs Dance Hall, Cherryspring. Besides Elvis and Cash, the bill included Floyd Cramer, Wanda Jackson, Jimmy Newman and Porter Wagoner.

10 October
Soldiers And Sailors Memorial Hall, Brownwood, Texas.

11 October
Fair Park Auditorium, Abilene, Texas.

12 October
High School Auditorium, Midland, Texas.

13 October
City Auditorium, Amarillo, Texas.

14 October
High School Field House, Odessa, Texas.

15 October
Fair Park Auditorium, Lubbock, Texas
The opening act at this show was Buddy (Holly) & Bobby.

17 November
Arkansas Municipal Auditorium, Texarkana, Arkansas.
This date coincides with Elvis's appearance on the Western Swing Jamboree Tour and although it is possible that Cash played other dates on this tour including Memphis, Forrest City, Sheffield, Camden, Longview and Gladewater it is more likely he only played this date as a replacement for Carl Perkins who missed the show.

26 November
"Cry, Cry, Cry" registers at #14 on the country charts on its only week on the chart.

12 December
National Guard Armory, Amory, Mississippi. Cash appears with fellow Sun recording artists Carl Perkins and Elvis Presley.

28 December
Cash plays as support for George Jones at a show in Texarkana.

29 December
Tyler, Texas.

December
"Folsom Prison Blues"/"So Doggone Lonesome" (Sun 232) released.

1956

7 January
Cash lands a regular Saturday night spot on the Louisiana Hayride, broadcast from the Auditorium in Shreveport, Louisiana.

3 February
San Angelo, Texas.

4 February
Odessa, Texas.

11 February
Both sides of Cash's latest single, "Folsom Prison Blues" and "So Doggone Lonesome" enter the country charts at #14 and will reach a high of #5 during their chart residency. They also receive BMI awards.

16 April
Cash's second daughter, Kathy, is born in Memphis.

May
"I Walk The Line"/"Get Rhythm" (Sun 241) released. "I Walk The Line" will go on to receive a BMI Award and a Gold Record.

May
Cash signs with Bob Neal's Stars Inc.

1 June
Overton Park Shell, Memphis, Tennessee. Also on the show are Warren Smith, Roy Orbison and Carl Perkins, all Sun artists.

2 June
Big D Jamboree, Dallas, Texas.

July
Tour of Florida with Jim Reeves, Hawkshaw Hawkins, Jean Shepard and Johnny T. Talley.

7 July
Grand Ole Opry, Nashville, Tennessee
Following six months on the Louisiana Hayride Cash is offered a regular spot on the Grand Ole Opry. He makes his first appearance on this day.

28 July
Grand Ole Opry, Nashville, Tennessee.
Cash performs "Get Rhythm" during the
9:30-10:00 p.m. segment sponsored by
Stephens, while on the 11:00-11:30 p.m.
Coca-Cola sponsored segment he sings "So
Dogonne Lonesome" and "I Walk The
Line".

July-August
Tour of Texas with Roy Orbison, Faron
Young and Johnny Horton. Dates in
Ontario, Canada were followed by another
tour through Florida.

September
"I Walk The Line" becomes Cash's first hit
on the pop charts when it reaches #19
during a run of 22 weeks. On the country
charts it had given him his second top five
country hit and during the incredible run of
43 weeks spent four weeks at # 2.

November
Sun Records release "Train Of Love"/
"There You Go" (Sun 258). Both songs will
receive BMI Awards.

4 December
Carl Perkins was recording his new single

at Sun Studios in Memphis with Jerry Lee
Lewis playing piano. Elvis Presley, who
was with RCA Records, dropped by as did
Johnny Cash. The resulting jam session has
since become known as the Million Dollar
Quartet. Photos were taken that included all
four artists but there is confusion over what
part Cash played. Tapes exists, and have
been released, but none of the material
featured Cash although it is possible he
appears on some of the remaining
unreleased material or is too far away from
the microphone to be heard. During a
concert tour of the UK in 1987 Cash had
this to say – "That particular session was a
Carl Perkins recording session and when I
went in Elvis Presley had just arrived and
the session practically ended when Elvis
walked in. He sat down at the piano and
then Jerry Lee Lewis came in later. Elvis
played the piano…and the microphone was
one of those old RCA Victor microphones
way down to Elvis's left. I was down at the
other end of the piano – that's the reason
you don't hear me much. But we sang Bill
Monroe songs and a little bit of everything
– mainly gospel – and then after a while
Jerry Lee Lewis sat down at the piano, and
nobody follows Jerry Lee Lewis at the
piano so we sang with Jerry for quite a
while. It was a big time, it took about two
hours of Carl Perkins' recording session
and we didn't know at the time it was being
recorded. I didn't leave, I was there for the
whole thing. I was singin' the high part, the
tenor part, I was singin' Bill Monroe's
part!"

1957

January-February
With "I Walk The Line" still in the top ten
Cash's new single "There You Go" and
"Train Of Love" register at # 2 in the
country charts.

3 January
Concert in Akron, Ohio.

19 January
Johnny Cash and the Tennessee Two appear on Jackie Gleason's TV Show. Also on the show are Johnny Horton, The McCormack Brothers, Lee Emerson, Marty Robbins, Ray Scott, Jimmie Skinner, Ray Lunsford, Phyllis & Billy Holmes, Jimmy Williams, Jeanne Hogan and The Lucky Pennies.

6 February
Pittsburgh, Pennsylvania.

8 February
Cincinatti, Ohio.

13 February
Iberia, Louisiana.

14 February
Alexandria, Louisiana.

15 February
Austin, Texas.

16 February
Tucson, Arizona.

17 February
San Diego, California.

18 February
Bakersfield, California.

19 February
Fresno, California.

20 February
Sacramento, California.

21 February
Richmond, California.

23 February
Oakland, California.

24 February
San Jose and Stockton, California.

24 March
A new tour opens with a show at the 'Grand Ole Opry', Topeka. Supporting acts on the tour will include The Louvin Brothers, Jerry Lee Lewis, Kitty Carson, George McCormick and Smiley Wilson.

31 March
Little Rock, Arkansas.

1 April
Monroe, Louisiana.

2 April
Sheffield, Alabama.

3 April
Jackson, Mississippi.

April
"Next In Line"/"Don't Make Me Go" (Sun 266) is released and gives Cash his fourth top ten country hit and the a-side just manages to scrape into the Pop Charts at #99. "Next In Line" gives Cash yet another BMI Award.

5 April
Tour continues in Odessa, Texas.

6 April
Dallas, Texas.

7 April
Abilene, Texas.

8 April
Texarkana, Arkansas.

9 April
Winnfield, Louisiana.

11 April
Cash makes an appearance on the Paul Winchell TV Show.

14 April
Tour continues with a show in Syracuse.

20 April
Minneapolis, Minnesota.

21 April
Saulte St. Marie, Ontario.

22 April
Sudbury, Ontario.

23 April
Pembroke, Ontario.

24 April
Ottawa, Ontario.

26 April
Fort Frances, Ontario.

27 April
Duluth, Minnesota.

28 April
Des Moines, Iowa.

29 April
Aberdeen, South Dakota.

30 April
Moorhead, South Dakota.

1 May
Winnipeg, Manitoba.

2 May
Saskatoon, Saskatchewan.

3 May
Calgary, Alberta.

4 May
Billings, Montana.

5 May
Camrose, Alberta.

6 May
Trail, British Columbia.

May/June
Tour of Georgia and the Jimmie Rodgers Memorial Day Picnic in Meridian, Mississippi.

1 July
Both "Give My Love To Rose" and "Home Of The Blues" are recorded and will be released later in the month as Sun 279.

4 August
A productive recording session that results in six masters being put on tape.

August
"Home Of The Blues"/"Give My Love To Rose" (Sun 279) is released and will spend the last four months of the year hovering in the top ten. "Home Of The Blues" also registers on the Pop Charts at #88.

31 August
Cash appears on the *Town Hall Party*, a live broadcast. Backstage Johnny Cash and Carl Perkins met Don Law, who inquired whether either artist would be interested in signing with Columbia at the expiration of their contract with Sun. Both said that they would. And Johnny Cash will sign a contract on 1 August, 1958.

Throughout the year Cash also makes regular appearances on *Western Ranch Party*. Other guests on the shows during the year included Tex Williams, Jimmy Newman, Eddie Dean, Jim Reeves, Bobby Helms, Gordon Terry, Wanda Jackson, Patsy Cline, Merle Travis and Carl Perkins.

10 September
Sun Records release Johnny Cash's first album *With His Hot And Blue Guitar* (Sun SLP-1220). This is the only album released during his time with the label, although in years to come many more would be issued. Tracks: "Rock Island Line", "I Heard That Lonesome Whistle", "Country Boy", "If The Good Lord's Willing", "Cry, Cry, Cry", "Remember Me", "So Doggone Lonesome", "I Was There When It Happened", "I Walk The Line", "Wreck Of The Old '97", "Folsom Prison Blues", "Doin' My Time".

16 October
Cash starts tour of Georgia with The Wilburns and follows with an appearance in Miami on a bill that included Jerry Lee Lewis. A tour with Jerry Lee Lewis and George Jones through Florida followed.

Late-October
Although the date is uncertain it was around this time that Cash had his tonsils removed. His doctor was worried that it might affect his singing voice but after a few weeks rest everything was fine. The last few days of recuperation were spent in Hollywood with his manager Bob Neal. During those few days they visited all the major movie studios and talked to the producers of the Western TV shows.

November
Luther Perkins and Marshall Grant receive the 'Best Instrumental Duo' Award from *Jamboree* magazine.

December
"Ballad Of A Teenage Queen"/"Big River" (Sun 283) released.

December
Cash undertakes a fifteen-day tour of Canada. Following the release of "Ballad Of A Teenage Queen" a contest is held at each city on the tour to find the local 'Teenage Queen.' At each city on the tour Cash would make local radio and TV appearances followed by a record signing at a local record outlet. During the signing a name would be drawn out and the winner in each city would be announced at that evening's concert. Just before the evening concert in Saskatoon the winner unfortunately died and the runner-up was crowned – the runner-up went on to become a successful singer/songwriter– Joni Mitchell!

1958

January
The year opens with a series of concert dates in Battle Creek, Michigan; Sault Ste. Marie, Ontario; Wichita Falls, Kansas and Toledo, Kansas.

6 January
Billboard magazine review Cash's latest single: "This is the most poppish try for Cash in a while. "Teenage Queen" tells a cute story that can appeal to teens, and the artist's approach is highly attractive. Flip. "Big River", has more of a traditional c&w flavour, but the rhythmic presentation can also appeal in pop marts. A dual-market contender".

February-March
Both sides of the latest single, "Big River" and "Ballad Of A Teenage Queen", register at #1 in the country charts. During the 22 week run "Ballad..." will stay on the top spot for eight weeks while "Big River" holds the #1 position for five weeks. "Ballad..." also manages a respectable #16 in the pop charts. Two more BMI Awards are also added to Cash's growing collection.

April
Dates in Hickory, North Carolina; Newburgh, New York; Newark, New Jersey; Fort Smith, Arkansas; Sulphur Spring, Texas and the Canadian Maritimes.

12 April
The British pop weekly *Disc* has this to say about Cash's new single: "Dark-voiced Johnny Cash has never quite pulled it off so far as customers are concerned on this side of the sea. On "Ballad Of A Teenage Queen" he may find the title is against him here...don't think our teenagers jump automatically at songs with this kind of name. Cash sounds like a youthful Tex Ritter as he treacles through this C and W half. "Big River" gets that new deep guitar noise into its backing and is a more hopeful half altogether. A more dramatic country effort it has something of the old blues flavour in it".

May
"Guess Things Happen That Way"/"Come In Stranger" (Sun 295) released. Following on from the success of his previous single this release also goes to the top of the country charts and registers on the pop charts as well.

15-28 May
Knowing Cash was planning to leave Sun Records, Sam Phillips and Jack Clement hold a series of recording sessions to stockpile tracks for future release. Over ten tracks are recorded including several Hank Williams songs.

June
Tour of California and Oregon.

June
Bob Neal folds Stars Inc.

1 July
Tour ends with a show in Vancouver.

17 July
Cash records his final session for Sun Records. Only two tracks are recorded - "Down The Street To 301" and "I Forgot To

Remember To Forget", both of which will be subject to overdubs before release.

24 July
Although he would not officially sign a contract for another week Cash holds his first recording session for his new label Columbia. At Owen Bradley Studios in Nashville the basic sound of Cash, Perkins and Grant is supported by a steel guitar player, piano and drums, as well as a vocal chorus.

29 July
A third daughter, Cindy, is born in Memphis. Her parents called her a "rockabilly baby" as she slept in a drawer for several weeks while the family finalised plans to move out of Memphis.

August
"The Ways Of A Woman In Love"/"You're The Nearest Thing To Heaven" (Sun 302) released.

1 August
Cash signs a contract with Columbia records.

September
Cash's first single for his new label "All

Over Again"/"What Do I Care" (Columbia 4-41251) is released. The a-side wins a BMI Award and also a Columbia Gold Guitar Award.

September–November
A busy period chartwise with "Guess Things Happen That Way" finishing its chart run, both sides of his latest Sun Records single registering in the top ten and his first single for his new label also making an appearance. On the pop charts it was a similar story with three of the tracks registering in the top 100.

September–November
Cash tours the mid-west with Carl Perkins, Sonny James and Mitchell Torok. The tour moves into Texas and picks up Bob Luman, Gordon Terry and Johnny Horton.

November
"It's Just About Time"/"I Just Thought You'd Like To Know" (Sun 309) released. Compared to recent singles this could be seen as a flop chartwise, with a stay of just one week in the charts at the start of 1959.

November
Cash attends the DJ Convention in Nashville.

November
Cash's first extended play album is released on the Sun Records label. *Sings Hank Williams* (SUN EP-111) featured four tracks from the pen of Hank Williams – "I Can't Help It (If I'm Still In Love With You)", "Hey Good Lookin'", "You Win Again" and "I Could Never Be Ashamed Of You". Another Hank Williams song "Cold, Cold Heart" was considered for this release but was not included and would remain unissued for several years. These tracks were heavily overdubbed before release. Between now and early 1960 five more extended play albums would be issued on the Sun label - *Johnny Cash*, also known as *Country Boy*, *I Walk The Line*, *Johnny Cash With The Tennessee Two*,

Home Of The Blues and *So Doggone Lonesome.*

November

Johnny Cash's first album for Columbia, *The Fabulous Johnny Cash* (CL-1253/CS-8122), is released.
Tracks: "Run Softly, Blue River", "Frankie's Man, Johnny", "That's All Over", "The Troubadour", "One More Ride", "That's Enough", "I Still Miss Someone", "Don't Take Your Guns To Town", "I'd Rather Die Young", "Pickin' Time", "Shepherd Of My Heart", "Suppertime".

It was common practice with record companies in the late fifties and early sixties to take an artist's latest album and release the material on three separate extended play releases. *The Fabulous Johnny Cash* was issued on three EPs, with each featuring a different cover shot from the same photo session. Initial sales of the album approached 400,000.

10 November

Although he is now a Columbia recording artist Sun Records continue to release his material on albums. *Songs That Made Him Famous* (Sun SLP-1235) is his second release on the label.
Tracks: "Ballad Of A Teenage Queen", "There You Go", "I Walk The Line", "Don't Make Me Go", "Guess Things Happen That Way", "Train Of Love", "Ways Of A Woman In Love", "Next In Line", "You're The Nearest Thing To Heaven", "I Can't Help It", "Home Of The Blues", "Big River".

15 November

Disc, the UK pop weekly, reviews Cash's first single for his new label: "The deep brown voice of Johnny Cash turns up now on the Philips label after a long spell with London. And Philips should be pleased, because Johnny might have one of his biggest successes on this side of the water with this coupling. "What Do I Care" is a rich, steady country romancer that lopes along in company with a rhythm group backing. Both songs on this release were written by Johnny himself. And it may be that "All Over Again" will turn out to be the bigger attraction of the pair. Quicker than the other side with some chorus work behind Cash, it's catchy stuff".

23 November

Benefit show in Memphis for Jay Perkins' wife. Also on the show are Jerry Lee Lewis and Charlie Feathers.

December

"Don't Take Your Guns To Town"/"I Still Miss Someone" (Columbia 4-41313) released.

8 December

The Fabulous Johnny Cash becomes Cash's first album chart success when it enters the pop charts at #20.

During the year Cash is voted Favourite Country And Western Artist by *Billboard* magazine. And for the second time *Cash Box* vote him Most Programmed Male Country Vocalist.

1959

13 January

During his time with Sun Records, Cash never had the chance to record gospel material, the only exceptions being "Belshazzar" and "I Was There When It Happened". On this day he recorded enough material for his first album of gospel songs, many written or arranged by Cash himself.

19 January

"Don't Take Your Guns To Town" enters the country charts at #20 and begins its 20 week run during which time it will hold the top spot for six weeks during March and April. In the pop charts it does less well peaking at #32.

February
"Luther Played The Boogie"/"Thanks A Lot" (Sun 316) released. Cash will receive BMI Awards for "Don't Take Your Guns To Town" and "Luther Played The Boogie".

9 February
The Fabulous Johnny Cash had spent three weeks in the chart at the end of 1958 and it re-entered the charts at #24 on this day and spent a further six weeks in the pop charts, peaking at #21. *Billboard* voted the album "Favourite C&W Album".

22 February
The half-hour western series *The Rebel* is broadcast for the first time. Produced by Goodson-Todman Productions it starred Nick Adams as the former Confederate soldier Johnny Yuma and the theme song was sung by Johnny Cash. The series would run until September 1961. Cash had appeared in other western series including *Wagon Train* and *Shotgun Slade* and would make a guest appearance on *The Rebel*. An extended play album released in 1960 featured the title song along with three other western themed tunes – "Remember The Alamo", "The Ballad Of Boot Hill" and "Lorena". This release came in a gatefold sleeve, rare for this period, and had notes about the show and the music.

March
"You Dreamer You"/"Frankie's Man Johnny" (Columbia 4-41371) released.

March
With his new producer Don Law at the controls, Cash records tracks for the *Songs Of Our Soil* album.

23 March
Cash takes a screen test for a possible western musical drama.

April
Cash undertakes a tour of Australia, his first appearances outside the United States. Although he would become known for wearing black during his concerts, in Sydney he wore a bright red sports jacket, black shirt with red flowers, powder blue slacks and white shoes.

18 April
Under the heading "Fabulous? Not On Your Life" the UK paper *Disc* prints a lukewarm review of his his latest album. "The sleeve-note hails Johnny Cash as "fabulous". I disagree. He is a good performer and I'll admit that he is a lot better than most in his field of singing. But "fabulous" — never. People are too free with flowing praise nowadays with the result that many adjectives have lost their meaning. "Fabulous" is one of the most overworked of all. This is a good album and the Cash boy has a rich voice which should make him pretty popular. He sounds a little like a young Ernie Ford but lacks the richness of that artist's voice".

May
Johnny Cash's first gospel album, *Hymns By Johnny Cash* (CL-1284/CS-8125), is released.
Tracks: "It Was Jesus", "I Saw A Man", "Are All The Children In", "The Old Account", "Lead Me Gently Home", "Swing Low Sweet Chariot", "Snow In His Hair", "Lead Me Father", "I Call Him", "These Things Shall Pass", "He'll Be A Friend", "God Will".

As with Johnny Cash's previous album this release was issued as three separate extended play albums, although this time the same photo appeared on each one.

4 May
Johnny Cash's first song book, *Song And Picture Folio, Number 1*, is published by Hill & Range Songs, Inc., based in New York. The 40-page book, selling at $1.50, includes the music and lyrics to 13 songs including "I Still Miss Someone", "One More Ride" and "I Walk The Line". The

cover featured a great colour publicity photo while inside another 11 pages of photos were included.

May-June
The recent Sun Records release and his latest Columbia release both register on the country charts. "Thanks A Lot" just misses the top ten, stalling at #12, while "Frankie's Man Johnny" goes three places higher.

June
Sun Records issue another single pairing, "Katy Too" and "I Forgot To Remember To Forget" (Sun 321) and it reaches #11 during its chart residency.

July
Columbia release "I Got Stripes"/"Five Feet High And Rising" (Columbia 4-41427).

August-September
"I Got Stripes" enters the country charts at #30, staying five weeks and reaching a peak of #9. It re-enters the chart on 14 September for another 15-week run, with six weeks locked in the #4 position. On the pop charts it peaks at #45. Cash had received a Gold Guitar Award for his first single on Columbia and he received another for his recording of "I Got Stripes", which also received a BMI Award.

September

Cash's third album for Columbia, *Songs Of Our Soil* (CL-1339/CS-8148), is released featuring mostly original material.

Tracks: "Drink To Me", "Five Feet High And Rising", "The Man On The Hill", "Hank And Joe And Me", "Clementine", "Great Speckled Bird", "I Want To Go Home", "The Caretaker", "Old Apache Squaw", "Don't Step On Mother's Roses", "My Grandfather's Clock", "It Could Be You (Instead Of Him)".

Again this was split into three extended play releases, each with four tracks and featuring the same cover photo.

September

Sun records release "You Tell Me"/ "Goodbye, Little Darlin" (Sun 331) and it registers on the country charts for just four weeks with a high of #22.

8 September

Cash plays the Jimmie Rodgers Show.

17 September

Cash makes his first appearance in the United Kingdom, on *Boy Meets Girls*, without the Tennessee Two who, under UK Musicians Union rules, were not allowed to accompany Cash.

19 September

Disc carries a review of Cash's latest single: "The kind of "Stripes" Johnny Cash has got in this quick-trotting Country and Western side are the prison stripes of his convicts uniform. Chains around his feet, too, in this gaol tale. Johnny sings his sad story most equably. It is quite tuneful, but it hasn't got the dejected mood that the lyric writer obviously sought! "Five Feet High And Rising" refers to the flood waters outside the farm house. Johnny sings it in question and answer form. Better all round than the other deck and including a wry pinch of humour".

October

"Little Drummer Boy"/"I'll Remember You" (Columbia 4-41481) is released.

Disc opened their review of Cash's latest single with this comment "Country and Western star, Johnny Cash, may seem an unlikely artist to find singing "Little Drummer Boy", but on reflection, why not?" They went on to say, "...Johnny sings the tale convincingly with a very effective pause before the closing phrases."

12 October

Sun Records release *Greatest Johnny Cash* (Sun SLP-1240).

Tracks: "Goodbye Little Darlin", "I Just Thought You'd Like To Know", "You Tell Me", "It's Just About Time", "I Forgot To Remember To Forget", "Katy Too", "Thanks A Lot", "Luther Played The Boogie", "You Win Again", "Hey Good Looking", "I Could Never Be Ashamed Of You", "Get Rhythm" .

25 October

Cash records German language versions of two of his recent hits. Both "Viel zu Spat (I Got Stripes)" and "Wo ist zu Hause Mama (Five Feet High And Rising)" will be released later in his career as a single in Germany.

November

"Bandana"/"Wabash Blues" (Columbia 4-41573) released. This instrumental is credited to The Tennessee Two.

November

Bob Neal, who had been co-managing Cash with Stew Carnall, returns to Tennessee. The professional relationship between Cash and Stew Carnall would only run for another eighteen months.

November

Johnny Cash and The Tennessee Two fly to Germany to play some shows at US Bases.

December

"Straight A's In Love"/"I Love You Because" (Sun 334) released. Both sides of this single will chart during February and March 1960.

December

Sessions begin for the *Ride This Train* album. This would be Cash's first concept album and along with the songs he would also record some narratives. Sessions will continue through to February 1960.

December

"Little Drummer Boy" spends just one week at #24 in the country charts while its success in the pop charts is only marginally better, with a high of #63 during a three-week run.

26 December

Disc opened their review of Cash's latest single with the comment "Country and Western star, Johnny Cash, may seem an unlikely artist to find singing "Little Drummer Boy", but on reflection, why not?" They went on to say, "And Johnny's sober performance of this Czech nativity story is very likeable indeed. While a drum beats in the background and a girl group supplies the rap-a-pa-bom-boms, Johnny sings the tale convincingly with a very effective pause before the closing phrases."

1960

1 January

Cash plays his first free concert for the inmates of the notorious San Quentin Prison in California. Future country music star Merle Haggard is in the audience.

February

"Don't Take Your Guns To Town"/"Five Feet High And Rising" (Columbia 4-33006) released.

17 February

A very productive day during which, in one three-hour session, Cash records all the tracks for the *Now There Was A Song* album.

March

"Seasons Of My Heart"/"Smiling Bill McCall" (Columbia 4-41618) released.

23 & 30 April

Cash appears on *Jubilee USA* on these two dates.

May-June

Both sides of Cash's latest single "Smiling Bill McCall" and "Seasons Of My Heart" chart. They will reach #10 and #13 respectively.

June

Filming takes place for Cash's first leading role in a movie, although he had featured previously in minor roles in television westerns. The Flower Films production *Five Minutes To Live* was based on a story by Palmer Thompson and Cash played a psychopathic killer, Johnny Cabot, who brings a reign of terror to a calm, quiet suburban community. The movie also starred Pamela Mason, James Mason's wife, Cay Forrester, Donald Wood, Vic Tayback and Merle Travis. The production ran out of money during shooting and Cash put approximately $20,000 into the project to keep it afloat. When released in December the movie's title was changed to *Door To Door Maniac*, condemning Cash's title song to be banished to the vaults where it stayed for several years. Over the years the film gained a cult following although at the time the press were less than enthusiastic — "A familiar but more than serviceable story is ruined by flabby direction and acting..." (*Monthly Film Bulletin*) and "Smartly plotted cops and robbers yarn with a novel twist; but feebly developed and tediously directed; acting over the top." (*The Daily Cinema*).

June

Both Columbia and Sun Records release

singles this month – "Second Honeymoon"/"Honky Tonk Girl" (Columbia 4-41707) and "Story Of A Broken Heart"/"Down The Street To 301" (Sun 343).

9 July

In it's review of "Hymns By Johnny Cash" *Disc* had this to say: "Here's a top pop and C and W exponent Johnny Cash in a new light performing hymns. He does an excellent job of it, too, his deep rich voice being ideally suited to this material. Johnny has selected a group of popular American hymns and added a few of his own composing for good measure. The new offerings blend admirably with the old-established items and few will be able to distinguish them. The hymns seem to have a C and W touch about them which does not seem out of place".

5 August

The Tennessee Two become The Tennessee Three when W. S. "Fluke" Holland, from Jackson, Tennessee, joins on drums.

22 August

"Second Honeymoon" charts at #21 and will peak at #15 during its 7 weeks on the chart.

September

"Loading Coal"/"Goin' To Memphis" (Columbia 4-41804) released. Neither this nor the recent Sun single manage to make any impression on the chart.

September

Ride This Train (CL-1464/CS-8255) is released.
Tracks: "Loading Coal", "Slow Rider", "Lumberjack", "Dorraine Of Ponchartrain", "Goin' To Memphis", "When Papa Played The Dobro", "Boss Jack", "Old Doc Brown".

12 October

Sun Records release the misleadingly titled *Sings Hank Williams* (Sun SLP-1240).

Despite the title only the first four tracks are from the pen of the great Hank Williams. Some of the tracks are overdubbed with a vocal chorus.

Tracks: "I Can't Help It", "You Win Again", "Hey Good Looking", "I Could Never Be Ashamed Of You", "Next In Line", "Straight A's In Love", "Folsom Prison Blues", "Give My Love To Rose", "I Walk The Line", "I Love You Because", "Come In Stranger", "Mean Eyed Cat".

October

"Mean Eyed Cat"/"Port Of Lonely Hearts" (Sun 347) released.

November

Concert dates in Germany.

5 November

Cash's friend Johnny Horton, who had a hit with "Battle Of New Orleans" and wrote "Girl from Saskatoon", dies in a head-on car crash in Milano, Texas.

13 November

Hammond Civic Center, Hammond, Indiana.

Late-November
Hill & Range Songs publish *Song And Picture Folio, Number 2*. Like the previous songbook published in 1959, this also contains 40-pages and has a colour portrait photo on the cover with 16 pages of photos from Cash's TV appearances, on stage, from the film *Door To Door Maniac* and with Luther & Marshall. The music and lyrics to 10 songs are included.

December
Now, There Was A Song! (CL-1463/CS-8254) is released.

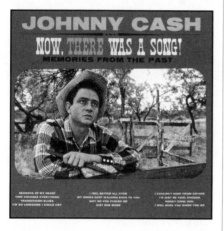

Tracks: "Seasons Of My Heart", "I Feel Better All Over", "I Couldn't Keep From Crying", "Time Changes Everything", "My Shoes Keep Walking Back To You", "I'd Just Be Fool Enough", "Transfusion Blues", "Why Do You Punish Me", "I Will Miss You When You Go", "I'm So Lonesome I Could Cry", "Just One More", "Honky-Tonk Girl".

By the end of 1960 the practice of taking an artist's current release and issuing it on extended play albums was coming to an end, and this would be the last Johnny Cash album to be released this way. It wouldn't be an end of extended plays as a format, and there would be several more in the years to come.

December
Another month when Sun and Columbia release singles at the same time – "Oh, Lonesome Me"/"Life Goes On" (Sun 355) and "Locomotive Man"/"Girl In Saskatoon" (Columbia 4-41920).

26 December
The recently released "Mean Eyed Cat" manages just one week on the charts.

1961

January
"Blues For Two"/"Jeri And Nina's Melody" (Columbia 4-41926) released. This is the second instrumental credited to The Tennessee Two. Jeri and Nina were Johnny Horton's children and the song was written especially for them.

28 January
The concept album "Ride This Train" is reviewed in *Disc*. Despite doubts about the commercial appeal in the UK the reviewer has nothing but praise for the album. "I don't think that this will be one of Johnny Cash's best-selling efforts with the British public, and that is a pity considering the thought and talent brought to bear in compiling this travelogue in story and song. Singer Cash takes the listener across America in story and winds up each instalment with a folksy offering in song to set off the mood perfectly. The accompaniement is excellent, the idea superb, and the performance immaculate. Let us hope my prediction proves to be wrong and that Johnny Cash has, in fact, come up with a best seller".

6 February
The material released by Sun Records continues to chart, and in many cases does better than the Columbia material. "Oh Lonesome Me" opens its nine-week run at #26 and will go on to peak at #13.

14 March
Houston, Texas.

27 April
At Owen Bradley Studios in Nashville Cash lays down tracks for his *Hymns From The Heart* release.

April
"Forty Shades Of Green"/"The Rebel-Johnny Yuma" (Columbia 4-41995) released.

May
Lure Of The Grand Canyon (CL-1622) released.
Cash appears on this album with an eleven minute narration entitled "A Day In The Grand Canyon".

17 May
Memorial Gardens, Guelph, Ontario.

29 May
It is reported that Johnny Cash has acquired the rights to the *Jimmie Rodger's Story* and will be filming it as an independent production.

June
"Sugartime"/"My Treasure" (Sun 363) released.

12 June
"The Rebel-Johnny Yuma" enters the chart at #21 and the following week moves up to #14.

July
Canadian promoter Saul Holiff, who had recently booked Cash on a concert tour, took over as his manager. This was a role he would undertake well into the early seventies.

27 September
Massey Hall, Toronto, Ontario.

1962

Early-1962
Tour of the Far East including military installations in Japan and Korea. At the Korakeum Auditorium in Tokyo Cash and the Tennessee Three play for a crowd of 3,000. In Korea they play 26 shows instead of the original scheduled 12, and the same applies during the shows at the military bases in Japan.

28 January
Concert at the KRNT Theatre Des Moines, Iowa. Following the show Gerald E. Bloomquist, manager of the theatre, was quoted as saying "It was a distinct privilege and a genuine pleasure to present at KRNT Theatre January 28, 1962, the Johnny Cash Show, which broke all our existing attendance records. The unaminous acclaim of the 11,000 dedicated fans who patronized the one-day three-performance engagement exemplifies the esteen and respect that Johnny Cash, a superb showman, commands throughout the country."

February
"Tall Man"/"Tennessee Flat-Top Box" (Columbia 4-42147) is released.

March
"The Big Battle"/"When I've Learned" (Columbia 4-42301) is released and enters the chart at the end of the month.

April
Sun Records issue another single – "Blue Train"/"Born To Lose" (Sun 376).

23 April
At the Columbia Studios in Nashville Cash records a version of "Bonanza".

10 May
Cash makes his debut at the famous Carnegie Hall in New York.

May
"In The Jailhouse Now"/"A Little At A Time" (Columbia 4-42425) released.

June
Hymns From The Heart (CL-1722/CS-8522), Cash's second album of gospel material, is released.
Tracks: "He'll Understand And Say Well Done", "God Must Have My Fortune Laid Away", "When I've Learned", "I Got Shoes", "Let The Lower Lights Be Burning", "If We Never Meet Again", "When I Take My Vacation In Heaven", "When He Reached Down His Hand For Me", "Taller Than Trees", "I Won't Have To Cross Jordan Alone", "My God Is Real", "These Hands".

June
Fifteen gospel songs are featured in *Hymns From The Heart*, the latest songbook published by Hill & Range Songs of New York. There were no photos inside and the cover used the same shot as on the album.

July
"Bonanza"/"Pick A Bale O' Cotton" (Columbia 4-42512) released.

July
Waterloo, Iowa.

7 July
Cash's latest album of gospel material receives a poor review from Owen Bryce in the UK pop weekly *Disc*. "I've got to admit that Johnny Cash's voice is quite something, but the scope of this record is sickening, and it's most definitely not for me. There's something quite awful about this class of material. It's bad enough to have all those cowboys singing songs about their lost loved ones...but as far as I'm concerned religion is a thing people ought to be happy about. Johnny Cash and his arrangers make it sound like the cattle-ranchers burden. You can be reverent and emotional without all that sob stuff. I realise that in the part of America where C

and W is most prominent religion does take on that severe, austere you-miserable-lot-of-sinners attitude...and it's more than likely that they'll go for this in a big way out there...if they're prepared to admit that God doesn't object to the pleasures of the phonograph!"

14 July
"In The Jailhouse Now" debuts at #26 and will peak at #8 during a chart residency of 10 weeks.

15 July
Cash appears at the Hollywood Bowl on a show billed as the *"First Giant Folk-Western-Bluegrass Spectacular."*

July-August
At a series of sessions held in the Columbia's Studio A in Nashville, Cash records tracks for his second concept album, *Blood, Sweat And Tears*.

August
Johnny Cash plays his first "real" show in the UK, at the Astoria Irish Club in Plymouth Grove, Manchester.

August
Sound Of Johnny Cash (CL-1802/CS-8602) released.
Tracks: "Lost On The Desert", "Accidentally On Purpose", "In The Jailhouse Now", "Mr Lonesome", "You Won't Have Far To Go", "In Them Old Cottonfields Back Home", "Delia's Gone", "I Forgot More Than You'll Ever Know", "You Remembered Me", "I'm Free From The Chain Gang Now", "Let Me Down Easy", "Sing It Pretty Sue"

31 August
Arnold's Park, Mason City, Iowa.

1 September
Danceland, Cedar Plains, Iowa.

2 September
Buck Lane Ranch, Angola, Indiana.

3 September
New River Ranch, Rising Sun, Maryland.

4 September
Dick Clark TV Show, Philadelphia, Pennsylvania.

6 September
Madison, Wisconsin.

7 September
Green Bay, Wisconsin.

8 September
Metropolitan Stadium, Minneapolis, Minnesota.

9 September
Kentucky State Fair, Louisville, Kentucky.

21–22 September
White Horse Academy, Trenton, New Jersey.

23 September
Lone Star Ranch, Reeds Ferry, New Hampshire.

29 September
East Moline High School, Moline, Illinois.

30 September
Civic Center, Hammond, Indiana.

November
"Peace In The Valley"/"Were You There (When They Crucified My Lord)" (Columbia 4-42615) released.

November
Cash volunteers to entertain the troops out in Korea. Over seven days he performed before 26,000 G.I.s, at 30 shows, although he was originally scheduled for 20 shows.

15 November
Sun Records release *All Aboard The Blue Train* (Sun SLP-1270), a themed collection of railroad songs.
Tracks: "Blue Train", "There You Go", "Train Of Love", "Goodbye Little Darlin'", "I Heard That Lonesome Whistle", "Come In Stranger", "Rock Island Line", "Give My Love To Rose", "Hey Porter", "Folsom Prison Blues", "Wreck Of The Old '97", "So Doggone Lonesome"

December
"Busted"/"Send A Picture Of Mother" (Columbia 4-42665) released.

1963

January
Blood, Sweat And Tears (CL-1930/CS-8730) is released.
Tracks: "Legend Of John Henry's Hammer", "Tell Him I'm Gone", "Another Man Done Gone", "Busted", "Casey Jones", "Nine Pound Hammer", "Chain Gang", "Waiting For A Train", "Roughneck".

In their review *Billboard* write "This is one of Johnny Cash's most exciting albums in a long time, featuring the country-pop chanter in a collection of folk-styled ditties, which he sings with spirit and fervor. One

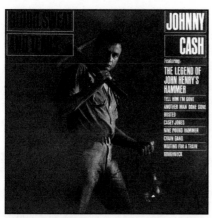

of the best sides is "Legend of John Henry's Hammer" which Cash sells in sock fashion. Also included are "Busted", "Casey Jones", "Nine-Pound Hammer" , "Chaingang" and "Roughneck." First rate Cash, and that's saying something!"

1 January
Johnny Cash, The Tennessee Three and June Carter play for the inmates of San Quentin Prison in California.

19 January
Mid-western tour with George Jones, Grandpa Jones, June Carter, Johnny Western, Georgie Riddle and Gordon Terry. Opening show is in Salina, Kansas.

20 January
Kansas City, Missouri.

21 January
Sioux City, Iowa.

22 January
Sioux Falls, South Dakota.

23 January
Pershing Auditorium, Lincoln, Nebraska.

24 January
Omaha, Nebraska.

25 January
Topeka, Kansas.

19 February
Wichita, Kansas.

25 February
KRNT Theater, Des Moines, Iowa.

16 March
Blood, Sweat And Tears becomes Cash's first pop chart entry for four years when it debuts at #134. A run of fifteen weeks will see it go no higher than #80.

25 March
Records the June Carter/Merle Kilgore composition "Ring Of Fire". Anita Carter had also recorded the song and Cash promised that he would not record his version for several months to give Anita's version a chance to hit. Apparently he dreamed he heard the song with Mexican trumpets and this is how his version was recorded, probably the first time that Mexican trumpets had been used on a Nashville recording session. A few weeks later he recorded a Spanish version with the title "Anillo de Fuego".

March
At various sessions held between March and September, tracks were recorded for Cash's first seasonal offering *The Christmas Spirit*.

April
"Ring Of Fire"/"I'd Still Be There" (Columbia 4-42788) released. Both tracks will appear on the album *Ring Of Fire*.

13 April
With just 3 weeks on the charts "Busted" peaks at #13.

18 April
Laramar Ballroom, Fort Dodge, Iowa.

19 April
Wharton Fieldhouse, Moline, Illinois.

20 April
Kintner Gymnasium, Decatur, Illinois.

21 April
Consistory Auditorium, Freeport, Illinois.

23 April
Coronado Theatre, Rockford, Illinois.

24 April
University of North Dakota, Grand Forks.

25 April
Municipal Auditorium, Fargo, North Dakota.

26 April
Armory, Duluth, Minnesota.

27 April
Civic Auditorium, Milwaukee, Wisconsin.

28 April
Arie Crown Theatre, Chicago, Illinois.

14 May
Dade Auditorium, Miami, Florida.

15 May
Auditorium, Orlando, Florida.

16 May
City Auditorium, Macon, Georgia.

17 May
Municipal Auditorium, Columbus, Georgia.

18 May
Township Auditorium, Columbia, South Carolina.

19 May
Greensboro, North Carolina.

23 May
New London, Connecticut.

24 May
Providence, Rhode Island.

25 May
Boston, Massachusetts.

26 May
Bangor, Maine.

8 June
"Ring Of Fire" debuts at #28 and becomes Cash's first #1 single since "Don't Take Your Guns To Town" in 1959. It reaches the summit on 27 August and holds the top spot for 7 weeks during a run of 26 weeks. On the pop charts it reaches #17. "Ring Of Fire" is voted Favourite Country Single and receives a Columbia Gold Guitar Award.

14 June
Ponce De Leon Ball Park, Atlanta, Georgia.

15 June
Municipal Auditorium, Shreveport, Louisiana.

16 June
Sam Houston Coliseum, Houston, Texas.

17 June
Fair Park Livestock Coliseum, Dallas, Texas.

18 June
Municipal Auditorium, Austin, Texas.

19 June
Municipal Auditorium, San Antonio, Texas.

20 June
Auditorium, Lubbock, Texas.

22 June
Hollywood Bowl, Hollywood.

23 June
4th Country Music Spectacular, Memorial Auditorium, Sacramento, California.

July
Ring Of Fire (CL-2053/CS-8853) is released. The album is basically a best-of compilation.
Tracks: "Ring Of Fire", "I'd Still Be There", "What Do I Care", "I Still Miss Someone", "Forty Shades Of Green",

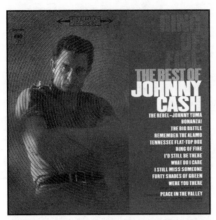

"Were You There (When They Crucified My Lord)", "The Rebel–Johnny Yuma", "Bonanza", "The Big Battle", "Remember The Alamo", "Tennessee Flat-Top Box", "Peace In The Valley".

25 July
Champaign County Fair, Urbana, Illinois.

26-28 July
Springlake Park, Oklahoma City, Oklahoma.

August
A special edition of *Country Music Report* has a feature on Cash's recent concert at the Hollywood Bowl and includes many rare photos.

13 August
Columbia place a full-page advert for the *Ring Of Fire* album in *Billboard* magazine.

September
"The Matador"/"Still In Town" (Columbia 4-42880) released.

30 September
Cash appears on ABC-TV's *Hootenanny* Show which started back in April.

3 October
Lakehead (now Thunderbay), Canada.

9 November
"The Matador" debuts at #20 and stops just short of the top spot with a run of 16 weeks.

16 November
Owen Bryce reviews Cash's latest album in *Disc*: "The title song "Ring Of Fire" I found highly attractive with its simple three trumpet brass figure repeated throughout. Johnny tends at times to be dramatic. He does it excellently, but it lacks the gay abandon of the best of C and W. In his favour, it must be said that the simple, sparse backings which he likes are most effective, though I didn't go for the choir on "Remember The Alamo". On the other hand, anything by the Carter family is interesting, and Johnny use them on "There'll Be Peace In The Valley" to good effect".

December
The Christmas Spirit (CL-2117/CS-8917), Cash's first album of Christmas songs, is released.
Tracks: "The Christmas Spirit", "I Heard The Bells On Christmas Day", "Blue Christmas", "The Gifts They Gave", "Here Was A Man", "Christmas As I Knew It", "Silent Night", "Little Drummer Boy", "Ringing The Bells For Jim", "We Are The Shepherds", "Who Kept The Sheep", "Ballad Of The Harpweaver".

1964-1967

"Gene Ferguson worked for Columbia Records in Nashville. I was visiting him one night, and he played *The Ballad Of Ira Hayes* by Peter La Farge for me, and he said, 'You should record this. It's a true story, and it's the kind of thing you should do.' So I did, and when I recorded it, I loved it so much, I had such a feeling for Ira Hayes. I had been to the Apache country out there, you know. I had seen the old women carrying the big bundle of sticks on their backs for their night's firewood and seen the poverty, and I had a feeling for it. So I really got into it there for a while. Then Peter La Farge himself came down and visited me and brought me more songs, so I decided to do a whole album of them. And Peter wrote half of them and I wrote three or four myself for the album."

Johnny Cash talking about *The Ballad Of Ira Hayes* 1980

1964

January
""Understand Your Man"/"Dark As A Dungeon" (Columbia 4-42964) released.

11 January
Today was the first time *Billboard* produced a chart for country albums and Johnny Cash was riding high at #1 with *Ring Of Fire*. The album would go on to spend an incredible 13 weeks at the top during its run of 31 weeks. On the pop charts it spends 68 weeks in the top 200 between July 1963 and November 1964.

9 February
Johnny Cash and the Tennessee Three, along with June Carter, Tex Ritter and Bill Monroe and the Bluegrass Boys, play a show at Kane's Ballroom, Niagara Falls.

22 February
"Understand Your Man" debuts at #30. The other side of the single, "Dark As A Dungeon", also charts for a single week on 7 March. BMI Awards go to both "The Matador" and "Understand Your Man".

March
"Fair And Tender Ladies"/"Keep On The Sunnyside" (Columbia 4-43004) released. This was a Carter Family single with Cash only appearing on "Keep On The Sunnyside".

5 March
Cash records the Peter La Farge composition "Ballad Of Ira Hayes". This told the true story of a Pima Indian, one of those who held the flag on Iwo Jima, who, although given a hero's welcome, died drunk and penniless in a ditch of water. This was strong material and a subject close to Cash's heart, but it would not be well received by the country music establishment.

9 March
The Statler Brothers join the Johnny Cash Show. In the years to come they would have a succession of hits including "Flowers On The Wall" and "Bed Of Roses".

21 March
Cash appears on the ABC-TV show Hootenanny, broadcast between 7:30-8:30pm.

2 April
University of Alabama, Tuscaloosa, Alabama.

4 April
Forum, Wichita, Kansas.

4 April
"Understand Your Man" reaches the #1 spot and stays there for 6 weeks.

5 April
Memorial Building, Kansas City, Kansas.

7 April
Municipal Auditorium, Topeka, Kansas.

8 April
Pershing Auditorium, Lincoln, Nebraska.

9 April
Civic Auditorium, Omaha, Nebraska.

10 April
Municipal Auditorium, Sioux City, Iowa.

11 April
Civic Auditorium, Minneapolis, Minnesota.

12 April
KRNT Theater, Des Moines, Iowa.

14 April
Memorial Hall, Salina, Kansas.

15 April
City Auditorium, St. Joseph, Missouri.
30 April
Memorial Coliseum, Fort Wayne, Indiana.

May
"Wide Open Road"/"Belshazzah" (Sun 392) released.

1 May
Civic Auditorium, South Bend, Indiana.

2 May
Central High School Auditorium, Kalamazoo, Michigan.

3 May
Olympia Stadium, Detroit, Michigan.

12 May
At the annual Grammy Award Ceremony Johnny Cash is nominated in the 'Best Country & Western Recording' category with "Ring Of Fire" although the award goes to "Detroit City" by Bobby Bare. The eligibility period for the awards is 1 December 1962 – 30 November 1963 and ceremonies are held at the Beverly Hilton Hotel in Los Angeles, the Waldorf-Astoria Hotel in New York and the Knickerbocker Hotel in Chicago.

13 May
University of Mississippi, Oxford, Mississippi.

14 May
Riverside Park Ballroom, Phoenix, Arizona.

15 May
University of New Mexico, Albuquerque, New Mexico.

16 May
Big 'D' Jamboree, Sportatorium, Dallas, Texas.

29 May
White Horse Bowling Academy, Trenton, New Jersey.

30 May
Boston Arena, Boston, Massachusetts.

June
"The Ballad Of Ira Hayes"/"Bad News" (Columbia 4-43058) released.

June
"The Wreck Of The Old '97"/"Hammers And Nails" (Columbia 4-43069) released. This was a Statler Brothers single with Cash featured on "Hammers And Nails" only.

3 June
Memorial Arena, Kitchener, Ontario.

4-6 June
Kiwanis Football Stadium, Chatham, Ontario.

29-30 June
Following his recording of "Ira Hayes", Cash records more Peter La Farge Indian songs and some of his own compositions for an album called *Bitter Tears*. In an interview years later Cash said about the album "Gene Ferguson worked for Columbia Records in Nashville. I was visiting him one night, and he played The Ballad Of Ira Hayes by Peter La Farge for me, and he said, 'You should record this. It's a true story, and it's the kind of thing you should do.' So I did, and when I recorded it, I loved it so much, I had such a feeling for Ira Hayes. I had been to the Apache country out there, you know. I had seen the old women carrying the big bundle of sticks on their backs for their night's firewood and seen the poverty, and I had a feeling for it. So I really got into it there for a while. Then Peter La Farge himself came down and visited me and brought me more songs, so I decided to do a whole album of them."

July
I Walk the Line (CL-2190/CS-8990), an album that included re-recordings of many of his early Sun recordings, is released.
Tracks: "I Walk The Line", "Bad News", "Folsom Prison Blues", "Give My Love To

Rose", "Hey Porter", "I Still Miss Someone", "Understand Your Man", "Wreck Of The Old '97", "Still In Town", "Big River", "Goodbye Little Darling", "Troublesome Waters"

In their Country Spotlight review *Billboard* wrote "Johnny is thought of first as a country artist. However, he consistently makes the pop charts with singles. Cash is more than just a singer of songs, he's a first rate balladier and musical interpreter of the saga of the West. One certainly doesn't have to be a country and western music fan to dig the deep baritone of Johnny Cash".

11 July

Johnny Cash's recording of the Peter La Farge track "Ballad Of Ira Hayes" debuts at #42 and with 20 weeks on the chart it will reach #3. The other side, "Bad News", also charts during this period. The record, however, never made the pop charts, which were dominated by The Beatles and the British invasion.

26 July

Johnny Cash appears at the Newport Folk Festival. He performs "Big River", "Folsom Prison Blues", "I Still Miss Someone", "Rock Island Line", Bob Dylan's "Don't Think Twice, It's Alright", "I Walk The Line", "The Ballad Of Ira Hayes" and "Keep On The Sunnyside". The show is recorded but does not find an official release for over thirty years, until Bear Family Records of Germany release it in a box set. "Johnny Cash, the Nashville star, closed the gap between commercial country and folk music with a masterly set of storytelling songs." – Robert Shelton (*New York Times*). *The Freewheelin' Bob Dylan* was one of Cash's favourite albums and backstage he met up with Bob Dylan. Over the next few years he would record several of Dylan's songs including "Mama, You've Been On My Mind", "It Ain't Me Babe" and "Don't Think Twice, It's Alright".

1 August
Auditorium, Milwaukee, Wisconsin

4 August
Omaha, Nebraska

5 August
Scottsbluff, Nebraska

6 August
Casper, Wyoming

7–8 August
Lagoon Ballroom, Salt Lake City, Utah

15 August
Soldier Field, Chicago, Illinois

22 August
Following the reluctance of radio stations to play his new single, "The Ballad Of Ira Hayes", Cash takes out a full-page ad in *Billboard* magazine lambasting their decision. The ad read:

DJs – station managers – owners, etc., where are your guts?

I'm not afraid to sing the hard, bitter lines that the son of Oliver LaFarge wrote...

Classify me, categorize me – STIFLE me, but it won't work...

I am fighting no particular cause. If I did, it would soon make me a sluggard. For as time changes, I change.

You're right! Teenage girls and Beatle-record buyers don't want to hear this sad story of Ira Hayes – but who cries more easily, and who always go to sad movies to cry??? Teenage girls.

Some of you 'Top Forty' DJs went all out for this at first. Thanks anyway. Maybe the program director or station manager will reconsider.

This ad (go ahead and call it that) costs like hell. Would you, or those pulling the strings for you, go to the mike with a new approach? That is, listen again to the record?

Regardless of the trade charts – the

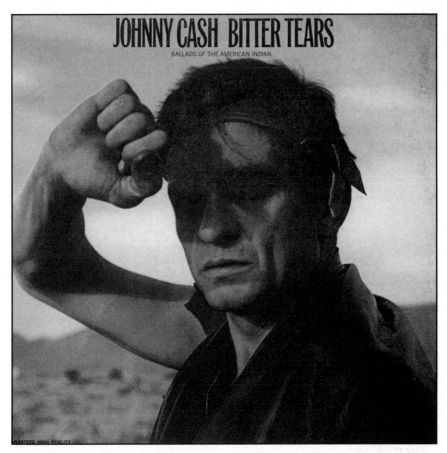

categorizing, classifying and restrictions of air play, this is not a country song, not as it is being sold. It is a fine reason though for the gutless to give it thumbs down.

"Ballad Of Ira Hayes" is strong medicine. So is Rochester—Harlem—Birmingham and Vietnam...

I've blown my horn now, just this once, then no more. Since I've said these things now, I find myself not caring if the record is programed or not. I won't ask you to cram it down their throats.

But... I had to fight back when I realized that so many stations are afraid of "Ira Hayes".

Just one question: WHY???

At the bottom of the ad was the Columbia Records tag line - *Nobody but nobody more original than Johnny Cash*. This attack was not well received by the country music establishment and there were demands that he be stripped of his membership of the Country Music Association.

September

Bitter Tears (CL-2248/CS-9048) is released.

Tracks: "As Long As The Grass Shall Grow", "Apache Tears", "Custer", "The Talking Leaves", "Ballad Of Ira Hayes", "Drums", "White Girl", "The Vanishing Race"

Robert Shelton of the *New York Times* wrote in his review – "...one of the best LP's to emerge from the 60's folk movement." The album went on to sell over 100,000 units. Under its Country Spotlight review section *Billboard* write "Cash, in narrative and song documents the tragic history of the American Indian".

Peter La Farge, who had written half of the tracks on the album, died in 1965.

8 September
Memorial Auditorium, Topeka, Kansas.

9 September
Arena, Sioux Falls, South Dakota.

10 September
Pershing Auditorium, Lincoln, Nebraska.

11 September
Municipal Auditorium, Sioux City, Iowa.

12 September
Forum, Wichita, Kansas.

13 September
Municipal Auditorium, Kansas City, Missouri.

14 September
Rochester, Minnesota.

16 September
Fargo, North Dakota.

17 September
Duluth, Minnesota.

18 September
Auditorium, Fort William
(now Thunderbay), Ontario.

19 September
Sault Ste. Marie, Ontario.
This is his fifth appearance at the town.

29 September
After hovering around the top ten for several weeks, the *I Walk The Line* album finally reaches #1 where it will stay for four weeks. It will spend a further fourteen weeks in the top twenty before finally dropping out at the end of December.

October
"It Ain't Me Babe"/"Time And Time Again" (Columbia 4-43145) released.

17 October
The new single is reviewed in *Billboard* magazine — "Cash swings on the harmonica on the first side and duets with mystery girl. Watch this for pop action too.

"It Ain't Me, Babe" 4-43145

a new song from Bob Dylan on a new single sung by Johnny Cash
On Columbia Records

Flip: Strong hand-clapper featuring great instrumental support".

November
Sun Records release their last Johnny Cash album – *Original Sun Sound* (Sun SLP-1275).
Tracks: "Belshazzah", "Born To Lose", "New Mexico", "I Forgot To Remember To Forget", "Two Timin' Woman", "Story Of A Broken Heart", "Always Alone", "Country Boy", "Goodnight Irene", "Wide Open Road", "Thanks A Lot", "Big River"

6-8 November
Annual Country Music Festival, Nashville, Tennessee

7 November
A full-page ad for the new single appears in *Billboard*: "A new song from Bob Dylan on a new single sung by Johnny Cash".

11 November
Cash headlines the *Hayloft Jamboree* in Providence, Rhode Island promoted by Station WRIB.

12 November
Fitchburg Theater, Fitchburg, Massachusetts.

13 November
Avalon Rollerdrome, Newburgh, New York.

14 November
Memorial Auditorium, Utica, New York.

14 November
Bitter Tears enters the country charts at #19 and will remain for 20 weeks, reaching a high of #2. On the pop charts it only manages to reach #47 during a 14-week stay in the top 200.

15 November
Convention Hall, Saratoga, New York.

16 November
Cash tapes an appearance on the Jimmy Dean TV Show, to be broadcast by ABC-TV on 26 November between 10:00-11:00pm. Other guests on the show included Floyd Cramer, Norm Crosby and Molly Bee.

30 November
The Johnny Cash Show featuring the Tennessee Three, Statler Brothers and Hank Williams Jnr. tours the Northern States and Canada. The tour opens with a show at the Auditorium, Winnipeg, Manitoba.

1 December
Exhibition Auditorium, Regina, Saskatchewan.

2 December
Stampede Corral, Calgary, Alberta.

3 December
The Gardens, Edmonton, Alberta.

4 December
Coliseum, Spokane, Washington.

5 December
Queen Elizabeth Auditorium, Vancouver, British Columbia.

6 December
Memorial Coliseum, Portland, Oregon.

7 December
Center Opera House, Seattle, Washington.

9 December
Ventura, California.

10 December
Monterey, California.
Hank Williams Jr. did not play on the last two dates of the tour.

1965

January
"Orange Blossom Special"/"All God's Children Ain't Free" (Columbia 4-43206) released.

13 January
Cash appears on *Shindig* and performs two songs.

30 January
"It Ain't Me Babe" had entered the chart in November 1964 but on this day it reached its highest position of # 4.

February
"I Just Don't Like This Kind Of Living"/"Rock Island Line" (Columbia 4-43228) released. This Johnny Horton single features Cash on *Rock Island Line*.

11 February
The album *Ring Of Fire* is certified gold by the RIAA (Record Industry Association of America).

20 February
"Orange Blossom Special" debuts at #44 and will eventually go on to reach #3 during a 16-week spell in the chart.

13 March
Johnny Cash winds up a tour with two full-houses at the Massey Hall, Toronto. This appearance makes ten one-nighters in recent years at this venue and it is reported in *Billboard* magazine under the heading *Johnny Cash winds up one of the best tours.*

March
The a-sides of two of Cash's recent singles are paired up and released – "Ring Of Fire"/"It Ain't Me Babe" (Columbia 4-33089).

March
Orange Blossom Special (CL-2309/CS-9109) is released and features three tracks that were recently issued as singles.
Tracks: "Orange Blossom Special", "Long Black Veil", "It Ain't Me Babe", "The Wall", "Don't Think Twice, It's Alright", "You Wild Colorado", "Mama, You've Been On My Mind", "When It's Springtime In Alaska", "All Of God's Children Ain't Free", "Danny Boy", "Wildwood Flower", "Amen".

March
Following months of research into the history of the American West, Cash records material for a forthcoming concept album of western songs.

17 March
Memorial Auditorium, Kitchener, Ontario.

18 March
Music Hall, Toronto, Ontario.

20 March
Shrine Mosque, Peoria, Illinois.

20 March
The *Orange Blossom Special* album starts its country chart run at #16 and will peak at #3 during its fourteen week stay. In the pop charts it spends thirteen weeks and reaches #49.

23 March
Bay Theater, Green Bay, Wisconsin.

24 March
Orpheum Theater, Madison, Wisconsin.

25 March
Coranado Theater, Rockford, Illinois.

26 March
Kintner Gymnasium, Decatur, Illinois.

27 March
Kiel Auditorium, St. Louis.

28 March
Arie Crown Theater, Chicago, Illinois.

13 April
Johnny Cash is nominated for Grammy Awards in two categories at the annual awards ceremony covering the eligibility period of 1 December 1963 – 30 November 1964. *Bitter Tears* is nominated in the 'Best Country & Western Album' category while "I Walk The Line" is up for the 'Best Country & Western Vocal Performance, Male' award. He is beaten in both cases by Roger Miller who takes the honours with *Dang Me/Chug-a-lug* and "Dang Me" respectively. Ceremonies are held at the Beverly Hilton Hotel in Los Angeles, the Astor Hotel in New York and at dinners held in Nashville and Chicago.

May
"Understand Your Man"/"It Ain't Me Babe" (Columbia 4-33091) released. This is the second time "Understand Your Man" has appeared on a single and the third time for "It Ain't Me Babe".

May

Although it was never used in the James Bond film Cash records a song called "Thunderball". It was a version by Tom Jones that was eventually chosen as the theme song for the film.

June

"Mister Garfield"/"The Streets Of Laredo" (Columbia 4-43313) released. Both titles are from the forthcoming *Ballads Of The True West* album.

3 June

Cash has his first UK hit when "It Ain't Me Babe" charts and reaches #28 during a run of eight weeks.

July

"The Sons Of Katie Elder"/"A Certain Kinda Hurtin'" (Columbia 4-43342) released.

July

An instrumental by The Tennessee Three is issued – "Cattle Call"/"Bill's Theme" (Columbia 4-43299).

10 July

"Mister Garfield" debuts at #46 and will remain on the charts for 13 weeks.

25 July

At the Newport Festival Bob Dylan shocks his audience by playing an electric guitar. Cash defended Dylan in *Broadside* magazine when he pointed out that it was what he said, not how he said it that mattered. Cash ended with the comment "Shut up and let him sing!"

29 July

American Legion Auditorium, Greeneville, Tennessee.

30 July

Columbus, Georgia.

31 July

Little Rock, Arkansas.

August

"I Walk The Line"/"Orange Blossom Special" (Columbia 4-33101) released.

1 August

Hot Springs, Arkansas.

14 August

Illinois State Fair, Springfield, Illinois.

16 August

Mary Baldwin College, Staunton, Virginia.

17–18 August

Fair, Roanoke, Virginia.

20 August

Gibson County Fair, Princeton, Indiana.

22 August

Mockingbird Hill Park, Anderson, Indiana.

24–25 August

Franklin Country Fair, Malone, New York.

27–28 August

Lagoon Park, Salt Lake City, Utah.

29 August

Red Rocks Theater, Denver, Colorado.

September

The double album *Ballads Of The True West* (C2L38/C2S838) is released.

Tracks: "Hiawatha's Vision", "Road To Kaintuck", "Shifting, Whispering Sands (Part 1)", "Narration", "Ballad Of Boot Hill", "I Ride An Old Paint", "Narration", "Hardin Wouldn't Run", "Narration", "Mister Garfield", "Streets Of Laredo", "Narration", "Johnny Reb", "A Letter From Home", "Bury Me Not On The Lone Prairie", "Mean As Hell", "Sam Hall", "Twenty-Five Minutes To Go", "The Blizzard", "Narration", "Sweet Betsy From Pike", "Green Grow The Lilacs",

"Narration", "Stampede", "Shifting, Whispering Sands (Part 2)", "Reflections"

4 September
"The Sons Of Katie Elder" enters the chart at #50 and during its chart run will reach #10.

October
Cash's dependence on pills finally lands him in trouble with the law. Crossing the Mexican border from Juarez into El Paso, Texas he is caught with hundreds of pills that he had stashed into his guitar case. He spends a night in jail and is bailed the next day.

October
"Happy To Be With You"/"Pickin' Time" (Columbia 4-43420) released.

2 October
Tour closes in Dallas, Texas.

29 October
Back in 1959 Cash had recorded foreign language versions of two of his hits and today he recorded more tracks in German. Unlike the previous session only one song is a Cash original - "Wer Kennt Den Weg" ("I Walk The Line") the other three being "In Virginia", "Kleine Rosmarie" and "Besser So, Jenny-Joe". The original backing for "Wer Kennt Den Weg" was used while German musicians were utilised for the other three tracks.

1966

January
The *Everybody Loves A Nut* album is recorded.

January
"The One On The Right Is On The Left"/"Cotton Pickin' Hands" (Columbia 4-43496) released.

January
During the month Carl Perkins would become a permanent member of the Johnny Cash Show.

1 January
Although it first charted back in November 1965, "Happy To Be With You" reaches its high of #9 on this day.

12 February
The humorous "The One On The Right Is On The Left" starts its 18-week run when it enters the chart at #45. It will go on to peak at # 2 in April.

March
Mean As Hell (CL-2446/CS-9246), a condensed version of the *Ballads Of The True West* album, is released.
Tracks: "Shifting, Whispering Sands (Part 1)", "I Ride An Old Paint", "Road To Kaintuck", "A Letter From Home", "Mean As Hell", "Twenty-Five Minutes To Go", "Mister Garfield", "The Blizzard", "Streets Of Laredo", "Sweet Betsy From Pike", "Stampede", "Bury Me Not On The Lone Prairie".

2 April
Mean As Hell enters the charts at #30. Considering the material had been released the previous year on *Ballads Of The True West* it does well when it reaches #4 during an 18-week run.

9 April
Des Moines, Iowa.

15 April
Rochester, Minnesota.

16 April
Minneapolis, Minnesota.

19 April
Rockford, Illinois.

22 April
Fargo, North Dakota.

23 April
Grand Forks, North Dakota.

24 April
Duluth, Minnesota.

May
"Everybody Loves A Nut"/"Austin Prison" (Columbia 4-43673) released. This is the second single to be lifted from the forthcoming *Everybody Loves A Nut* album and it will spend nine weeks on the charts in July and August, reaching a high of #17.

5–6 May
Johnny Cash, June Carter and manager Saul Hollif arrive at London Airport for the start of their British tour. The next day a press conference is held at the Pickwick Club in Gt. Newport Street, London.

7 May
UK tour opens with a show at the Empire, Liverpool.
The Statler Brothers opened each show, followed by June Carter, and then Johnny Cash and the Tennessee Three took the stage. Songs performed on this tour included: "Big River", "Busted", "Rock Island Line", "I Still Miss Someone", "Streets Of Laredo", "Joe Bean", "Orange Blossom Special", "Remember The Alamo", "I Walk The Line", "It Ain't Me Babe", "Waiting For A Train", "Ring Of Fire", "Guess Things Happen That Way",

"Ballad Of A Teenage Queen", "Were You There (When They Crucified My Lord)", "Forty Shades Of Green", "I Got Stripes", "Five Feet High And Rising", "The One On The Right Is On The Left", "Gotta Travel On", "Supper Time", "Dark As A Dungeon" and "I Ride An Old Paint".

8 May
City Hall, Birmingham.

11 May
Throughout April and May Bob Dylan is playing a series of concerts in Europe and across the United Kingdom. During his show at Sofia Gardens in Cardiff Cash, on a day off from his own tour, meets Dylan backstage. An impromptu recording of "I Still Miss Someone" with Dylan on the piano is included in the documentary about the tour, *Eat The Document*, which remains unreleased.

12 May
City Hall, Sheffield.

13 May
Odeon, Glasgow.

14 May
Palace, Manchester.

15 May
Odeon, Hammersmith.

17 May
Adelphi, Dublin.

20 May
A.B.C. Theatre, Belfast.

22 May
Granada, Walthamstow.

Following the tour and on his return to the States Cash wrote to the UK Appreciation Society: "It was a wonderful trip for us all. In most places during the three weeks in England, Scotland and Ireland the attendance and enthusiasm was far more than we had expected it to be. We will always have a warm spot in our hearts for your country, and we are anxious for the scheduled return."

June

Everybody Loves A Nut (CL-2492/CS-9292) is released.
Tracks: "Everybody Loves A Nut", "The One On The Right Is On The Left", "A Cup Of Coffee", "Bug That Tried To Crawl Around The World", "Singing Star's Queen", "Austin Prison", "Dirty Old Egg-Sucking Dog", "Take Me Home", "Please Don't Play Red River Valley", "Boa Constrictor", "Joe Bean"

June

Throughout the month Cash plays concerts in Baltimore, Washington, Brooklyn, Knoxville, Nashville and Memphis. While in New York he appears on Pete Seeger's TV Show.

June

Souvenir Picture And Songbook, another Hill & Range Songs publication, features the music and lyrics to nine of Cash's songs including "Forty Shades Of Green", "Tennessee Flat Top Box" and "Were You There (When They Crucified My Lord)". Although published in 1966 the cover shot was an early live photo. Inside was a further 14 pages of photos.

July

More concerts in Dallas, Oklahoma City, Tulsa, St. Louis, and Chicago.

August

Columbia release "Boa Constrictor"/ "Bottom Of A Mountain" (Columbia 4-43763).

August

The *Everybody Loves A Nut* album spends all of August on the country chart and also enters the pop charts.

10 August

Auditorium, Lubbock, Texas.

12 August

Auditorium, Colorado Springs, Colorado.

13 August

Lagoon Ballroom, Salt Lake City, Utah.

14 August

Red Rocks Theatre, Denver, Colorado.

10 September

"Boa Constrictor" was probably one comedy single too many and it only manages to spend five weeks in the charts with a high of #39.

20 September

Capitol Theatre, Ottawa, Canada.

22 September

Forum, Montreal.

23 September

T. C. Williams High School, Alex, Virginia.

24 September

Coliseum, Winston-Salem, North Carolina.

25 September

Memorial Auditorium, Norfolk, Virginia.

30 September

Charleston, West Virginia.

1 October

Coliseum, Knoxville, Tennessee.

2 October

Mosque, Richmond, Virginia.

8 October

Municipal Auditorium, Birmingham, Alabama.

14 October

Memorial Auditorium, Greenville, North Carolina.

15 October
Memorial Auditorium, Grensboro, North Carolina.

16 October
Auditorium, Asheville, North Carolina

November
Happiness Is You (CL-2537/CS-9337) is released.
Tracks: "Happiness Is You", "Guess Things Happen That Way", "Ancient History", "You Comb Her Hair", "She Came From The Mountains", "For Lovin' Me", "No One Will Ever Know", "Is This My Destiny", "A Wound Time Can't Erase", "Happy To Be With You", "Wabash Cannonball"

November
"You Beat All I Ever Saw"/"Put The Sugar To Bed" (Columbia 4-43921) released.

November
Folsom Prison, California.

November
Proposed dates in the UK are cancelled.

5 November
Auditorium, Oakland, California.

10 November
Swing Auditorium, San Bernardino, California.

12 November
"Happiness Is You" enters the country charts at #40 and during a chart run of 26 weeks, taking it through to May 1967, the album will reach a high of #10.

13 November
Civic Auditorium, Bakersfield, California.

22 November
Cash performs "Bottom Of A Mountain" and "Orange Blossom Special" on *Swinging Country*.

1 December
Dallas, Texas.

2 December
Little Rock, Arkansas.

3 December
Shreveport, Louisiana.

4 December
San Antonio, Texas.

13 December
Mississippi.

24 December
"You Beat All I Ever Saw" makes its chart debut at #66. It will manage to reach the top twenty early in 1967.

1967

January
"The One On The Right Is On The Left"/"Boa Constrictor" (Columbia 4-33109) released. Both tracks, which are taken from the *Everybody Loves A Nut* album, have been released on singles previously.

11 January
Johnny Cash and June Carter record the duet "Jackson". More sessions followed during which time they recorded the *Carryin On...* album and Cash would also record tracks for the *Sea To Shining Sea* album.

14 January
Chattanooga, Tennessee.

18 January
Auditorium, Atlanta, Georgia.
19 January
Albany, Georgia.

20 January
Savannah, Georgia.

21 January
Township Auditorium, Columbia, South Carolina.

22 January
Ft. Homer Hesterly Armory, Tampa, Florida.

26 January
Dade County Auditorium, Miami, Florida.

February
"Jackson"/"Pack Up Your Sorrows" (Columbia 4-44011) released. Both sides of this single feature June Carter and in the eighties Cash would say about the song "June and I had probably been singing Jackson for about three years before we ever recorded it."

14 February
Municipal Auditorium, Fort Smith, Arkansas.

15 February
Shrine Mosque, Springfield, Missouri.

16 February
Civic Center Music Hall, Oklahoma City, Oklahoma.

17 February
Assembly Center, Tulsa, Oklahoma.

18 February
Memorial Hall, Salina, Kansas.

19 February
Memorial Building, Kansas City, Kansas.

20 February
Municipal Auditorium, Sioux City, Iowa.

21 February
Coliseum, Sioux Falls, South Dakota.

22 February
Municipal Auditorium, Topeka, Kansas.

24 February
Cortillion Ballroom, Wichita, Kansas.

25 February
Pershing Auditorium, Lincoln, Nebraska.

26 February
Music Hall, Omaha, Nebraska.

March
From Sea To Shining Sea (CL-2647/CS-9447) is released.
Tracks: "From Sea To Shining Sea", "Whirl And The Suck", "Call Daddy from The Mine", "Frozen Four-Hundred-Pound Fair-To-Middlin' Cotton Picker", "Walls Of A Prison", "The Masterpiece", "You And Tennessee", "Another Song To Sing",

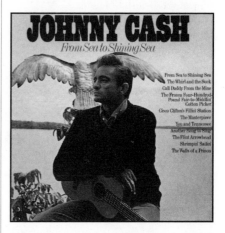

"Flint Arrowhead", "Cisco Clifton's Fillin' Station", "Shrimpin' Sailin'", "From Sea To Shining Sea".

4 March
The Johnny Cash and June Carter duet "Jackson" debuts at #71. During its 17-week residency on the chart it will stop just short of the top spot, stalling at #2.

1 April
Auditorium, Minot, North Dakota.

2 April
Civic Auditorium, Winnipeg, Manitoba.

3 April
Two shows at the Auditorium, Regina, Saskatchewan.

4 April
Arena, Saskatoon, Saskatchewan.

6 April
Corral, Calgary, Alberta.

7 April
Gardens, Edmonton, Alberta.

8 April
Arena, Victoria, British Columbia.

9 April
Two shows at the Queen Elizabeth Theatre, Vancouver, British Columbia.

20 April
Mayo Civic Center, Rochester, Minnesota.

21 April
Two shows at the Auditorium, Waterloo, Iowa.

22 April
Two shows at the Auditorium, Minneapolis, Minnesota.

23 April
KRNT Theatre, Des Moines, Iowa.

26 April
Two shows at the Grand Theatre, Warsaw, Wisconsin.

27 April
Two shows at the Capitol Theatre, Madison, Wisconsin.

28 April
Memorial Auditorium, Burlington, Iowa.
29 April
Two shows at the War Memorial Building, Cedar Rapids, Iowa.

April-May
Around this time Cash purchases a new house on the edge of Old Hickory Lake in Hendersonville, near Nashville, Tennessee

May
"Long Legged Guitar Pickin' Man"/"You'll Be Alright" (Columbia 4-44158) released. Both sides feature June Carter.

10 June
Lagoon Ballroom, Salt Lake City, Utah.

16 June
Opera House, Seattle, Washington.

17 June
Coliseum, Portland, Oregon.

18 June
Coliseum, Spokane, Washington.

July
With several hits under his belt the time is right to release *Greatest Hits* (CL-2678/CS-9478).
Tracks: "Jackson", "I Walk The Line", "Understand Your Man", "Orange Blossom Special", "The One On The Right Is On The Left", "Ring Of Fire", "It Ain't Me Babe", "Ballad Of Ira Hayes", "The Rebel-Johnny Yuma", "Five Feet High And Rising", "Don't Take Your Guns To Town".

14 July
The album *I Walk The Line* is certified gold by the RIAA (Record Industry Association of America).

22 July
Two shows at the Moultire-Douglas County Fair, Arthur, Illinois.

23 July
Three shows at the Buck Lake Ranch, Angola, Indiana.
22 July
Greatest Hits enters the country charts at #35. It spends three weeks at the top of the charts during its 35-week residency. Sixteen weeks on the pop charts will see it peak at #83.

24 July
"Long Legged Guitar Pickin' Man" starts its 17-week chart run, during which it will reach #6.

August
"Outside Lookin' In"/"Spanish Harlem" (Columbia 4-44264) released. Both sides were instrumentals credited to the Tennessee Three.

20 August
State Fair, Sedalia, Missouri

26 August
State Fair, DuQuoin, Illinois

September
"The Wind Changes"/"Red Velvet" (Columbia 4-44288) released. Following the recent chart successes this single is a relative failure, reaching only #60 during a six-week chart spell.

September
Carryin' On With Johnny Cash And June Carter (CL-2728/CS-9528) is released.
Tracks: "Long-Legged Guitar Pickin' Man", "Shantytown", "It Ain't Me, Babe", "Fast Boat To Sidney", "Pack Up Your Sorrows", "I Got A Woman", "Jackson", "Oh, What A Good Thing We Had", "You'll Be All Right", "No, No, No", "What'd I Say".

This album and the earlier release *From Sea To Shining Sea* were the last to be produced by Don Law, who resigned in the spring of 1967. Bob Johnston took over and his first album *Johnny Cash At Folsom Prison*, recorded and released in 1968, was an idea that Don Law had been trying to get off the ground.

September-December
With his *Greatest Hits* album still in the charts Cash has another chart album with *Carryin' On With Johnny Cash And June Carter* which, while only reaching #5, spends 17 weeks in the top forty.

3-4 September
Two shows each day at the State Fair, Detroit, Michigan.

16 September
Two shows at the Consistory Auditorium, Freeport, Illinois.

17 September
Two shows at the Masonic Temple, Davenport, Iowa.

18 September
Hilltopper Football Stadium, Ft. Leonard Wood, Missouri.

19 September
Memorial Hall, Salina, Kansas.

20 September
Memorial Building, Joplin, Missouri.

21 September
Springfield, Missouri.

23 September
Two shows at the Jamboree Hall, Wheeling, West Virginia.

24 September
Two shows at the Auditorium, Norfolk, Virginia.

October
Bob Johnston takes over as producer at Cash's sessions.

17 October
I.M.A. Auditorium, Flint, Michigan.

18 October
L.C. Walker Arena, Muskegon, Michigan.

19 October
Civic Auditorium, Grand Rapids, Michigan.

20 October
Central High School, Kalamazoo, Michigan.

21 October
Morris Civic Auditorium, South Bend, Indiana.

22 October
Civic Center, Lansing, Michigan.

24 October
Scottish Rite Building, Ft. Wayne, Indiana.

25 October
Stambaugh Auditorium, Youngstown, Ohio.

26 October
Montgomery County Memorial Auditorium, Dayton, Ohio.

27 October
H. McMorran Arena, Pt. Huron, Michigan.

28 October
Franklin Memorial Building, Columbus, Ohio.

29 October
Two shows at the Auditorium, Saginaw, Michigan.

November
"Rosanna's Going Wild"/"Roll Call" (Columbia 4-44373) released.

November
Californian tour including dates in San Diego, San Carlos and Los Angeles.

December
"Jackson"/"Long Legged Guitar Pickin' Man" (Columbia 4-33120) released. Both sides of this single featuring June Carter had been released earlier in the year.

23 December
"Rosanna's Going Wild" sees a return to form when it debuts at #44 and goes on to hit #2 in early 1968.

1968-1971

"The concert recorded at Folsom Prison in February, 1968, was our second appearance at Folsom. Back in 1966, Rev. Gressett had asked me on behalf of the inmates he had met and counselled there to come and give a performance. Because of the response, I had talked for two years about possibly recording an album in a prison. After the first concert, I was invited to come back any time and do the recorded concert."

from *MAN IN BLACK* by Johnny Cash 1976

1968

3 January
The year starts with the news that Vivian Liberto has been granted a decree nisi. After 14 years their marriage is over.

10 January
Cash and the rest of the band members travel to Sacramento.

11-12 January
The whole troupe, who are booked into a motel a few miles from Folsom, run through the complete show in preparation for the next day's concert and recording. Near midnight Rev. Gressett turned up at the motel with a tape of a song written by inmate Glen Sherley. Cash was so impressed with the song, "Greystone Chapel", that he spent the next few hours learning the lyrics.

13 January
Cash performs a concert for the inmates at the infamous Folsom Prison in California. On stage with Cash are the Tennessee Three (Luther Perkins, Marshall Grant and W. S. "Fluke" Holland), Carl Perkins, June Carter, The Carter Family and The Statler Brothers.

Throughout his career Cash had given concerts for inmates in some of America's most notorious prisons. He appeared at San Quentin as early in his career as 1960. For a long time he had wanted to record an album inside Folsom but, unfortunately, Columbia had not been keen on the idea. It was only when Bob Johnston took over from Don Law as Cash's producer that Johnston managed to persuade Columbia to give the project the go ahead. The result was one of Cash's best and most moving albums.

Folsom held over 2,000 inmates and from the album it sounds like a good proportion of them were present for the one-hour

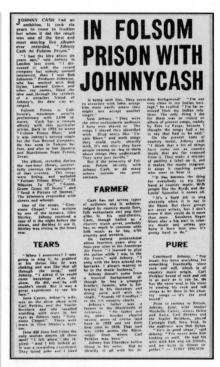

IN FOLSOM PRISON WITH JOHNNY CASH

JOHNNY CASH had an ambition. It took six years to come to fruition but when it did the result was one of the best and most moving live albums ever recorded. "Johnny Cash At Folsom Prison."

"I had the idea about six years ago," said Johnny in London last week. "I discussed it with the record company but nobody seemed interested, then I met Bob Johnston." Producer Johnston, who has worked with Bob Dylan, Leonard Cohen and other top names, liked the idea and, through the crevices of a preacher friend of Johnny's, the date was arranged.

Folsom Prison is California's maximum security penitentiary with 2,690 inmates. Cash has a certain affinity with this particular prison. Back in 1954 he wrote "Folsom Prison Blues" and it was Johnny's second single for the Sun Record Company. He has sung in Folsom before, and also in San Quentin and Hutchinson State Prison, Texas.

The album, recorded during the one-hour shows, successfully conveys the atmosphere of that evening. The songs were fitting, and included "Folsom Prison Blues," "25 Minutes To Go," "Green Grass Of Home" and "Send A Picture Of Mother." The prisoners responded with cheers and whoops.

One of the songs, "Greystone Chapel" was written by one of the inmates, Glen Shirley. Johnny received a tape of it the night before the shows, and decided to use it. Shirley was sitting in the front row.

TEARS

"When I announced I was going to sing it, he grabbed at his throat like he was choking and was like that all through the song," said Johnny. "I asked if he could come backstage after the show. He did, and he still couldn't speak. But it was a great experience to see his face."

June Carter, Johnny's wife, was on the show along with Carl Perkins and the Statler Brothers and she recalled standing with tears in her eyes as Johnny sang "Greystone Chapel." "There were tears in Glen Shirley's eyes," too.

How did June feel being the only woman among all those men? "I felt alone," she replied. "And I felt looked at. It was a rewarding experience. They loved John and I liked

it being with him. They seem to associate with John, accept him more easily where they might not accept another singer."

Said Johnny, "They were the most enthusiastic audience I have ever played to. The songs I played they identified with. Drug songs, like "Cocain Blues" and work songs with, it's not often they have people coming to them about things they understand. They were just terrific."

But if the prisoners of Folsom Prison identify with Johnny Cash, so do many others outside the penitentiary.

FARMER

Cash has cut across types of audience and is acknowledged by country music fans, folk enthusiasts and pop fans alike. In his mid-thirties, Cash, though hailed as a country music great, probably has as much in common with folk music as he has with country and western.

He turned professional about fourteen years after a four-year stint in the American Air Force. "I learned to play the guitar while I was in the Air Force," said Johnny. "I sang with the boys around the barracks. I always wanted to be in the music business."

Johnny doesn't come from a musical background although he has a younger brother, Tommy, who is following in his footsteps and doing quite well with his single, "Sounds Of Goodbye," in the U.S. country charts.

Johnny's father was a farmer in the Blacklands of Arkansas. "My father and my older brother cleared twenty acres of cotton land back in 1935 and set their first crop in 1936. That land was, right across, the Mississippi from where Carl Perkins was born."

Johnny has Cherokee Indian blood in his veins. Did he identify at all with his In-

dian background? "I'm not very close to my Indian heritage," he replied. "I'm far removed from my Indian relatives. The only thing I did for them was to record an album of protest songs, mainly by Pete La Farge, because I thought the songs had a lot to say that had to be said."

On the present state of country music, Johnny said: "I think that a lot of things have come out as country music that are far removed from it. They make a mistake of putting a label on it, and it makes the music stagnate. It stops it reaching people who want to hear it.

"It has become the thing for everybody to try their hand at country music. With people like the Byrds and the Lovin' Spoonful it comes off.

PURE

"It's a hard job to sing sincerely when it is not in the blood. But these groups are great artists, but I don't know if they could do it more than once. Southern Negro blues play a big part in country music and unless you have it born into you, it's pretty hard to do."

Continued Johnny: "Pop music has been searching for something frantically since rock and roll, which is of country music origin. Carl Perkins' brand of rock and roll is as pure as it can be. He has the same soul in his since in singing his rock and roll songs as he does in his country songs — it's the soul sound."

Prior to coming to Britain, Johnny, June, with Mother Maybelle Carter, sisters Helen and Anita, Carl Perkins and the Statler Brothers, played Carnegie Hall, New York. In the audience was Bob Dylan. "He's in good shape," said Johnny. "I've never seen him looking so well. He had his wife with him and six friends, and we went to dinner together." — TONY WILSON

show. "They were the most enthusiastic audience I have ever played to. The songs I played they identified with. They were just terrific," said Cash after the show and in his sleevenotes for the album he wrote "So for the fourth time I have done so in California, I brought my show to Folsom. Prisoners are the greatest audience that an entertainer can perform for."

February
Cash proposes to June Carter in London, Ontario. At an award ceremony later in the month, Cash announces "This will be a fine wedding present" during his acceptance speech. Up to that point nobody knew the wedding was going ahead.

2 February
Cash visits several hospitals in Memphis and later in the day entertains the sick and wounded at the Navy Hospital in Millington, Tennessee, many of whom had just returned from Vietnam.

3 February
Today is designated Homecoming Day for Johnny Cash in Memphis and he is given the key to the city. In the evening he appears before a crowd of 12,500 people, the biggest audience ever to attend a country show in the Memphis and mid-south area.

4 February
Another Homecoming Day, this time in Dyess, Arkansas where a crowd of over 4,000 turn out to see him. The scheduled one show had to be extended to two in order to cope with the capacity crowd of friends who turned up. The Mayor of Dyess called it "The biggest crowd Dyess has seen since 1936 when Eleanor Roosevelt came to dedicate the community."

10 February
From Sea To Shining Sea starts its 14-week chart run when it enters at #34.

February
Johnny Cash spends most of February on the road.

16 February
Stanley Warner Theatre, Jersey City, New Jersey.

17 February
Kleinhans Music Hall, Buffalo, New York.

18 February
Two shows at the Auditorium Theatre, Rochester, New York.

19 February
Two shows at the Massey Hall, Toronto, Ontario.

20 February
Civic Centre, Brantford, Ontario.

21 February
Tapes C.B.C. Special *O'Keefe Presents*.

22 February
The Gardens, London, Ontario.

23 February
Two shows at the Warner Theatre, Erie, Pennsylvania.

24 February
Two shows at the Civic Theatre, Akron, Ohio.

25 February
Two shows at the Masonic Temple, Scranton, Pennsylvania.

29 February
Cash finally wins a Grammy Award at the annual awards show covering the period 2 November 1966-1 November 1967. "Jackson", his duet with June Carter, takes the honours in the 'Best Country & Western Performance Duet, Trio or Group (Vocal or Instrumental)' category.

1 March
At 3.00 pm Johnny Cash and June Carter marry at a small private ceremony at the Methodist Church in Franklin, Kentucky. Merle Kilgore was best man and Micky Brooks was June's Matron of Honour. A reception follows at their house in Hendersonville.

9 March
Following his recent wedding Johnny Cash hits the road again for a series of concert dates, opening with a show at the Virginia Polytechnic Institute in Blacksburg, Virginia.

11 March
Corn Palace, Mitchell, South Dakota.

12 March
Two shows at the Coliseum, Sioux Falls, South Dakota.

13 March
Pershing Auditorium, Lincoln, Nebraska.

14 March
Municipal Auditorium, Topeka, Kansas.

15 March
Two shows at the Cotillion Ballroom, Wichita, Kansas.

16 March
Shrine Mosque, Springfield, Missouri.

17 March
Memorial Building, Kansas City, Kansas.

15 April
Mary Sawyer Auditorium, La Crosse, Wisconsin.

16 April
Two shows at the Shrine Auditorium, Rockford, Illinois.

17 April
Two shows at the Orpheum Theatre, Madison, Wisconsin.

18 April
Mayo Civic Centre, Rochester, Minnesota.

19 April
Two shows at the Veterans Memorial Coliseum, Cedar Rapids, Iowa.

20 April
Auditorium, Minneapolis, Minnesota.

21 April
Three shows at the KRNT Theatre, Des Moines, Iowa.

April
"Folsom Prison Blues"/"The Folk Singer" (Columbia 4-44513) is released. The a-side is lifted from the *Johnny Cash At Folsom Prison* album and features the trademark intro - "Hello, I'm Johnny Cash."

2–3 May
The Johnny Cash Show arrives in the UK for a series of concerts. Before the tour starts a press conference is held.

4 May
Cash opens his UK tour with a show at the Free Trade Hall in Manchester.

5 May
Two shows at the Guildhall, Portsmouth.

6 May
US Military Installation, Mildenhall, Newmarket.

7 May
Capitol, Cardiff, Wales.

8 May
Colston Hall, Bristol.

9 May
Royal Albert Hall, London.

10 May
Granada, Kingston, Surrey.

10 May
During the day a special session was taped at the BBC studios in Piccadilly featuring Cash, June Carter-Cash, Carl Perkins and The Tennessee Three. Opening with "Big

River", Cash performed several songs before handing over to Carl Perkins who kicked off his section with "Lake County Cotton Country" and followed with several of his hits. Cash returned to perform a selection of material from his *Folsom Prison* album after which June Carter joined to finish the show with a selection of duets and gospel numbers.

11 May
Granada, Walthamstow, London.

12 May
Liverpool Empire.

13 May
Town Hall, Birmingham.

14 May
Granada, Bedford.

15 May
Cash played another show at a US Military Installation.

16 May
Odeon, Glasgow, Scotland.

17 May
Usher Hall, Edinburgh, Scotland.

18 May
ABC Cinema, Carlisle.

19 May
Newcastle.

June
The recent live prison recordings are issued as *Johnny Cash At Folsom Prison* (CL-2839/CS-9639).
Tracks: "Folsom Prison Blues", "Dark As A Dungeon", "I Still Miss Someone", "Cocaine Blues", "Twenty-Five Minutes To Go", "Orange Blossom Special", "Long Black Veil", "Send A Picture Of Mother", "The Wall", "Dirty Old Egg–Sucking Dog", "Flushed From The Bathroom Of Your Heart", "Jackson", "Give My Love To

Rose", "I Got Stripes", "Green, Green Grass Of Home", "Greystone Chapel"

Hill & Range Songs publish the *Johnny Cash At Folsom Prison* songbook, selling at $2.95. Within the 40 pages are the lyrics and music to 13 of the songs featured on the album, along with 6 pages of photos.

1 June
After entering the US country charts at #47 the single "Folsom Prison Blues" spends four weeks at #1 during its 18-week chart residency. During a 12-week spell on the pop charts it manages to reach #32.

6 June
Two shows at the Municipal Auditorium, Fort Smith, Arkansas.

7 June
Memorial Hall, Joplin, Missouri.

8 June
Assembly Centre, Muskogee, Oklahoma.

9 June
Coliseum, Oklahoma City, Oklahoma.

10 June
Convention Hall, Enid, Oklahoma.

11 June
Sports Arena, Hutchinson, Kansas.

12 June
Memorial Hall, Salina, Kansas.

13 June
Municipal Auditorium, Sioux City, Iowa.

14 June
Two shows at the Music Hall, Omaha, Nebraska.

15 June
City Auditorium, St. Joseph, Missouri.

15 June
The live prison album *At Folsom Prison* enters the country chart at #24. It will spend more than 90 weeks on the chart peaking at #1 for three weeks in July-August. The success of the album pushes sales of other Cash product, resulting in *Greatest Hits* spending a further 16 weeks on the charts. The same story unfolds on the pop charts with *Folsom Prison* registering an incredible 122 weeks in the top 200, much of it spent in the top half of the chart.

16 June
Hilltopper Stadium, Ft. Leonard Wood, Missouri.

29 June
The special show recorded by the BBC during Cash's recent UK tour is broadcast at 9.00pm on Radio 2.

6 July
Old Golden Throat peaks at number 37 in the UK. The album is a mixture of tracks dating back to 1958, early sixties leftovers and recent recordings, including two instrumental tracks credited to The Tennessee Three. In their review *Record Mirror* said "Interesting selection—for all Cash addicts, even the most recent converts." A second album, *More Of Old Golden Throat*, will also be released but will fail to chart.

July-August
Cash records tracks for his forthcoming religious set *The Holy Land*. Narration for the album was recorded by Cash and June on a portable tape machine during a recent trip to the Holy Land. As they travelled across the Holy Land various sites of Biblical importance were pointed out in the narratives. Among the tracks recorded was the Carl Perkins composition "Daddy Sang Bass".

6 July
Two shows at the WWVA Jamboree, Wheeling, West Virginia.

7 July
Two shows at the Frontier Ranch Park, Columbus, Ohio.

9 July
Rapid City, South Dakota.

10 July
Idaho Falls, Idaho.

11 July
Boise, Idaho.

12 July
Twin Falls, Idaho.

13 July
Two shows at the Lagoon Ballroom, Salt Lake City, Utah.

24-28 July
Rehearsals and taping for the *Summer Brothers Smothers Show*.

28 July
Two shows at the Buck Lake Ranch, Angola, Indiana.

4 August
Two shows at the Sangamon Park, Monticello, Illinois.

5 August
Guitarist Luther Perkins dies from his injuries sustained during a fire at his home. Two days earlier he had fallen asleep with a

lighted cigarette and was rushed to Vanderbilt Medical Center with 50% burns. Perkins, who was 40, leaves a wife, Margie, and four daughters. Ralph Emery summed up everybody's feelings when he said "It will be hard to adjust to a world without Luther. He was loved by everyone."

7 August
The funeral service for Luther Perkins is held in Hendersonville. Pallbearers include Johnny Cash, Marshall Grant, W. S. Holland and Carl Perkins.

11 August
Two shows at the Frontier City, Onsted, Michigan.

14 August
Arena, Glace Bay, Nova Scotia.

15 August
Two shows at the Capitol Theatre, Halifax, Nova Scotia.

16 August
Arena, Moncton, New Brunswick.

17 August
Beaverbrook Arena, Fredericton, New Brunswick.

18 August
Two shows at the Lone Star Ranch, Reeds Ferry, New Hampshire.

4 September
Municipal Auditorium, Austin, Texas.

5 September
Two shows at the Municipal Auditorium, Beaumont, Texas.

6 September
Sportatorium, Dallas, Texas.

7 September
Two shows at the Municipal Auditorium, Shreveport, Louisiana.

8 September
Two shows at the Hemis Fair Arena, San Antonio, Texas.

11 September
Municipal Auditorium, Amarillo, Texas.

12 September
Auditorium, Lubbock, Texas.

13 September
Coliseum, El Paso, Texas.

14 September
City Auditorium, Colorado Springs, Colorado.

15 September
Auditorium, Denver, Colorado.

20 September
Following Luther's death, Carl Perkins, no relation, had been filling in as lead guitarist on Cash's shows. On this day they were due

to play a show in Fayetteville, Arkansas. Marshall and Carl had been delayed on their flight from Memphis due to bad weather and just before showtime there was only Cash, June and W.S.Holland. It was then that a young man introduced himself to Cash. "You need me. I can play all your songs", commented Bob Wootton. When Cash asked him "Do you play like Luther", he replied "Nobody can do that. But I'll try if you want me to". "Get out and plug your guitar in" said Cash and Wootton, who knew every song, found himself on stage in front of a crowd of more than 7,000 people. Following the show Cash offered him a job and a few days later he became a permanent member of The Tennessee Three.

21 September
Coliseum, Charlotte, North Carolina.

22 September
Auditorium, Norfolk, Virginia.

28 September
State Fair Grounds, Memphis, Tennessee.

17 October
At the annual Country Music Association awards ceremony Cash wins the 'Best Album' award for *Johnny Cash At Folsom Prison*.

23 October
Cash appears at the famous Carnegie Hall. A full house greeted Cash and among the sold out crowd sat Bob Dylan and Janis Joplin. In his review Robert Shelton, *New York Times* music critic, wrote "Soul music of a rare kind - country soul from the concerned and sensitive white south — that Northerners tend to forget — was heard Wednesday night at Carnegie Hall as Johnny Cash made a stirring comeback to New York."

25 October
Cash undertakes his second UK tour of the year. The opening date is at the Odeon, Manchester. Also on the show were

regulars The Tennessee Three, June Carter, The Statler Brothers and Carl Perkins.

26 October
Liverpool Empire.

27 October
Palladium, London. Plans were made to tape the show for future release but they did not materialise.

30 October
Johnny Cash At Folsom Prison is certified gold by the RIAA (Record Industry Association of America).

November
"Daddy Sang Bass"/"He Turned The Water Into Wine" (Columbia 4-44689) released. The a-side is a track written by Carl Perkins and both tracks are taken from the *The Holy Land* album.

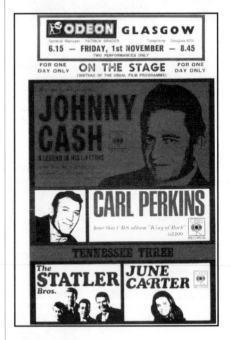

1 November
Odeon, Glasgow.

2 November
Granada, Walthamstow.

3 November
Theatre, Birmingham.

10 November
Two shows at the Masonic Temple, Davenport, Iowa.

11 November
Two shows at the Bay Theatre, Green Bay, Wisconsin.

12 November
Two shows at the Craig Senior High School Auditorium, Janesville, Wisconsin.

14 November
Two shows at the Senior High School Gym, Jacksonville, North Carolina.

15 November
Municipal Auditorium, Charleston, West Virginia.

16 November
Two shows at the Civic Auditorium, Kingsport, Tennessee.

17 November
Two shows at the Kiel Auditorium, St. Louis, Missouri.

30 November-8 December
Northwest US and Canadian Tour.

7 December
"Daddy Sang Bass" debuts at #50 on the country chart and will eventually hold the top spot for 6 weeks while registering a total of 20 weeks. Ten weeks on the pop chart sees it peak at #42. This is the start of a very successful spell of chart activity for Cash that will run through to late 1970.

9 December
As far back as 1964 Cash had publicly spoken about the plight of the American Indian and had released an album of songs - *Bitter Tears* - that was ignored by the majority of the music press. For several months he had wanted to put on a benefit show for the Sioux Indians and his chance came on this day. The show was held at the St. Francis Indian Mission, St. Francis, South Dakota, and a film crew from New York filmed the show and the events that followed for an hour-and-a-half-long documentary on Cash for transmission in early 1969. During the show he performed several songs from the *Bitter Tears* album, including "Custer", "Drums" and "As Long As The Grass Shall Grow". The highlight of the show was his rendition of "The Ballad Of Ira Hayes". Before singing the song he told the audience "Let's have the house lights turned up so we can look each other in the eye and tell it like it really is." After the show the locals put on some dances and gave out gifts to the performers and this was followed by a small get-together.

The next day the troupe drove the 100 miles to the Wounded Knee Battlefield. It was here that nearly 300 bodies, mainly women and children, were buried following the massacre by white soldiers back in 1890. Again they met up with a group of Indians and after finding out that they had been unable to travel to the show the previous night proceeded to give an impromptu performance.

December
The year was one of the most successful for Cash since the fifties and the end-of-year polls reflect this. The following list details just some of his achievements of 1968:

TOP COUNTRY SINGLES
No. 5   Folsom Prison Blues
No. 29   Rosanna's Going Wild

TOP COUNTRY ALBUMS
No. 23   Johnny Cash At Folsom
                   Prison
No. 27   Johnny Cash's Greatest
Hits - volume one
No. 38   From Sea To Shining Sea

TOP COUNTRY SINGLES ARTISTS
No. 10   Johnny Cash
                (Male Vocalist)

TOP COUNTRY ARTISTS - ALBUMS
No. 6   Johnny Cash

ARTISTS DISCOGRAPHY - SINGLES
No. 5   Johnny Cash

ARTISTS DISCOGRAPHY - ALBUMS
No. 5   Johnny Cash

1969

9-29 January
Johnny Cash and June Carter leave Los Angeles for a three-week tour of the Far East. Scheduled appearances include Tokyo, Okinawa, Manila and Vietnam, where they play for the U.S. Forces at the Long Binh Air Force Base in Saigon. During their time in Vietnam they often played more than ten shows a day for the troops.

15 January
The *Kraft Music Hall* TV show, taped the previous December, is broadcast.

18 February
Following a session on the 17th, Cash records tracks with folk hero Bob Dylan. Of the tracks recorded only one will find an official release. "Girl from The North Country" appears on Dylan's *Nashville Skyline*, an album that would win Cash yet another Grammy Award, for his sleeve notes. The remaining tracks are not considered good enough for release and stay in the vaults. Other tracks recorded at the session included "I Walk The Line", "Big River", "'T' For Texas", "You Are My Sunshine" and a version of "Careless Love" which runs for over six minutes. The tracks do find a release on bootleg and are snapped up by both Cash and Dylan fans. At the time rumours were rife that Columbia were intending to release the material on a joint Dylan/Cash album, and that promoter Mervyn Conn was trying to arrange a tour featuring both artists.

22 February–3 March
Concert dates in California. These are the first concerts promoted by Lou Robin and Allen Tinkley.

24 February
Following the success of the Folsom Prison recordings, Columbia decided to repeat the exercise at another California state penitentiary, this time San Quentin. A crew from the British TV station Granada were also present to film the show for transmission later in the year. The producer, Jo Durden-Smith, said of San Quentin "It is the most evil place I have ever been in."

One of the highlights of the show is "A Boy Named Sue", the amusing story of a boy saddled with a girl's name, which Cash only learnt the night before. It was written by Shel Silverstein, a former cartoonist for *Playboy* magazine. Cash called it "the most cleverly written song I've ever heard." For release the song had the "son of a bitch" line bleeped.

February
The religious set *The Holy Land* (KCS-9726) is released.
Tracks: "Prologue", "Land Of Israel", "A Mother's Love", "This Is Nazareth", "Nazarene", "Town Of Cana", "He Turned The Water Into Wine", "My Wife June At The Sea Of Galilee", "Beautiful Words", "Our Guide Jacob At Mt. Tabor", "The Ten Commandments", "Daddy Sang Bass", "At The Wailing Wall", "Come To The Wailing Wall", "In Bethlehem", "In The Garden Of Gethsemane", "The Fourth Man", "On The Via Dolorosa", "Church Of The Holy Sepulchre", "At Calvary", "God Is Not Dead".

Hansen Publications, based in Miami, Florida, publish *The Holy Land* songbook to tie in with the albums release. At $2.95

this 64-page book, with an identical cover, featured the music and lyrics to every song and narration from the album. Illustrated with over 26 pages of photos taken in the Holy Land, it came with an additional 20-page book with lyrics to nine of the tracks.

4 March
Coliseum Arena, Oakland, California. Cash sells out this 13,800 seater venue. Also on the bill are Marty Robbins, June Carter-Cash, The Carter Family and The Statler Brothers. With tickets scaled at $2.50 and $5.00 the gross for the show amounted to nearly $50,000.

12 March
Cash is a winner in the 'Best Country Solo Vocal, Male' category with "Folsom Prison Blues" and also takes the 'Best Album Notes (Annotator's Award)' for the album *Johnny Cash At Folsom Prison* at the annual Grammy Awards ceremonies held at the Beverly Hilton Hotel in Los Angeles, the Astor Hotel in New York and at dinners held in Nashville and Chicago. The awards covered an eligibility period of 2 November 1967 – 1 November 1968.

April
The Holy Land reaches #6 on the charts, not bad for an album of religious material. It spends a respectable 25 weeks in the chart. It also makes an appearance on the pop chart.

16 April
Cash's first ABC-TV Show is filmed with guests Jeannie C. Riley, The Rouse Brothers, Joe Tex and Ron Carey. Glen Campbell is also scheduled to appear but his section is filmed later. Although this show is taped first it is actually broadcast as Show # 5. The first show broadcast is due to be taped during the first week of May.

17 April
The UK TV magazine TV Times runs a four-page article on *Johnny Cash In San Quentin*.

Mid–April
Johnny Cash is given an *Honorary Life Sentence* at Cummins Prison Farm in Arkansas. His show is filmed by KATV (ABC) in Little Rock for broadcast later in the year.

Mid-April
During the month Cash appears on the *Joey Bishop Show* (15 April), the *Kraft Music Hall* (16 April) and the *Glen Campbell Show* (23 April).

May
The a-sides of Cash's last two singles are paired up and issued as a new single – "Folsom Prison Blues"/"Daddy Sang Bass" (Columbia 4-33153).

4 May
Cobo Arena, Detroit.
This show with Hank Williams Jnr. attracted a crowd of over 23,000 and box office receipts of $93,000.

June
Johnny Cash At San Quentin (CS-9827) is released.

Tracks: "Wanted Man", "Wreck Of The Old '97", "I Walk The Line", "Darling Companion", "Starkville City Jail", "San Quentin #1", "San Quentin #2", "A Boy Named Sue", "Peace In The Valley", "Folsom Prison Blues".

CASH RECORDS SMASH IN JAIL

JOHNNY CASH: AT SAN QUENTIN (CBS mono and stereo 63629; 37s. 6d.).

DESTINED to become a classic, this is Johnny's second "live" prison album, the first being his Folsom LP which was a world-wide smash. It is, in fact, one of the best things he has ever recorded.

He has a rapport with the prisoners which is quite fantastic — here they support him like the more exuberant Glasgow Rangers' fans.

His chat to them about prison life gets them going at the outset, and he goes straight into Bob Dylan's Wanted Man which is a good choice. Backed by the Tennessee Three, Johnny rips and roars the number, then belts on with the famous Wreck Of The Old 97, ends and asks the prisoners what they want to hear; the result is a mighty unanimous roar of I Walk The Line which still sounds as good as ever, but with an added electricity in the atmosphere.

The album was recorded at the end of Johnny's show, which includes his wife, June Carter, Carl Perkins and the Statler Brothers. It is June and Carl that Johnny calls onto stage to join in on Darling Companion and the show had obviously been a good one because the whole place erupts. The album is so natural that even Johnny's asides to the guards are included, plus a few beeps when his language gets too fruity for the record.

He puts himself in the place of the prisoners for San Quentin which he describes as a living Hell and, after some sort of disturbance, sings again! He gets Carl and the entire Carter Family to join in on Folsom Prison Blues, a good number to end on. This is by far one of the best albums I've heard in a long, long time. All praise to everyone concerned, not forgetting the producer, Bob Johnston. RG.

Other tracks: Starkville City Jail, A Boy Named Sue, Peace In The Valley.

June

Jackson Coliseum, Jackson, Tennessee.

7 June

The first ABC-TV *Johnny Cash Show* is broadcast. Cash had been apprehensive about starring in his own networked TV series, but despite his reservations the series became a big hit and would run through to 1971. The show's format permitted Cash to move in and out of the performer's circle as the shows progressed. He appeared in certain numbers along with his guests, in addition to being featured in special production numbers. Specially shot film was sometimes used to illustrate visually the songs he sang. Regulars on all the shows were The Tennessee Three, June Carter, The Statler Brothers, The Carter Family and Carl Perkins. Most of the shows were taped at the famous Ryman Auditorium in Nashville, with the first 13 being taped back in April–May. On this first show his guests are Bob Dylan, Doug Kershaw and Joni Mitchell. The show featured the following songs sung by Cash: "I Walk The Line", "Big River", "Ring Of Fire", "Orange Blossom Special", "I Still Miss Someone", "Come Along And Ride This Train Medley", "Girl From The North Country", "Don't Take Your Guns To Town", "Dirty Old Egg-Sucking Dog", "It Ain't Me Babe", "Daddy Sang Bass".

Note: The following dates shown for the ABC-TV shows are broadcast dates.

14 June

The Johnny Cash Show #2 with special guests Dan Blocker, Gordon Lightfoot and Joey Scarborough.

Songs: "Hey Porter", "For Lovin' Me", "Come Along And Ride This Train Medley", "Folsom Prison Blues", "Get Rhythm", "There You Go", "Still In Town", "The One On The Right Is On The Left", "Swing Low Sweet Chariot"

14 June

Columbia place a full-page ad in *Billboard* Magazine advertising Johnny Cash's latest release. The ad read:

"San Quentin may you rot and burn in hell."

It only takes one night in San Quentin to feel that way.

Not long ago Johnny Cash spent a night in there, singing for the boys.

That's what he felt, and that's what he sang. Cash came by his hatred of prisons the hard way.

That's why he goes back. First to Folsom Prison, now San Quentin.

That's why there's this tremendous affinity with the prisoners.

And that's why there's so much feeling in the music.

Johnny Cash At San Quentin. The brilliant follow-up to Folsom Prison. On Columbia Records

21 June

The Johnny Cash Show #3 with special guests Linda Ronstadt and Eddie Albert.

Songs performed: "Wanted Man", "I Never

Will Marry", "Come Along And Ride This Train Medley", "Sloop John B", "Detroit City", "Rock Island Line", "Cry, Cry, Cry", "I Tremble For You", "Darlin' Companion", "He's Got The Whole World In His Hands".

July

"A Boy Named Sue"/"San Quentin" (Columbia 4-44944) released. The a-side is written by Shel Silverstein who would later record a song called "A Front Row Ticket To Hear Old Johnny Sing". Both tracks are taken from the *San Quentin* live album.

5 July

The Johnny Cash Show #4 with special guests Buffy St. Marie, Doug McLure and The Cowsills.
Songs performed: "I Guess Things Happen That Way", "Custer", "Come Along And Ride This Train Medley", "Cowboy Buckaroo", "Children Go Where I Send Thee", "Cocaine Blues", "Blistered", "Ballad Of A Teenage Queen", "You Beat All I Ever Saw".

5 July

Johnny Cash's second prison album, *San*

Quentin, starts its 48-week chart run when it enters at #38.

12 July

The Johnny Cash Show #5 with special guests Jeannie C. Riley and Glen Campbell. Songs performed: "Folsom Prison Blues", "Bad News", "Come Along And Ride This Train Medley", "I've Been Everywhere", "By The Time I Get To Phoenix", "Folsom Prison Blues", "Galveston", "Abilene", "Arkansas", "I Got Stripes", "I Still Miss Someone", "Jackson", "These Hands"

19 July

The Johnny Cash Show #6 with special guests Joni Mitchell, The Monkees, Roy Clark and Ed Ames.
Songs performed: "Ring Of Fire", "Long Black Veil", "Come Along And Ride This Train Medley", "Love Of The Common People", "Everybody Loves A Nut", "Frankie's Man Johnny", "Sing It Pretty Sue", "The Rebel-Johnny Yuma", "Lead Me Father".

26 July

A Boy Named Sue opens its 14 week chart run when it enters at #54. It goes on to hit the top spot on 22 August, where it will stay for five weeks.

26 July

The Johnny Cash Show #7 with special guests Marty Robbins and Dale Robertson. Songs performed: "Orange Blossom Special", "Streets Of Laredo", "Come Along And Ride This Train Medley", "The Wayward Wind", "Doin' My Time", "I'd Just Be Fool Enough To Cry", "Billy Christian", "He Turned The Water Into Wine".

July-September

Cash holds a series of sessions to record tracks for his next album *Hello, I'm Johnny Cash*. Songs recorded include "See Ruby Fall", "Blistered", "Route 1 Box # 44" and "I've Got A Thing About Trains". His new producer Bob Johnston is at the controls.

August

The Record Industry Association of America (RIAA) give *Johnny Cash At San Quentin* a gold award. The single "A Boy Named Sue" achieves gold status, as does the album *Johnny Cash's Greatest Hits*.

1 August

At San Quentin hits the top spot for its first week in a long run.

2 August

The Johnny Cash Show #8 with special guests Merle Haggard and O. C. Smith.

Songs performed: "Big River", "Sing Me Back Home", "Come Along And Ride This Train Medley", "It Was A Very Good Year", "Bummin' Around", "I've Got Five Dollars And It's Saturday Night", "Country Boy", "What Do I Care", "Long Legged Guitar-Pickin' Man", "Walk With Your Neighbour".

9 August

The Johnny Cash Show #9 with special guests Diana Trask and Pat Boone.

Songs performed: "Understand Your Man", "The Last Thing On My Mind", "Come Along And Ride This Train Medley", "Peace In The Valley", "Train Of Love", "Drums", "Worried Man Blues", "Steal Away".

16 August

The Johnny Cash Show #10 with special guests Melanie and O. C. Smith Jnr.

Songs performed: "Wreck Of The Old '97", "Silver Threads And Golden Needles", "Come Along And Ride This Train Medley", "Hickory Holler's Tramp", "So Doggone Lonesome", "Seasons Of My Heart", "Pack Up Your Sorrows", "The Old Account".

16 August

The Johnny Cash Show #11 with special guests Odetta and Roger Miller.

Songs performed: "I Got Stripes", "Shame And Scandal On The Family", "Come Along And Ride This Train Medley", "King Of The Road", "Tennessee Flat Top Box", "Delia's Gone", "Outside Looking In", "Luther Played The Boogie", "How Great Thou Art".

23 August

San Quentin peaks at number 1 on the pop charts, his only number 1 on this chart, but on the country charts it spends an incredible 20 weeks at the top. Meanwhile the single "A Boy Named Sue" cannot repeat its success on the country charts and stalls at number 2. Both are certified million-sellers. In the UK the album and single will give Cash his biggest hits so far when they reach number 2 and number 4 respectively.

September

With all the renewed interest in Cash's career, Shelby Singleton, owner of all the Sun Records catalogue, releases a flood of singles on his Sun International label. Called 'Summer Cash' the campaign will see all of Cash's original Sun releases re-issued — twenty singles from "Cry Cry Cry"/ "Hey Porter" through "Belshazah"/ "Wide Open Road". This wasn't the end of what seemed to be 'Cashing in' on his career. Over the next couple of years Singleton would compile and release a series of albums including 2 volumes of *Original Golden Hits* (SUN 101 & 102), *Story Songs Of Trains And Rivers* (SUN 104), *Get Rhythm* (SUN 105), *The Singing Storyteller* (SUN 115) and an album that led buyers to believe they were getting a live album, *Showtime* (SUN 106), when in fact it was just a compilation of eleven previously released tracks overdubbed with applause.

September-December

The recent success of both *Folsom Prison* and *San Quentin* and the flood of re-issues by Shelby Singleton result in a virtual stranglehold on the country charts. Throughout this four-month period the top forty will include both prison albums, *Original Golden Hits Vol 1*, *Original*

Golden Hits Vol 2, *Showtime*, *Get Rhythm* and *Story Songs Of Trains And Rivers*. A similar story is unfolding on the pop charts, with nine different albums registering in the top 200.

6 September
The Johnny Cash Show #12 with special guests Charlie Pride.
Songs performed: "Country Boy", "I Can't Help It", "Your Cheating Heart", "Kaw-Liga", "Come Along And Ride This Train Medley", "A Boy Named Sue", "Mister Garfield".

15-18 September
New Mexico State Fair in Albuquerque. Cash broke all previous attendance records during his four days and more than 1,000 fans had to be turned away on the last day.

20 September
The Johnny Cash Show #13 with special guests Ramblin' Jack Elliott, Mama Cass Elliott and Tommy Cash.
Songs performed: "Goin' To Memphis", "Take Me Home", "Come Along And Ride This Train Medley", "Gentle On My Mind", "Little Green Apples", "Honey", "Release Me", "Born To Lose", "I'm Sorry", "Gentle On My Mind", "Come In Stranger", "Do What You Do Well", "Were You There (When They Crucified My Lord)"

27 September
Sold-out show at the Hollywood Bowl.

27 September
The Johnny Cash Show #14 with special guests Roy Orbison and Phil Harris.
Songs performed: "I Walk The Line", "Pretty Woman", "Come Along And Ride This Train Medley", "Folsom Prison Blues", "Cisco Clifton's Filling Station", "Flesh And Blood", "Jackson", "Battle Hymn Of The Republic".
This was the last ABC-TV show of the first series.

October
Cash's new single "Blistered"/"See Ruby Fall" (Columbia 4-45020) is released.

October
Cash is awarded five out of the ten awards at the Country Music Association Awards Ceremony. He takes the top honour in the following categories: 'Entertainer Of The Year', 'Male Vocalist Of The Year', 'Singles Disc Of The Year' with "A Boy Named Sue", 'Vocal Group Of The Year' with June Carter and 'Album Of The Year' for *San Quentin*. The headlines in the trade papers read "Cash sweeps CMA Awards at Biggest-Ever Convention."

Early October
John is cast in a leading role in a made-for-TV film. He plays the part of John Ross in *Trail Of Tears*, the story of the Cherokee Removal of 1838, when the tribe was forced to leave its homeland in northern Georgia and emigrate to Oklahoma. Thousands died during the journey. Most of the filming is done in Georgia.

4 October
The Andy Williams Show, featuring a guest appearance by Cash, is broadcast.

4 October
University of Illinois, Champaign, Illinois.

10 October
Two shows at the Symphony Hall, Newark, New Jersey.

11 October
RPI Field House, Troy, New York.

11 October
Riding on the back of Cash's recent chart success the re-issued "Get Rhythm" spends 12 weeks on the chart, reaching #23. Meanwhile both sides of his latest Columbia single chart and eventually peak at #7 in early 1970.

12 October
Two shows at the Kleinhans Music Hall, Buffalo, New York.

18 October
An article in the *Nashville Banner* points out that Cash is now selling more records than any other recording artist or act in the world – including The Beatles. The information came from Clive Davis, president of Columbia Records, who was quoted as saying "The man Cash is phenomenal in the true sense of the word. For instance his Folsom Prison album which went on sale a year-and-half ago has sold 1,750,000 and his San Quentin album, released only the past summer, has sold 1,300,000 – and both are still selling at the rate of 60,000 weekly."

19 October
Cash entertained music executives at a Columbia Records Luncheon and received a standing ovation.

20-21 October
Shreveport, Louisiana.

23 October
The Forum, Montreal, Quebec.

24 October
Two shows at the National Arts Center, Ottawa, Ontario.

25 October
War Memorial, Rochester, New York.

26 October
Two shows at the Civic Center, Akron, Ohio.

29 October
Cash makes a guest appearance on the Glen Campbell Show.

November
It is announced that Cash has been nominated in the following categories in the Grammy Awards Ceremony to be held in March 1970:
Album Of The Year (*San Quentin*)
Record Of The Year ("A Boy Named Sue")
Best Country Vocal Performance Male ("A Boy Named Sue")
Best Album Notes - Annotator's Award (Bob Dylan's *Nashville Skyline*)

7 November
Two shows at the Bushnell Auditorium, Hartford, Connecticut.

8 November
CYC Auditorium, Scranton, Pennsylvania.

9 November
More than 9,000 pack the Public Hall in Cleveland for Cash's show.

9 Novemeber
The Tom Jones Show is broadcast featuring Cash performing "A Boy Named Sue".

10 November
Cash breaks the attendance record at the Maple Leaf Gardens, Toronto, playing before 18,106 people. The record gross of $93,000 outdistanced even the Beatles. It was the largest indoor crowd that Cash had performed for. The show received no newspaper advertising, only an on-air comment on country station CFGM about his appearance, yet the show was still an early sell-out.

12 November
Memorial Auditorium, Bangor, Maine.

13 November
Two shows at the Music Hall Theatre, Boston, Massachusets.

14 November
War Memorial, Syracuse, New York.

15 November
R. I. Auditorium, Providence, Rhode Island.

16 November
Two shows at the Gannon Auditorium, Erie, Pennsylvania.

22-25 November
Kraft Music Hall, New York City.

28 November
Oklahoma City, Oklahoma.

29 November
Dallas, Texas.

30 November
Houston, Texas.

Late–November
The entire Johnny Cash Show tape a *Kraft Music Hall* Show.

December
Life magazine runs a special Johnny Cash issue.

December
"If I Were A Carpenter"/ "'Cause I Love You" (4-45064) released. The second single to feature tracks from the forthcoming *Hello, I'm Johnny Cash* album.

December
"San Quentin"/"A Boy Named Sue" (Columbia 4-33177) released.

1 December
Jackson, Mississippi.

2 December
Mobile, Alabama.

5 December
Cash appears at Madison Square Garden, New York. The show is a joint presentation by Cash and Radio Station WJRZ in New Jersey.

6 December
His new single "Blistered" hits number 50 while in the UK *Greatest Hits volume 1* peaks at number 23 and has a chart run of six months.

10 December
The *Kraft Music Hall* Show taped at the end of November is broadcast.

Topping off a year where Cash received countless awards both "Folsom Prison Blues" and "Daddy Sang Bass" receive B.M.I. Awards, while he is voted Man Of The Year by Metronome.

1970

January
Hello, I'm Johnny Cash (KCS-9943) is released.
Tracks: "Southwind", "The Devil To Pay", "'Cause I Love You", "See Ruby Fall", "Route #1, Box 144", "Sing A Travelling Song", "If I Were A Carpenter", "To Beat The Devil", "Blistered", "Wrinkled, Crinkled, Wadded Dollar Bill", "I've Got A Thing About Trains", "Jesus Was A Carpenter".

A songbook was published by Hansen Publications in Miami to accompany the album. Retailing at $3.95 the book contained music and lyrics to the album tracks along with a handful of other material, and included 42 pages of photos.

21 January
Following the success of the previous series of Johnny Cash Shows ABC-TV broadcast the first of the new series.

The Johnny Cash Show #15 with special guests Bobbie Gentry and Jose Feliciano.

Songs performed: "I Walk The Line", "Big River", "Orange Blossom Special", "Folsom Prison Blues", "On The Banks Of The Old Ponchartrain", "Come Along And Ride This Train Medley", "Guess Things Happen That Way", "Blistered", "Sing A Travelling Song", "Lonesome Valley", "Worried Man Blues", "If I Were A Carpenter".

28 January
The Johnny Cash Show #16 with special guest Glen Campbell.
Songs performed: "Five Feet High And Rising", "Country Boy", "Five Feet High And Rising", "Come Along And Ride This Train Medley", "Tennessee Flat Top Box", "Orange Blossom Special", "Don't It Make You Wanna Go Home", "South Wind", "No One's Gonna Miss Me", "Peace In The Valley".

29 January
The recently released album *Hello, I'm Johnny Cash* qualifies for a gold award from the RIAA.

4 February
The Johnny Cash Show #17 with special guests Kirk Douglas and Rod McKuen.
Songs performed: "Understand Your Man", "Sugar Time", "Understand Your Man", "I Walk The Line", "Come Along And Ride This Train Medley", "South Wind", "Life Is Like A Mountain Railway", "Doesn't Anybody Know My Name", "Folsom Prison Blues", "I Still Miss Someone", "This Old House", "The Rebel-Johnny Yuma".

11 February
The Johnny Cash Show #18 with special guests Tammy Wynette, Neil Diamond and Ray Charles.
Songs performed: "I Got Stripes", "Doin' My Time", "I Got Stripes", "Old Red River Flows", "Come Along And Ride This Train Medley", "Hey Porter", "Wrinkled, Crinkled, Wadded Dollar Bill", "Busted",

"Rock Island Line", "Flesh And Blood", "Roll In My Sweet Baby's Arms", "He Turned The Water Into Wine".

14 February
Cash's domination of the country charts which started back in September 1967 continues unabated. With five albums still on the chart his latest release *Hello, I'm Johnny Cash* joins at #26. Once again the chart action is repeated on the top 200 pop chart.

16 February
Johnny Cash - The Man, His World, His Music has its UK premiere at the Fairfield Halls in Croydon.

18 February
The Johnny Cash Show #19 with special guests Jerry Lee Lewis, Vicky Carr and Jimmie Rogers.
Songs performed: "Cry, Cry, Cry", "Get Rhythm", "Cry, Cry, Cry", "Scarborough Fair", "I Never Will Marry", "Come Along And Ride This Train Medley", "Keep On The Sunnyside", "Danny Boy", "Cocaine Blues", "What Do I Care", "The Old Account", "'Cause I Love You".

25 February
The Johnny Cash Show #20 with special guests Mama Cass Elliott, Kenny Rogers and Bob Hope.
Songs performed: "For Lovin' Me", "Hey Porter", "Country Pie", "Reuben James", "Come Along And Ride This Train Medley", "Waiting For A Train", "Sunday Morning Coming Down", "Gather Around The Fire", "Train Of Love", "A Boy Named Sue", "Keep On The Sunnyside", "Jesus Was A Carpenter".

February
The flood of reissues of Cash's Sun material continues with the release of "Rock Island Line"/"Next In Line" (Sun International 1111). During its brief chart spell it manages to rise to #35.

March
"What Is Truth"/"Sing A Travelling Song"
(Columbia 4-45134) released.

3 March
John and June's first son, John Carter-Cash, is born in Nashville.

4 March
The Johnny Cash Show #21 with special guest Roger Miller and Pete Seeger.
Songs performed: "Ballad Of A Teenage Queen", "Come Along And Ride This Train Medley", "Preachin', Prayin', Sinin'", "Home", "A Boy Named Sue", "Devil To Pay", "Greystone Chapel", "Were You There (When They Crucified My Lord)".

7 March
"If I Were A Carpenter" peaks at #2.

11 March
The annual Grammy Awards Ceremonies covering the eligibility period 2 November 1968 – 1 November 1969 are held at the Century Plaza Hotel in Los Angeles, the Alice Tully Hall in New York and at dinners held in Nashville and Chicago. Johnny Cash is nominated in four categories: 'Album Of The Year' with *Johnny Cash At San Quentin*, 'Record Of The Year' and 'Best Country Vocal Performance, Male' with "A Boy Named Sue" and 'Best Album Notes (Annotator's Award), for Bob Dylan's *Nashville Skyline*. Although he is beaten by *Blood, Sweat And Tears* ('Album Of The Year) and the 5th Dimension with "Aquarius"/"Let The Sun Shine In" ('Record Of The Year') he does take the honours in the other two categories. "A Boy Named Sue" also won 'Best Country Song (Songwriter's Award)' for Shel Silverstein while Waylon Jennings and The Kimberleys won 'Best Country Performance, Duo Or Group' for their recording of "MacArthur Park".

11 March
The Johnny Cash Show #22 with special guests Linda Ronstadt, Hank Williams Jr.,
L. Reynolds and O. C. Smith.
Songs performed: "The One On The Right Is On The Left", "Walk A Mile In My Shoes", "Waitin'", "Come Along And Ride This Train Medley", "You Beat All I Ever Saw", "Jesus Was A Soul Man", "Poem For The Elderly", "If I Were A Carpenter".

18 March
The Johnny Cash Show #23 with special guests Merle Haggard and Tommy Cash.
Songs performed: "Ring Of Fire", "'T' For Texas", "Women Make A Fool Out Of Me", "Come Along And Ride This Train Medley", "Wreck Of The Old '97", "I Love You Because", "Do What You Do Well", "Mister Garfield", "What Is Truth", "Come Along And Ride This Train Medley", "You Beat All I Ever Saw", "Jesus Was A Soul Man", "Poem For The Elderly", "If I Were A Carpenter".

25 March
The Johnny Cash Show #24 with special guests Jackie DeShannon, Waylon Jennings and Michael Parks.
Songs performed: "Guess Things Happen That Way", "No Light Will Shine On Me", "Waylon's Back In Town", "Come Along And Ride This Train Medley", "Oklahoma Hills", "Bad News", "Love's Been Good To Me", "Seeing Nellie's Home", "Old Doc Brown".

April-September
The motion picture *Johnny Cash - The Man, His World, His Music* has a series of 'one day only' showings throughout England and Scotland. The schedule includes screenings at the following cinemas:
Adelphi, Slough (2 April)
ABC, Glasgow (8 April)
Essoldo, Newcastle (12 April)
Odeon, Swiss Cottage, London (14 April)
Whiteladies, Bristol (15 April)
Granada, East Ham, London (20 April)
Odeon, Blackpool (6 May)
ABC, Southend (6 May)
Essoldo, Loughborough (10 May)

Century, Bedford (12 May)
Winter Gardens, Bournemouth (13 May)
ABC, Sheffield (20 May)
ABC, Sunderland (20 may)
Odeon, Preston (18 June)
Odeon, Aberdeen (19 June)
Fairfields Hall, Croydon (21 September)
Odeon, Leeds (24 September)

1 April
The Johnny Cash Show #25 with special
guests Shel Silverstein and Kenny Rogers
and the First Edition.
Songs performed: "Rock Island Line", "A
Boy Named Sue", "Come Along And Ride
This Train Medley", "When I'm On My
Journey", "I Got Stripes", "Long Black
Veil", "Billy Christian", "How Great Thou
Art".

8 & 27 April
Soundtrack sessions for the Gregory
Peck/Tuesday Weld film *I Walk The Line*
and the Robert Redford cult movie *Little*

Fauss And Big Halsy. Both albums have several instrumental tracks featuring The Tennessee Three along with Carl Perkins.

8 April

The Johnny Cash Show #26 with special guests Tony Joe White and Patti Page.
Songs performed: "Wanted Man", "Polk Salad Annie", "Come Along And Ride This Train Medley", "My Elusive Dreams", "Cross Over The Bridge", "Detour", "Gentle On My Mind", "Blistered", "Sunday Morning Coming Down", "Smile On Your Brother", "Ten Commandments".

The Ride This Train segment consisting of "Six Days On The Road", "There Ain't No Easy Run" and "Sailor On A Concrete Sea" was used on the live album *The Johnny Cash Show*.

15 April

The Johnny Cash Show #27 with special guest Judy Collins.
Songs performed: "Frankie's Man Johnny", "Come Along And Ride This Train Medley", "Money", "White Trash", "Pickin' Time", "Blue Moon Of Kentucky", "Turn, Turn, Turn", "Wrinkled, Crinkled, Wadded Dollar Bill", "Flesh And Blood", "If I Were A Carpenter", "Jackson", "Poem On Drugs", "What Is Truth".

17 April

At the invitation of President Nixon, Cash performs before 250 guests at *An Evening In The White House*. During the performance he sang "What Is Truth", "Five Feet High And Rising", "Folsom Prison Blues" and a selection of gospel material. Nixon had requested that Cash perform "Welfare Line" and "Okie From Muskogee" but Cash declined.

22 April

The Johnny Cash Show # 27 with special guests Burl Ives and Lynn Anderson.
Songs performed: "South Wind", "I've Been Everywhere", "Come Along And Ride This Train Medley", "Mary Don't You Weep", "Eating Gober Peas", "Lorena", "Give My Love To Rose", "Darlin' Companion", "Children Go Where I Send Thee".

29 April

The Johnny Cash Show #28 with special

guests Chet Atkins, Doug Kershaw, Loretta Lynn, Kris Kristofferson and Rick Nelson. Songs performed: "Orange Blossom Special", "Louisiana Man", "Come Along And Ride This Train Medley", "Hey Porter", "No One Will Ever Know", "The Pilgrim", "It Ain't Me Babe".

May

Dial Press of New York publish the most comprehensive songbook so far. *Songs Of Johnny Cash* is an incredible 240 page book with the words and music to fifty-nine songs covering his entire career. With an additional sixty-eight pages of black and white photos, the book was well worth the $4.95 price tag.

During the year two other songbooks were published - *I Walk The Line And Other Johnny Cash Hits* and *Johnny Cash Motion Picture Songs*, both by *Hill & Range Songs, Inc.* The former contained 30 songs within its 56 pages and although the front and back cover carried photos the inside did not. The second book with 43 pages and again no photos included 18 songs which, strangely, did not bear any relevance to his motion pictures! Three songs - "Blue Suede Shoes", "Bread And Gravy" and "The Last Thing On My Mind" were never recorded by Cash in a studio.

1 May

The National Education Television two-hour film *Trail Of Tears* is broadcast. Filmed back in October 1969 Cash plays the role of Chief John Ross in the story of the Chrokee removal of 1838. Cash also recorded a version of the story at the request of the Historic Landmarks Associatioin for use in their talking library series. This version was broadcast on radio.

6 May

The Johnny Cash Show #29 with special guests Merle Haggard, Brenda Lee and Charlie Pride.
Songs performed: "One More Ride", "Wreck Of The Old '97", "One More

Ride", "Wreck Of The Old #9", "In The Jailhouse Now", "Bad News", "Come Along And Ride This Train Medley", "Long, Long Texas Road", "Abilene", "Back To Houston", "Long, Long Texas Road", "Long Legged Guitar-Pickin' Man", "Life Is Like A Mountain Railway", "I'm Gonna Try To Be That Way".

"I'm Gonna Try To Be That Way" was used on the live album *The Johnny Cash Show*.

9 May

Another Shelby Singleton compilation *Singing Storyteller* (SUN-115) spends a couple of weeks in the country charts.

13 May

The Johnny Cash Show #30 with special guests Marty Robbins, Roy Acuff, Tex Ritter and Carrie Cash.
Songs performed: "I Walk The Line", "I Ride An Old Paint", "Streets Of Laredo", "I Ride An Old Paint", "Come Along And Ride This Train Medley", "Wabash Cannonball", "Hey Porter", "Home Of The Blues", "If I Were A Carpenter", "Keep On The Sunnyside", "Uncloudy Day".

Johnny Cash's mother Carrie also appeared on this show and they duetted on "Uncloudy Day". This was the last show in the current series.

18 May

"What Is Truth" debuts at #37 and will eventually peak at # 3. In the UK it reaches #21 and spends 11 weeks on the chart.

23 May

Billboard magazine includes a 28 page supplement - *Spotlight On Johnny Cash*.

24 May

Johnny Cash appears at the Billy Graham Crusade in Knoxville, Tennessee. His appearance was so successful that Graham asked Cash to appear with him at his New York Crusade to be held at Shea Stadium.

25 May

Bob Wootton, Marshall Grant and W. S. Holland record an instrumental selection of Johnny Cash hits as a tribute to Luther Perkins who tragically died in a house fire. The released album will be called *The Sound Behind Johnny Cash.*

June

Location filming for *A Gunfight,* an offbeat western about two ageing gunfighters, Cash and Kirk Douglas,takes place at the J. W. Eaves Movie Ranch in New Mexico. Further filming is scheduled to take place in Hollywood and possibly Spain. The The movie was financed by the Jicarilla Apaches of New Mexico. "A most intelligent and original version of the now familiar theme of the gunfighters who find themselves out of work in a changing society. Kirk Douglas gives an interesting, controlled performance as the more volatile of the two; but the big surprise of the film is the assurance with which singer Johnny Cash handles the demanding role of Abe Cross." – *Today's Cinema.*

6 June

The World Of Johnny Cash, a compilation, enters at #45. It will spend the rest of the year, and into January 1971, in the charts.

28 June

Taking a break from the filming schedule John and June entertain inmates of the New Mexico State Penitentiary in Santa Fe.

July

Two tracks from the forthcoming album *The Johnny Cash Show* are released as a single – "Sunday Morning Coming Down"/"I'm Gonna Try To Be That Way" (Columbia 4-45211). The a-side was a song written by Kris Kristofferson who had been working as a janitor at Columbia Records and had been warned not to talk to the artists or pitch songs. He was a songwriter and they told him if you want to work you don't pitch songs to Johnny Cash. He made several attempts to get material to Cash by passing tapes to June during sessions. Nothing ever happened but one day Kristofferson took drastic measures and landed a helicopter in Cash's garden. He

AG-13-17

approached Cash with a tape in his hand saying 'I thought the best way to do it would be to land in your yard. You wouldn't forget that, would you?' They remained friends and the song he pitched to him that day, "Sunday Morning Coming Down", would be a major hit for Cash.

September
Two tracks that have both been issued recently as singles are paired up as a new single – "If I Were A Carpenter"/"What Is Truth" (Columbia 4-33182).

September
Shelby Singleton continues to re-package Cash's Sun material. This month sees the release of *Sunday Down South* (SUN-119) with side one featuring Cash and side two material from Jerry Lee Lewis. The following month *Rough Cut King Of Country Music* (SUN-122) is issued. This

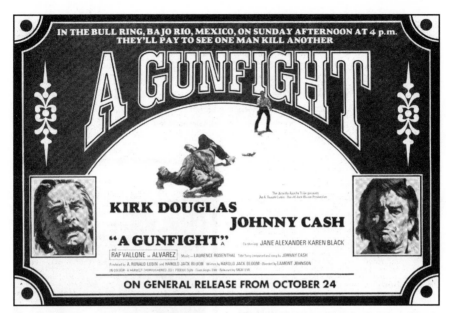

IN THE BULL RING, BAJO RIO, MEXICO, ON SUNDAY AFTERNOON AT 4 p.m.
THEY'LL PAY TO SEE ONE MAN KILL ANOTHER

A GUNFIGHT

KIRK DOUGLAS

JOHNNY CASH

"A GUNFIGHT" Co-starring JANE ALEXANDER KAREN BLACK

RAF VALLONE as ALVAREZ Music—LAURENCE ROSENTHAL Title Song Composed and sung by JOHNNY CASH
Produced by A. RONALD LUBIN and HAROLD JACK BLOOM Written by HAROLD JACK BLOOM Directed by LAMONT JOHNSON
IN COLOUR · A HARVEST THOROUGHBRED JOEL PRODUCTION · From Anglo-EMI · Released by MGM-EMI

ON GENERAL RELEASE FROM OCTOBER 24

would not be the end of the constant repackaging of Cash's early tracks.

5 September
The Kris Kristofferson penned "Sunday Morning Coming Down" debuts on the chart at #30. It spends 15 weeks on the chart with a two-week spell at #1.

23 September
The Johnny Cash Show #31 with special guests Ray Charles and Arlo Guthrie.
Songs performed: "One More Ride", "Hey Porter", "Orange Blossom Special", "Folsom Prison Blues", "I Walk The Line", "Oklahoma", "Come Along And Ride This Train Medley", "Help Me Make It Through The Night", "Peace In The Valley".

30 September
The Johnny Cash Show #32 with special guests Jackie DeShannon and Dennis Hopper.
Songs performed: "Rock Island Line", "This Old House", "Alabama Chattanooga Shoeshine Boy", "Come Along And Ride This Train Medley", "Going Up Going Down", "A Boy Named Sue", "Daddy Was

An Old Time Preacher Man", "Here Was A Man".

October
Once again two old singles are repackaged together and re-issued - this time its "See Ruby Fall"/"Blistered" (Columbia 4-33186).

October
The Johnny Cash Show (KC-30100), an album of material taken from his ABC-TV Shows is released.
Tracks: "Sunday Morning Coming Down", "Come Along And Ride This Train"–"Six Days On The Road", "There Ain't No Good Chain Gang", "Sailor On A Concrete Sea", "These Hands", "I'm Gonna Try To Be That Way", "Come Along And Ride This Train", "Mississippi Delta Land", "Detroit City", "Uncloudy Day", "No Setting Sun", "Mississippi Delta Land", "Here Was A Man"

This was released to tie in with the current run of the *Johnny Cash Show* on ABC-TV.

7 October
The Johnny Cash Show #33 with special

guests George Lindsey and Joni Mitchell.
Songs performed: "Southwind", "Don't It
Make You Wanna Go Home", "Girl From
The North County", "Come Along And
Ride This Train Medley", "Everybody
Loves A Nut", "Big River", "Poison Red
Berries", "Wings Of A Dove", "The Loving
Gift".

14 October
The Johnny Cash Show #34 with special
guests Jose Feliciano, Bobby Bare, Mac
Davis and Linda Ronstadt.
Songs performed: "Five Feet High And
Rising", "Come Along And Ride This Train
Medley", "Keep On The Sunnyside",
"These Hands".

21 October
The Johnny Cash Show #35 with special
guests the Guess Who, Marty Robbins,
Peggey Lee and Tommy Cash.
Songs performed: "Mama Tried", "Come
Along And Ride This Train Medley", "Just
A Closer Walk With Thee", "What Is
Truth", "Hand Me Down World".

24 October
A Gunfight, the movie starring Johnny Cash
and Kirk Douglas, goes on general release.

28 October
The Johnny Cash Show #36 with special
guest Tennessee Ernie Ford.
Songs performed: "Ring Of Fire", "Come
Along And Ride This Train Medley",
"Children Go Where I Send Thee", "I'll
Have A New Life".

November
Two soundtrack albums are released *Little
Fauss And Big Halsy* (S-30385).
Tracks: "Rollin' Free", "Ballad Of Little
Fauss And Big Halsy", "Ballad Of Little
Fauss And Big Halsy (instrumental)", "706
Union (instrumental)", "The Little Man",
"The Little Man (instrumental)", "Wanted
Man", "Rollin' Free (instrumental)", "True
Love Is Greater Than Friendship".
and *I Walk The Line* (S-30397).

Tracks: "Flesh And Blood", "I Walk The
Line", "Hungry", "This Town", "This Side
Of The Law", "Flesh And Blood
(instrumental)", "'Cause I Love You",
"'Cause I Love You (instrumental)", "The
World's Gonna Fall On You", "Face Of
Despair", "Standing On The Promises/
Amazing Grace".

Sheriff Tawes walks the line between duty and desire,
between law and violence, between honor and shame.

November
Two tracks lifted from the *I Walk The Line*
soundtrack album are released as Cash's
new single. "Flesh And Blood"/"This Side
Of The Law" (Columbia 4-45269).

4 November
The Johnny Cash Show #37 with special
guest Burl Ives.
Songs performed: "This Side Of The Law",
"Come Along And Ride This Train
Medley", "Don't Go Near The Water",
"Johnny Horizon", "Doin' My Time", "Roll
In My Sweet Baby's Arms", "Suppertime".

11 November
The Johnny Cash Show #38 with special
guests Stevie Wonder, Bill Monroe, Ian &

Sylvia and George Gobel.

Songs performed: "Destiny's Child", "Get Rhythm", "Come Along And Ride This Train Medley", "I Got Stripes", "Big Midnight Special", "Blowin' In The Wind".

14 November

The live album taken from his TV shows enters the country chart at #20. Over the Christmas period the album will hit the top spot.

18 November

The Johnny Cash Show #39 with special guest Mama Cass Elliott, Lorne Green, Maybelle Carter and Sara Carter.

Songs performed: "Allegheny", "Everybody Loves A Nut", "Act Naturally", "Come Along And Ride This Train Medley", "Way Out West In The Old Days", "Sing A Travelling Song", "I'll Be Satisfied", "I Saw A Man".

25 November

The Johnny Cash Show #40 with special guest Glen Campbell.

Songs performed: "Workin' Man Blues", "Folsom Prison Blues", "Arkansas", "Come Along And Ride This Train Medley".

2 December

The Johnny Cash Show #41 with special guests Homer & Jethro, Merle Haggard, Anne Murray and Bonnie Owens.

Songs performed: "Twenty Five Minutes To Go", "Guess Things Happen That Way", "Portrait Of My Woman", "Daddy Sang Bass", "Sing Me Back Home", "Mama Tried", "Swinging Doors", "Sing Me Back Home", "Come Along And Ride This Train Medley", "Put Your Hand In The Hand".

10 December

It is reported that Apollo 14 astronauts Alan Shepard Jr., Edgar Mitchell and Stuart Rosa will be entertained by Johnny Cash's singing during their flight to the moon that is scheduled to blast off on 31 January 1971. At a press conference Cash told reporters that he had recorded eight songs for the astronauts with the understanding that they would be played during the flight. In the end they were not used and were held over for release on the *America - A 200 Year Salute* album.

16 December

The Johnny Cash Show #42 with special guest Al Hirt.

Songs performed: "A Thing Called Love", "Remember Me", "Old Time Religion", "I Walk The Line", "Come Along And Ride This Train Medley".

19 December

I Walk The Line, the soundtrack to the Gregory Peck and Tuesday Weld film, charts at #44 and during its stay will creep into the top ten.

23 December

The Johnny Cash Show #43 with special guests The Everly Brothers, Tommy Cash and Ray & Carrie Cash.

Songs performed: "Twelve Days Of Christmas", "Do What You Do Well", "I Never Picked Cotton", "Turn Around", "Silent Night", "Little Drummer Boy".

1971

January

While the reissued "Big River" on Sun fails to make much impression on the chart, Cash's latest single "Flesh And Blood" repeats the success of "Sunday Morning Coming Down" by hitting the top spot, albeit for just one week.

6 January

The Johnny Cash Show #44 with special guests Derek And The Dominoes, Eric Anderson and Jack Elliot.

Songs performed: "Big River", "Ballad Of Little Fauss And Big Halsy", "Waltzing Matilda", "Matchbox", "Come Along And Ride This Train Medley", "The Needle".

The "Ride This Train" segment was a

repeat of that shown on 11 February 1970.

13 January

The Johnny Cash Show #45 with special guests Jane Morgan, Gordon Lightfoot, Bill Anderson and Jan Howard.

Songs performed: "When Uncle Bill Quit Dope", "Come Along And Ride This Train Medley", "Amazing Grace", "In The Sweet By And By", "Are We Washed In The Blood Of The Lamb", "Bringing In The Sheep", "A Boy Named Sue", "A Girl Named Cash", "Engine 143", "One More Ride".

Possibly January

During the taping of one of his TV Shows Cash is interrupted by his wife June – "Hey, John. John, I don't want to interrupt you, but I'd like to just for a minute if you don't mind. I want you to meet a good friend of mine all the way from California. Ralph, would you mind to come on out? This is a good friend..." Ralph Edwards walks out on stage and after asking if he can borrow the stage for a minute announces "We need to because, you see, we have brought a whole staff out here from Hollywood and a whole lot of surprising people to Nashville to tell the story of a poet, a troubadour, a musician, a dreamer, a man of great strength, courage and deep faith." To great applause he then goes on to say *"Johnny Cash, This Is Your Life."* The show, which will feature guests going back to Cash's early days, is filmed there and then. Both Billy Graham and Reverend Floyd Gressett pay tribute to Johnny Cash the man, although Graham's contribution is via a televised message. From his early days his High School teacher, Ruby Cooley, talks about his days as a student and his early singing career. Stu Carnell, his early manager, and Marshall Grant talk about the early days and a real surprise is an appearance of Reed Cummings and B. J. Carnahan, former air force buddies and members of The Landsberg Barbarians, the group Cash formed during his time stationed in Germany. Sheriff Ralph Jones

and Doctor Nat Winston, two people responsible for helping Cash kick his addiction to prescribed drugs, recall those days. Cash's daughters Rosanne, Kathy, Cindy and Tara all send a message while his parents Carrie and Ray, his son John and other members of the Cash and Carter families bring the show to a close.

20 January

The Johnny Cash Show #46.

Songs performed: "Ring Of Fire", "Orange Blossom Special", "There You Go", "The Prisoner Song".

This was the first program in a two-part show devoted to the history of Country Music.

27 January

The Johnny Cash Show #47.

Songs performed: "Jackson", "The Old Account", "Old Time Religion", "The Fourth Man".

This was the second show devoted to the history of Country Music.

3 February

The Johnny Cash Show #48.

Songs performed: "I Ride An Old Paint", "Mean As Hell", "The Streets Of Laredo", "Come Along And Ride This Train Medley", "Shifting, Whispering Sands", "Bury Me Not On The Lone Prairie", "Heading For The Last Roundup".

10 February

The Johnny Cash Show #49 with special guests Jim Nabors, Archie Campbell and Ferlin Husky.

Songs performed: "The One On The Right Is On The Left", "Everybody Loves A Nut", "Please Don't Play Red River Valley", "We Got Married", "May The Bird Of Paradise Fly Up Your Nose".

This show had comedy as its theme and included songs from Cash's album *Everybody Loves A Nut.*

16 February

At the Columbia Studios in Memphis Cash records the song "Man In Black."

17 February

The Johnny Cash Show #50 with special guests James Taylor, Linda Ronstadt, Neil Young and Tony Joe White.

Songs performed: "A Boy Named Sue", "Flesh And Blood", "Man In Black", "Oh Susannah", "Sunday Morning Coming Down", "Mama Don't Allow".

This show was filmed on the campus at Vanderbilt University in Nashville and was broadcast with the title *Johnny Cash On Campus*. During the show Cash was seen talking to students and the show also featured the first performance of the song *Man In Black*.

24 February

The Johnny Cash Show #51 with special guests The Blackwood Brothers, Edwin Hawkins, Staples Singers, The Oakridge Boys and Billy Graham.

Songs performed: "Everybody Is Going To Have Religion In Glory", "Praise The Lord", "The Preacher Said, 'Jesus Said'", "The Nazarene", "He Turned The Water Into Wine", "Come To The Wailing Wall", "God Is Not Dead", "When the Saints Go Marching In"

26-28 February

Cash appears at the Domes Stadium during the Houston Livestock and Rodeo Show. Both Glen Campbell and B. J. Thomas appear during the four-day event.

Late-February

"Man In Black"/"Little Bit Of Yesterday" (Columbia 4-45339) is released. Talking about the song in an interview held in the eighties Cash said "People had been asking me why I wear black all the time, and I just decided I'd answer them by pointing up some of the problems and some things that needed doing — some changes that needed to be made in our country — and pointed

the finger at myself as one of those responsible for doing it. I wasn't pointing at others; I was pointing at me, too. I tried to answer why I wear black in that way, by pointing up — I wear it, you know, because I'm concerned, and I care."

March

The Sound Behind Johnny Cash (C-30220) is released. This instrumental album by the Tennessee Three (Marshall Grant, Bob Wootton and W. S. Holland) was dedicated to Luther Perkins.

Tracks: "A Boy Named Sue", "Daddy Sang Bass", "Folsom Prison Blues", "I Walk The Line", "Understand Your Man", "Ring Of Fire", "Wreck Of The Old '97", "Cry, Cry, Cry", "I Still Miss Someone", "Tennessee Flat-Top Box", "Forty Shades Of Green".

March

Cash makes his second visit to Australia.

3 March

The Johnny Cash Show #52.

Songs performed: "The Very Biggest Circus Of Them All", "Old Shep", "Big Rock Candy Mountain", "Boa Constrictor", "Jesus Loves Me", "I'll Fly Away"

10 March

The Johnny Cash Show #53.

Songs performed: "The Legend Of John Henry", "You'll Be All Right", "These Men With Broken Hearts", "It Ain't Me Babe", "I'll Fly Away", "Man In Black".

16 March

The Grammy Awards ceremony is broadcast live by ABC from the Hollywood Palladium in Los Angeles, the first time they had been televised live. Johnny Cash is nominated for two awards at the ceremony covering an eligibility period of 2 November 1969 – 15 October 1970. "Sunday Morning Coming Down" is beaten by Ray Price's "For The Good Times" in the 'Best Country Vocal Performance, Male' while "If I Were A Carpenter" -

Johnny Cash & June Carter takes the 'Best Country Vocal Performance By A Duo Or Group' award.

17 March
The Johnny Cash Show #54.
Songs performed: "Folsom Prison Blues", "If Not For Love", "Singing In Vietnam Talking Blues", "June Makes The Flowers Grow", "Belshazzah".

24 March
The Johnny Cash Show #55 with special guest Mother Maybelle Carter.
Songs performed: "Starkville City Jail", "The World You Gave Me", "We Wouldn't Trade It All", "Greystone Chapel", "Melba's Wine", "May The Good Lord Bless And Keep You".

27 March
The single *Man In Black* debuts at #40 and will rise to #3 during its chart run.

31 March
The Johnny Cash Show #56 with special guests June Carter, Anita Carter and Mother Maybelle Carter. This was the final ABC-TV Johnny Cash Show.
Songs performed: "I Walk The Line", "Darlin' Companion", "If I Were A Carpenter", "Jackson", "Sing, Sing, Sing", "Sunday Morning Coming Down", "Come Along And Ride This Train Medley", "I'll Take You Home Again Kathleen", "He'll Understand And Say Well Done".

The "Ride This Train" segment used in this show was originally broadcast on 4 November 1970. This 56th show was the last of the series.

May
"Singing In Vietnam Talking Blues"/ "You've Got A New Light Shining" (Columbia 4-45393) is released and will hit #18 in July.

14 May
John is a guest on the BBC's David Frost Show where he talks about his career and performs "Man In Black" and "If I Were A Carpenter".

June
The album *Man In Black* (C-30550) is released.
Tracks: "The Preacher Said, 'Jesus Said'", "Orphan Of The Road", "You've Got A New Light Shining", "If Not For Love", "Man In Black", "Singing In Vietnam Talking Blues", "Ned Kelly", "Look For Me", "Dear Mrs.", "I Talk To Jesus Every Day".

July
"A Song To Mama"/"One More Summer In Virginia" (Columbia 4-45428) released. This was a Carter Family single which featured Cash on the a-side only. It manages to reach #37 during its 11-week spell on the chart.

24 July
Cash's latest album, *Man In Black*, reaches #1. It will spend two weeks at the top and a further 22 weeks on the chart.

August
"No Need To Worry"/"I'll Be Loving You" (Columbia 4-45431) released. Both sides of the single feature June Carter-Cash.

August
A performance in Copenhagen is taped for future television broadcast.

7 August
Cash appears at an engagement to celebrate the Carter Family in Virginia.

13-14 August
Allentown Fair, Allentown, Pennsylvania.

23-24 August
Lansdowne Park, Ottawa, Ontario.

26-27 August
C. N. E., Ontario.

September
"Papa Was A Good Man"/"I Promise You"
(Columbia 4-45460) released.

2-3 September
Ohio State Fair, Columbus, Ohio.

11 September
The "No Need To Worry" single begins its
chart life at #51 and will work its way up to
#15 over the coming weeks.

16 September
NEMS Enterprises Ltd and CBS Records
present Johnny Cash in Concert with the
opening show at Green's Playhouse,
Glasgow.

17 September
Belle Vue, Manchester.

18 September
Royal Festival Hall, London.

19 September
Odeon Cinema, Birmingham.

28 September
In recognition of his good deeds for his
fellow man Gardner-Webb College in
North Carolina awards Cash an honorary
Doctor Of Humanities degree.

October
Sessions start for the *Gospel Road*
album/film project. Produced by Larry
Butler, the sessions will run through to the
middle of 1972.

16 October
"Papa Was A Good Man" debuts at #57 at
the start of its 11-week run and goes on to
hit the #16 spot.

22 October
Southern Illinois University.

23 October
South Bend, Indiana.

24 October
Milwaukee.

29 October
Minneapolis, Minnesota.

30 October
Bradley University.

2-24 November
John and June leave Nashville for Tel Aviv.
They spend the month in Israel filming
scenes for the movie *The Gospel Road*.

2 December
Greensboro, North Carolina.

3 December
Charleston, West Virginia.

4 December
Richmond, Virginia.

5 December
Roanoake, Virginia.

23 December
The World Of Johnny Cash receives gold
classification from the RIAA.

1972-1979

"I got so excited writing the songs in this album that you'd think I just started in the music business. It's something I always wanted to do, write an album of all my own songs and for some reason, I just never got around to it."

from sleevenotes to *Ragged Old Flag* 1974

1972

January

"A Thing Called Love"/"/Daddy" (Columbia 4-45534) is released and enters the charts at #71. A stay of 16 weeks will see it rise to #2.

January

A second volume of Cash's *Greatest Hits* charts. Although it couldn't repeat the success of *Volume One* it does manage to scrape into the top ten.

28 January

Indiana University, Bloomington, Indiana

29 January

Shreveport, Louisiana

30 January

Louisiana State University, Baton Rouge, Louisiana

1-3 February

Atlanta Civic Center, Atlanta, Georgia

4 February

Abilene, Texas

5 February

Waco, Texas.

6 February

San Antonio, Texas.

7 February

Tucson, Arizona.

Late-February

Cash is in Europe.

26 February

Cash appears at the Edison Award Gala in Amsterdam.

March

A Thing Called Love (KC-31332) is released.
Tracks: "Kate", "Melva's Wine", "A Thing Called Love", "I Promise You", "Papa Was A Good Man", "Tear Stained Letter", "Mississippi Sand", "Daddy", "Arkansas Lovin' Man", "The Miracle Man".

14 March

The Johnny Cash & June Carter-Cash duet "No Need To Worry" is nominated at the Grammy Awards in the 'Best Country Vocal Performance, Duo Or Group' category but the honour goes to "After The Fire Is Gone" by Conway Twitty & Loretta Lynn. Broadcast live by ABC from the Felt Forum in New York, the awards cover the eligibility period of 16 October 1970 – 15 October 1971.

30 March-5 April

The Hilton Hotel, Las Vegas, Nevada.

April

A new state of the art recording studio is opened at the House of Cash in Hendersonville.

April

Two more tracks from *A Thing Called Love* are lifted for single release – "Kate"/"The Miracle Man" (Columbia 4-45590).

15 April
"A Thing Called Love" enters the UK singles chart and eventually reaches #4. It makes another appearance in the top 50 in July.

20 April
Auditorium, Bangor, Maine.

21 April
Gardens, Boston, Massachusets.

22 April
Memorial Auditorium, Buffalo, New York.

23 April
Civic Auditorium, Cleveland, Ohio.

28 April
Coliseum, Jacksonville, Florida.

29 April
Civic Auditorium, Miami Beach, Florida.

29 April
The album *A Thing Called Love* enters the country charts at #31. During a 24-week residency it will peak at #2.

30 April
Nassau County Coliseum, Hempstead, New York.

6 May
The single "Kate" repeats the success of "A Thing Called Love" by reaching #2.

19 May
Dane County Coliseum, Madison, Wisconsin.

20 May
Arena, Sioux Falls, South Dakota.

21 May
Arena Auditorium, Duluth, Minnesota.

25 May
Brown County Memorial Auditorium, Green Bay, Wisconsin.

26 May
McElroy Auditorium, Waterloo, Iowa.

27 May
Masonic Temple Auditorium, Davenport, Idaho.

28 May
Mayo Civic Auditorium, Rochester, Minnesota.

June
"If I Had A Hammer"/"I Got A Boy And His Name Is John" (Columbia 4-45631) released.

10 June
Swan Ball, Cheekwood Mansion, Nashville, Tennessee.

13-15 June
Arie Crown Theatre-McCormick Place, Chicago, Illinois.

16 June
Civic Arena, Pittsburgh, Pennsylvania.

17 June
Cash performs "A Thing Called Love" and "I See Men Walking As Trees" at the Jesus Musical Festival Explo '72 in Dallas, Texas. The show will be broadcast on 3 August.

18 June
Veterans Memorial Auditorium, Des Moines, Iowa.

24 June
Arena, Harrisburg, Pennsylvania.

25 June
Performing Arts Center, Saratoga, New York.

27 June
Montego Bay, Jamaica.

28 June
Kingston, Jamaica.

July
America (KC-31645) is released. Some of the tracks included were originally recorded for the Apollo 14 space mission. Track: "Opening Dialogue", "Paul Revere", "Begin Westward Movement", "The Road To Kaintuck", "To The Shining Mountains", "Battle Of New Orleans", "Southwestward", "Remember The Alamo", "Opening Of The West", "Lorena", "Gettysburg Address", "The West", "Big Foot", "Like A Young Colt", "Mister Garfield", "A Proud Land", "The Big Battle", "On Wheels And Wings", "Come Take A Trip In My Airship", "Reaching For The Stars", "These Are My People".

July
The latest issue of *Country* magazine runs an article entitled *The Johnny Cash Story*.

July
"Oney"/"Country Trash" (Columbia 4-45660) released.

15 July
"If I Had A Hammer", the recent single that featured June Carter-Cash, debuts at #47 for a short 7-week spell, during which it goes no higher than 29.

27 July
Cash records tracks for his second Christmas offering. Guests on the album include June Carter-Cash and Tommy Cash.

August
"The World Needs A Melody"/"A Bird With Broken Wings Can't Fly" (Columbia 4-45679) released. This is a Carter Family release which features Cash on the a-side. It makes the singles chart in October, managing to climb to #35

4-5 August
Merryweather Pavilion, Columbia, Maryland.

10 August
Lou Robin of Artists Consultants Productions Inc. takes over as Cash's manager from Saul Holiff.

11 August
Farm Show Arena, Harrisburg, Pennsylvania.

12 August
The Johnny Cash Country & Gospel Festival at the Pocono International Raceway, Mt. Pocono, Pennsylvania.

18-19 August
Central Canada Exhibition, Ottawa, Ontario.

26 August
State Fair, Indianapolis, Indiana.

27 August
Fair, DuQuoin, Illinois.

2 September
The *America* album enters at #32 and will spend nineteen weeks in the chart.

4 September
Muscular Dystrophy Show, Nashville, Tennessee.

8 September
Utica.

9 September
Wilmington, Delaware.

10 September
Raleigh, North Carolina.

20 September
European tour kicks off with a show at the Deutschlandhalle in Berlin, Germany.

21 September
Stadthalle, Bremen, Germany.

22 September
Sporthalle, Cologne, Germany.

23 September
Westfalenhalle, Dortmund, Germany.

26-28 September
Royal Albert Hall, London.

26 September
"Oney" enters the charts and during the course of its 15 weeks finds Cash hitting the #2 spot again.

29 September
Scandinavium, Gothenburg, Sweden.

30 September
Baltiskahallen, Malmo, Sweden.

2 October
Kungliga Tennishallen, Stockholm, Sweden.

3 October
Osteraker Prison, Sweden.
This concert is recorded and released in 1974 as *På Osteraker* in Europe only.

6 October
Auditorium, Nashville, Tennessee.

18 October
Civic Center, Saginaw, Michigan.

19 October
Mary Sawyer Auditorium, La Crosse, Wisconsin.

20 October
Oshkosh State University Field House, Oshkosh, Wisconsin.

21 October
Rock Valley College Field House, Rockford, Illinois.

22 October
Scope Coliseum, Norfolk, Virginia.

27 October
Oral Roberts University Center, Tulsa, Oklahoma.

28 October
Tarrant County Convention Center, Fort Worth, Texas.

November
"Any Old Wind That Blows"/"Kentucky Straight" (Columbia 4-45740) released.

November
Johnny Cash Family Christmas (KC-31754) is released.
Tracks: "Opening Dialogue", "King Of Love", "Dialogue", "Jingle Bells", "Dialogue", "That Christmassy Feeling", "Dialogue", "My Merry Christmas Song", "Dialogue", "Merry Christmas Mary", "Dialogue", "Christmas Time's A-Comin'", "Dialogue", "Christmas With You", "Christmas As I Knew It", "Dialogue", "When You're Twenty-One", "Dialogue", "Old Fashioned Tree", "Dialogue", "Silent Night".

7 November
Los Angeles, California.

8-10 November
An appearance on the *Flip Wilson Show* is taped in Los Angeles, California. The show is broadcast a few days later on the 14 November.

16 November
Roberts Auditorium, Evansville, Indiana.

17 November
Memorial Field House, Huntington, West Virginia.

18-19 November
Cash plays two shows each day at the Capital Music Hall, Wheeling, West Virginia.

23 November
Coliseum, Providence, Rhode Island.

24 November
Coliseum, Springfield, Massachussets.

25 November
Coliseum, New Haven, Connecticut.

26 November
Portland, Maine.

30 November
Coliseum, Jackson, Mississippi.

December
"Help Me Make It Through The Night"/"The Lovin' Gift" (Columbia 4-45758) released. Both sides feature June Carter-Cash.

1 December
Coliseum, Monroe, Louisiana.

2 December
Auditorium, New Orleans, Louisiana.

3 December
Old Plantation Music Park, Lakeland, Florida.

14 Decemberr
The *Flip Wilson Show* taped back in November is broadcast.

1973

January
Any Old Wind That Blows (KC-32091) is released.
Tracks: "Any Old Wind That Blows", "Kentucky Straight", "The Loving Gift", "The Good Earth", "Best Friend", "Oney", "Ballad Of Annie Palmer", "Too Little, Too Late", "If I Had A Hammer", "Country Trash", "Welcome Back Jesus"

12 January
Municipal Auditorium, Austin, Texas.

13 January
Memorial Coliseum, Corpus Christi, Texas.

14 January
Robinson Auditorium, Little Rock, Arkansas.

15 January
Municipal Auditorium, Springfield, Missouri.

16 January
Colorado Springs, Colorado.

17 January
Arena, Denver, Colorado.

18 January
Pershing Municipal Auditorium, Lincoln, Illinois.

19 January
Municipal Auditorium, Sioux City, Iowa.

20 January
Civic Arena, Bismarck, North Dakota.

21 January
North Dakota Field House, Fargo, North Dakota.

3 February
The album *Any Old Wind That Blows* enters the chart at #36. During its 14-week run it will reach a high of #5.

2 February
San Diego, California.

3 February
San Bernadino, California.

4 February
Sacramento, California.

7 February
Tucson, Arizona.

8 February
Phoenix, Arizona.

9 February
Anaheim, California.

10 February
New Mexico State, Las Cruces, New Mexico.

11 February
Coliseum, Oakland, California.

12 February
Fresno, California.

3 March
The Grammy awards ceremony is broadcast live by CBS from the Auditorium in Nashville, Tennessee and covers the period 16 October 1971 – 15 October 1972. The Johnny Cash & June Carter-Cash duet "If I Had A Hammer" is nominated for 'Best Country Vocal Performance By A Duo Or Group' but "Class Of '57" by The Statler Brothers, who are regulars on the Johnny Cash Show, takes the award.

10 March
"Any Old Wind That Blows" hits #3 after gradually climbing following its first appearance at #48 back in December 1972.

13 March
Honolulu, Hawaii.

16 March
Christchurch, New Zealand.

17 March
Wellington, New Zealand.

18 March
Auckland, New Zealand.

20-21 March
Melbourne, Australia.

23 March
Brisbane, Australia.

24 March
Sydney, Australia.

25 March
Hobart, Tasmania. The show also includes The Hawking Brothers, jan Howard and Carl Perkins.

27 March
Adelaide, Australia.

28 March
Perth, Australia.

22-30 March
While in Australia he films sequences in Kalgoorlie for use in a TV special tentatively called *Cash Down Under* and plays other dates.

April
The soundtrack album *The Gospel Road* (KG-32253) is released. The double album contains songs and dialogue.
Tracks: "Praise The Lord", "Introduction", "Gospel Road–Part One", "Jesus' Early Years", "Gospel Road–Part Two", "John The Baptist", "Baptism Of Jesus", "Wilderness Temptation", "Follow Me, Jesus", "Gospel Road–Part Three", "Jesus Announces His Divinity", "Jesus' Opposition Is Established", "Jesus' First Miracle", "He Turned The Water Into Wine–Part One", "State Of The Nation", "I See Men As Trees Walking", "Jesus Was A Carpenter–Part One", "Choosing Of Twelve Disciples", "Jesus' Teachings", "Parable Of The Good Shepherd", "Two Greatest Commandments", "Greater Love Hath No Man", "John The Baptist's Imprisonment And Death", "Jesus Cleanses Temple", "Jesus Upbraids Scribes And Pharisees", "Jesus In The Temple", "Come Unto Me", "The Adulterous Woman", "Help–Part One", "Jesus And Nicodeumus", "Help–Part Two", "Sermon On The Mount", "Blessed Are", "The Lord's Prayer–Amen Chorus", "Introducing Mary Magdalene", "Mary Magdalene Speaks", "Follow Me", "Magdalene Speaks Again", "Crossing The Sea Of Galilee", "He Turned The Water Into Wine–Part Two", "He Turned The

Water Into Wine–Part Three", "Feeding The Multitude", "He Turned The Water Into Wine–Part Four", "More Jesus Teaching", "The Living Water And The Bread Of Life", "Gospel Road–Part Four", "Jesus And Children", "Children", "Four Months To Live", "Help–Part Three", "Help–Part Four", "Raising Of Lazarus", "Jesus' Second Coming", "Jesus' Entry Into Jerusalem", "Burden Of Freedom", "Jesus Wept", "Burden Of Freedom", "Jesus Cleanses Temple Again", "Feast Of

The Passover", "Lord, Is It I", "The Last Supper", "John 14:1–3", "And Now He's Alone", "Agony In Gethsemane", "Jesus Before Ciaphas, Pilate And Herod", "Burden Of Freedom", "Crucifixion", "Jesus' Last Words", "Jesus' Death", "Earthquake And Darkness", "He Is Risen", "Mary Magdalene Returns To Galilee", "Jesus Appears To Disciples", "The Great Commission", "Ascension–Amen Chorus", "Jesus Was A Carpenter–Part Two".

A full page ad appears in the music press:

The Gospel according to Johnny Cash
'The Gospel Road' is a film of the life of Jesus, which Johnny Cash produced, scored and narrated. He calls it "my life's proudest work."
Such a special film required an equally special soundtrack, and Johnny selected a group of outstanding songs by some of America's most gifted songwriters, including Kris Kristofferson, John Denver, Joe South and Johnny Cash himself. Eight new songs were written just for the production.

April
"Children"/"The Last Supper" (Columbia 4-45786) released. Both tracks are taken from the double album *The Gospel Road* and the single charts in late April, eventually reaching #30.

13 April
Dayton, Ohio.

14 April
Indiana State University.

15 April
University of Kentucky.

27 April
Cash opens a week-long engagement at the Hilton in Las Vegas.

5 May
The soundtrack album *Gospel Road* opens

its chart run at #39. A 14 week chart run follows during which it will reach # 12.

13 June
Arena, Minneapolis, Minnesota.

14 June
Arena, Duluth, Minnesota.

15 June
Arena, Winnipeg, Manitoba.

16 June
Saskatoon Centennial, Saskatoon, Saskatchewan.

17 June
Centre Of The Arts, Regina, Saskatchewan.

19-20 June
Arena, Anchorage, Alaska.

22 June
Arena, Portland, Oregon.

23 June
Seattle, Washington.

24 June
Spokane, Washington.

July
"Praise The Lord And Pass The Soup"/"The Ballad Of Barbara" (Columbia 4-45890) released.

4 July
John & June guest on *Happy Birthday USA* in Jonesboro, Tennessee. The show was first held back in 1971 and had been the idea of the Statler Brothers.

27 July-2 August
Sahara Tahoe, Lake Tahoe, Nevada.

4 August
The second single taken from *The Gospel Road* album fails to repeat the moderate success of "Children". A high of #57 is all that "Praise The Lord" could manage.

5 August
Cash sticks to a religious repertoire for an appearance at the opening of the First All-Lutheran Youth Gathering in Houston. Paul Simon is also on the show which attracts a crowd of nearly 20,000.

8 August
Blossom Music Center.

10-11 August
Pine Knob.

12 August
Providence, Rhode Island.

13-18 August
Graden State.

September
The compilation album *Sunday Morning Coming Down* (KC-32240) released.
Tracks: "Folsom Prison Blues", "Orange Blossom Special", "It Ain't Me Babe", "Big River", "I'm Gonna Try To Be That Way", "Green, Green Grass Of Home", "Understand Your Man", "If I Were A Carpenter", "The Long Black Veil", "Don't Think Twice, It's Alright", "Sunday Morning Coming Down".

September
Johnny Cash And His Woman (KC-32443) is released.
Tracks: "Colour Of Love", "Saturday Night In Hickman County", "Allegheny", "Life Has It's Little Ups And Downs", "Matthew 24 (Is Knocking At The Door)", "City Of New Orleans", "Tony", "The Pine Tree", "We're For Love", "Godshine".

September
"Allegheny"/"We're For Love" (Columbia 4-45929) released. June Carter-Cash appears on both tracks. The single debuts on the chart at #95 and climbs steadily to #69.

1 September
30,100 people fill Wembley Stadium in London for the closing service of SPRE-E. Taking part were Johnny Cash, June Carter-Cash, Billy Graham and the Swedish musical group Choralerna.

2 September
Town Hall, Birmingham, London.

3 September
Free Trade Hall, Manchester, England.

4 September
City Hall, Newcastle, England.

5-6 September
Apollo Centre, Glasgow, Scotland.

29 September
Cash's latest album *Johnny Cash And His Woman* and the compilation *Sunday Morning Coming Down* make their debuts in the chart at #40 and #43 respectively. They both remain on the charts throughout October, November and December although neither of them go higher than #32.

October
"Pick The Wildwood Flower"/"Diamonds In The Rough" (Columbia 4-45938) released. Both sides of the single feature Mother Maybelle Carter. A high of #34 is reached early in 1974.

3 October
Boise State.

4 October
Coliseum, Spokane, Washington.

5 October
Mini Dome, Idaho State University, Pocatello, Idaho.

6 October
Fieldhouse, University of Wyoming, Laramie, Wyoming.

7 October
Calgary, Alberta.

8 October
Vancouver, British Columbia.

9 October
Arena, Victoria, British Columbia.

12 October
University of Montana, Missoula, Montana.

13 October
Montana State University, Bozeman, Montana.

15 October
Cash hosts the 7th Annual Country Music Association Awards from Nashville.

28 October
Dane County Arena, Madison, Wisconsin.

29 October
Milwaukee Auditorium, Milwaukee, Wisconsin.

30 October
Walker Sports Arena, Muskegon, Michigan.

1 November
Kitchener Memorial Auditorium, Kitchener, Ontario.

2 November
Maple Leaf Gardens, Toronto, Ontario.

3 November
London Gardens, London, Ontario.

7 November
Jackson, Mississippi.

8 November
Indianapolis, Indiana.

9 November
Lansing, Michigan.

10 November
Grand Rapids, Michigan.

14 November
San Jose, California.

15 November
San Antonio, Texas.

16 November
Denver, Colorado.

17 November
Houston, Texas.

22-25 November
Sahara Tahoe, Lake Tahoe, Nevada.

27 November
Taping the *Merv Griffin Show* in Los Angeles, California.

29 November-2 December
Hilton, Las Vegas, Nevada.

7 December
Coliseum, Roanoke, Virginia.

8 December
Capitol Center Coliseum, Washington, DC.

10-11 December
Filming an NBC Special at Studio 8H in the Rockefeller Center, New York.

12 December
New York City, New York.

17 December
Sacramento, California.

18 December
San Francisco, California.

19 December
Bakersfield, California.

December
"That Christmasy Feeling"/"Christmas As I Knew It" (Columbia 4-45979) released. Cash's brother Tommy appears on the a-side but this doesn't help the single and it fails to chart.

1974

Early 1974
Children's Album (C-32898) released.
Tracks: "Nasty Dan", "One And One Makes Two", "I Gotta Boy And His Name Is John", "Little Magic Glasses", "Miss Tara", "Dinosaur Song", "Tiger Whitehead", "Call Of The Wild", "Little Green Fountain", "Old Shep", "The Timber Man".

The album fails to make any impression on the charts.

January
"Orleans Parish Prison"/"Jacob Green" (Columbia 4-45997) released. An 8-week chart run will see it rise to #52.

9 January
Binghamton, New York.

10 January
Syracuse, New York.

11 January
Niagara Falls, New York.

Mid-January
Cash flies out to California to begin shooting a special guest appearance on the TV detective show *Columbo* starring Peter Falk.

25 January
Louisville, Kentucky.

26-27 January
Wheeling, West Virginia.

29-30 January
Atlanta, Georgia.

31 January
Savannah, Georgia.

1 February
Charleston, South Carolina.

2 February
Birmingham, Alabama.

3 February
Alexandria, Louisiana.

5 February
University of Mississippi.

23 February
A 90-minute Country Music Special recorded in New York is aired.

25 February
Saginaw, Michigan.

26 February
Toledo, Ohio.

27 February
Kalamazoo, Michigan.

1 March
Davenport, Iowa.

2 March
Moline, Illinois.

3 March
University of Illinois, Champaign, Illinois.

3 March
Johnny Cash is a special guest in an episode of *Columbo* entitled *Swan Song*. He plays the role of a musical star who murders his wife, an evangelist who has been exploiting his talents to finance her own religious crusade. The show, starring Peter Falk in the title role, is broadcast under the heading *NBC Mystery Movie*.

27 March
Corpus Christi, Texas.

28 March
San Antonio, Texas.

29 March
Dallas, Texas.

30 March
Lake Charles, Louisiana.

31 March
Austin, Texas.

April
Radio stations throughout the country start broadcasting a 12-hour documentary series on Johnny Cash. *Railroads Are Forever* profiles many of Cash's songs in depth.

April
Ragged Old Flag (KC-32917) is released. Tracks: "Ragged Old Flag", "Don't Go Near The Water", "All I Do Is Drive", "Southern Comfort", "King Of The Hill", "Pie In The Sky", "Lonesome To The Bone", "While I've Got It On My Mind", "Good Morning Friend", "I'm A Worried Man", "Please Don't Let Me Out", "What On Earth Will You Do (For Heaven's Sake)".

April
"Ragged Old Flag"/"Don't Go Near The Water" (Columbia 4-46028) released.

2-7 April
Music Theater, Houston, Texas.

12 April
During the afternoon Cash plays a free show in Hendersonville and in the evening another free concert for inmates at the Tennessee State Prison in Nashville.

15-17 April
Taping for a Grand Ole Opry special.

19 April
Benefit Show in Johnson City, Tennessee.

20 April
Benefit Show in Chattanooga, Tennessee.

26 April
Country Comes Home, celebrating the opening of the new Grand Ole Opry Building at the Opryland Complex in Nashville, is broadcast.

27 April
The patriotic "Ragged Old Flag" single debuts at #81. A 13-week spell and a high of #31 is an improvement on recent chart action.

30 April-6 May
A week of concerts in Las Vegas, Nevada.

11 May
A hospital dedication in Decatur, Alabama.

12 May-9 June
John and June take a well deserved vacation.

13 June
During sessions for his new album, being recorded at the House of Cash Studios, Cash records a new version of his 1959 hit single "Don't Take Your Guns To Town".

15 June
The *Ragged Old Flag* album enters the chart at #39 at the start of an 11-week stay during which it peaks at #16.

20 June
At an Awards Dinner in Washington Cash receives the Youth Award.

21 June
Lynchburg, Virginia.

22 June
Greensboro, North Carolina.

23 June
Another Benefit Show in Grandfather Mountain, North Carolina.

24 June
Asheville, North Carolina.

25 June
Knoxville, Tennessee.

29 June
Saratoga, New York.

5-11 July
A week of shows in Lake Tahoe, Nevada.

18 July
Parchman, Mississippi.

19 July
Chicago, Illinois.

20 July
Summer Festival, Milwaukee, Wisconsin.

21 July
Davenport, Iowa.

22-28 July
Music Theater, Warwick, Rhode Island.

August
"The Junkie And The Juicehead"/"Crystal Chandeliers And Burgundy" (Columbia 3-10011) released and fails to register on the charts.

5-11 August
Cash plays more shows at the Hilton in Las Vegas, Nevada.

19 August
State Prison, McAllister, Oklahoma.

20 August
Missouri State Fair, Sedalia, Missouri.

24 August
Two shows at the Ohio State Fair, Columbus, Ohio.

26-31 August
Nanuet, New York.

September
Backing tracks for a new album are laid down at Devonshire Studios in Hollywood. Cash's vocals will be overdubbed later in Nashville.

September
Junkie And The Juicehead (Minus Me) (KC-33086) is released.
Tracks: "Junkie And The Juicehead (Minus Me)", "Don't Take Your Guns To Town", "Broken Freedom Song", "I Do Believe", "Old Slewfoot", "Keep On The Sunnyside", "Father And Daughter (Father And Son)", "Crystal Chandeliers And Burgundy", "Friendly Gates", "Billy And Rex And Oral And Bob", "J–E–S–U–S", "Lay Back With My Woman".

2 September
Telethon, Nashville, Tennessee.

13 September
Portales, New Mexico.

14 September
Odessa, Texas.

15 September
El Paso, Texas.

16 September
Albuquerque, New Mexico.

18 September
Phoenix, Arizona.

19 September
San Bernadino, California.

20 September
Sports Arena, San Diego, California.

21 September
Convention Center, Anaheim, California.

22 September
Convention Center, Fresno, California.

25-30 September
Circle Theater, San Francisco, California.

October
"Don't Take Your Guns To Town"/"Father And Daughter" (Columbia 3-10048) released. The a-side is a re-recording of his 1960 hit while the b-side features Rosey Nix. Both tracks are lifted from the *Junkie And The Juicehead (Minus Me)* album. Like the previous single, this one fails to make any impression chartwise.

14 October
The 8th Annual Country Music Association Award ceremony is once again hosted by Johnny Cash.

25 October
Lansing, Michigan.

26 October
Indianapolis, Indiana.

27 October
Muncie, Indiana.

28 October
Grand Rapids, Michigan.

30 October
Eau-Claire, Wisconsin.

31 October
La Crosse, Wisconsin.

November
"The Lady Came From Baltimore"/ "Lonesome To The Bone" (Columbia 3-10066) released.

1 November
Fargo, North Dakota.

2 November
Jamestown, North Dakota.

3 November
Bismarck, North Dakota.

4 November
Aberdeen, South Dakota.

5 November
Sioux City, Iowa.

6 November
Kearney, Nebraska.

7 November
Lincoln, Nebraska.

8 November
McElroy Auditorium, Waterloo, Iowa.

9 November
Peoria, Illinois.

9 November
Junkie And The Juicehead spends all of the month hovering just inside the top fifty.

10 November
St. Louis, Missouri.

19-25 November
Las Vegas, Nevada.

14 December
"The Lady Came From Baltimore" enters the chart at #80. The next few months will see the single climb to #14.

December
Johnny Cash Pa Osteraker (CBS 65308) released.
Tracks: "Orleans Parish Prison", "Jacob Green", "Me And Bobby McGee", "The Prisoner's Song", "The Invertebrates", "Silver Haired Daddy Of Mine", "City Jail", "Life Of A Prisoner", Looking Back

In Anger", "Nobody Cared", "Help Me Make It Through The Night", "I Saw A Man"

Bear Family Records of Germany would later release the album as *Live In A Swedish Prison* (BFX-15092).

Exact Dates Unknown

The *Ridin' The Rails* special was filmed during a 25-day period at 12 different locations. The opening sequence of John driving the *4501* was filmed in Decatur, Alabama while in Zebulon, Georgia, the race between a horse and a locomotive was shot. At Stone Mountain in Georgia Cash sang many of the protest songs, while in Big Shanty the exciting scene of the chase and capture of the Civil War locomotive *The General* was recreated. Moving west, more filming took place at Promontory, Utah, with the driving of the golden spike linking East and West. Other scenes were filmed in Canon City, Colorado (the cattle drive), Stone Man Rock Crusher Rock

Quarry in Rossville, Georgia and the Tennessee Valley Outdoor Railroad Museum (the legendary story of the steel-drivin' man John Henry), Griffin, Georgia (the story of Casey Jones) and the Colorado Outdoor Railroad Museum (the 1918 station farewell). Nashville's Union Station was the setting for the return of soldiers in World War II and the closing sequences were filmed at Radnor Yard in Nashville.

In 1975 *Ridin' The Rails* received a Bronze Award from the International Film & Television Festival of New York.

1975

January

Precious Memories (C-33087), a collection of gospel material, is released.
Tracks: "Precious Memories", "Rock Of Ages", "Old Rugged Cross", "Softly And Tenderly", "In The Sweet By And By", "Just As I Am", "Farther Along", "When The Roll Is Called Up Yonder", "Amazing Grace", "At The Cross", "Have Thine Own Way Lord"

16 January
Greensville, South Carolina.

17 January
Columbus, Georgia.

18 January
Macon, Georgia.

19 January
Columbia, South Carolina.

21 January
Gainsville, Florida

22 January
Sarasota, Florida

23 January
West Palm Beach, Florida

24 January
Miami Beach, Florida

25 January
Lakeland, Florida

26 January
Orlando, Florida

28 January
Tallahassee, Florida

29 January
Mobile, Alabama

30 January
Dothan, Alabama

31 January
Birmingham, Alabama

January-February
Appalachian Pride, June Carter-Cash's solo album, is recorded during sessions held at the House of Cash Studios in Hendersonville, Tennessee.

1 February
Jackson, Tennessee

2 February
Memphis, Tennessee

27 February
Robarts Sports Arena, Sarasota, Florida

28 February
Miami Beach Auditorium, Miami, Florida

1 March
Civic Center, Lakeland, Florida.

2 March
University of Florida, Gainesville, Florida.

3 March
Municipal Auditorium, Columbus, Georgia.

7 March
Hershey Park Arena, Hershey, Pennsylvania.

8 March
Civic Center, Philadelphia, Pennsylvania.

10 March
Broome County Veterans Memorial Arena, Binghampton, New York.

11 March
Memorial Auditorium, Utica, New York.

12 March
Crete Memorial Civic Center, Plattsburg, New York.

13 March
Civic Center, Burlington, Vermont.

14 March
Civic Center, Hartford, Connecticut.

15 March
Symphony Hall, Boston, Massachusetts.

16 March
Civic Center, Augusta, Maine.

19 March
Civic Center, Johnstown, Pennsylvania.

20 March
Erie County Fieldhouse, Erie, Pennsylvania.

21 March
Allen County Memorial Coliseum, Fort Wayne, Indiana.

22 March
Capital Plaza, Frankfort, Kentucky.

24 March
Von Braun Civic Center, Huntsville, Alabama.

31 March
Oral Roberts TV show in Tulsa, Oklahoma.

April

John R. Cash (KC-33370) is released. Tracks: "My Old Kentucky Home", "Hard Times Comin'", "The Lady Came From Baltimore", "Lonesome To The Bone", "The Night They Drove Old Dixie Down", "Clean Your Own Tables", "Jesus Was Our Saviour", "Reason To Believe", "Cocaine Carolina", "Smokey Factory Blues".

April

"My Old Kentucky Home"/"Hard Times Comin'" (Columbia 3-10116) released. This second single from the *John R. Cash* album reaches #42 during a nine weeks on the chart.

2-12 April

Concerts at the Hilton, Las Vegas, Nevada.

19 April

Miami Beach Convention Centre, Miami, Florida.

7 May

American Freedom Train Taping in Nashville, Tennessee.

10 May

Benefit Show in Eudora, Mississippi.

12 May

Cash appears at the Billy Graham Crusade in Jackson, Mississippi.

16-17 May

Forum, Halifax, Nova Scotia.

18 May

Coliseum, Moncton, New Brunswick.

19 May

Kennedy Coliseum, Charlottetown, P.E.I.

20 May

Forum, Glace Bay, Nova Scotia.

22 May

Memorial Gardens Arena, Campbellton, New Brunswick.

23 May

Arena, Bathurst, New Brunswick.

24 May

Beaverbrook Rink, Fredericton, New Brunswick.

26-31 May

O'Keefe Centre for the Performing Arts, Toronto, Ontario.

1 June

Akron, Ohio.

14 June

Barton Coliseum, Little Rock, Arkansas.

16 June

Coliseum, Jackson, Tennessee.

23-28 June

Garden State Arts Centre, Holmdel, New Jersey.

30 June

Taping the *Today Show* in New York City, New York.

July

"Look At Them Beans"/"All Around Cowboy" (Columbia 3-10177) released. A high of #17 is achieved by this single during a run of 12 weeks.

2 July

Taping the *Mike Douglas Show* in Philadelphia, Pennsylvania.

3-6 July

Westchester Premier Theatre, Tarrytown, New York.

15-23 July

Another week of concerts at the Las Vegas Hilton, Las Vegas, Nevada.

18 July

Centennial Concert Hall, Winnipeg, Manitoba, Canada.

19 July
Exhibition Stadium, Regina, Saskatchewan, Canada.

20 July
Exhibition Pavilion, Lethbridge, Alberta, Canada.

21 July
Exhibition Center, Edmonton, Alberta, Canada.

23 July
Cash appears on the *Dinah Shore* and *Merv Griffin* TV shows, both taped in Los Angeles on this day.

24 July
Cash attends a Christian Bookseller's Convention at the Anaheim Convention Centre, Anaheim, California.

August
Johnny Cash's autobiography *Man In Black* is published by Zondervan. Cash called it a "spiritual odyssey... his own story in his own words."

2-3 August
Allentown Fair, Allentown, Pennsylvania.

4-10 August
Melody Fair Theatre, North Tonawanda Music Theatre, Buffalo, New York.

23 August
Colorado State Fair, Pueblo, Colorado.

24 August
Oregon State Fair, Salem, Oregon.

26 August-1 September
Sahara Tahoe, Lake Tahoe, Nevada.

September
Look At Them Beans (KC-33814) is released.
Tracks: "Texas '47", "What Have You Got Planned Tonight Diana", "Look At Them Beans", "No Charge", "I Hardly Ever Sing

Beer Drinking Songs", "Down The Road I Go", "I Never Met A Man Like You Before", "All Around Cowboy", "Gone", "Down At Drippin' Springs".

7 September
Civic Center, Springfield, Massachusetts.

9 September
Cash's European tour opens with a concert at the Stadthalle, Vienna, Austria.

10 September
Festhalle, Berne, Switzerland.

12 September
Deutsches Museum, Munich, Germany.

13 September
Jahrhunderthalle, Frankfurt, Germany.

14 September
Philipshalle, Dusseldorf, Germany.

15 September
Deutschlandhalle, Berlin, Germany.

17 September
Usher Hall, Edinburgh, Scotland.

18 September
Apollo, Glasgow, Scotland.

20 September
Royal Festival Hall, London, England.

21 September
Palladium, London, England.
Both the 6.00pm and 8.30pm shows are recorded for future release. A bomb scare during one performance meant that the venue had to be cleared and the concert halted. When released as *Strawberry Cake*, material from both shows was used and the announcement regarding the bomb scare was also included.

22 September
Royal Albert Hall, London, England.

24-25 September
Carlton, Dublin, Ireland.

3 October
Super Dome, New Orleans, Louisiana.

9 October
Brown County Arena, Green Bay, Wisconsin.

10 October
Dane County Arena, Madison, Wisconsin.

11 October
Bradley University Gym, Peoria, Illinois.

11 October
Cash's previous release *John R. Cash* had failed to chart but his latest effort *Look At Them Beans* spends the rest of the year in the charts, peaking at #38 at the start of November.

13-19 October
State Fair Music Hall, Dallas, Texas.

20 October
Concert Theatre, Honolulu, Hawaii.

20 October
An appearance on the *Dinah Shore* TV Show is broadcast.

25 October
Sun Plaza Hall, Tokyo, Japan.

28 October
Kobe Kokusai Hall, Kobe, Japan.

29 October
Koseninenkin Hall, Osaka, Japan.

30 October
Public Hall, Nagoya, Japan.

31 October
Budokan, Tokyo, Japan.

November
The second single from the *Look At Them Beans* album, "Texas '47"/"I Hardly Ever Sing Beer Drinking Songs" (Columbia 3-10237) is released and climbs to #35.

1-2 November
West High School Auditorium, Anchorage, Alaska.

14-16 November
Capitol Music Hall, Wheeling, West Virginia.

17-23 November
Shady Grove Music Fair, Silver Springs, Maryland.

25 November-4 December
Cash ends the year with another round of concerts at the Hilton in Las Vegas, Nevada.

Late-1975
Destination Victoria Station (VS-150) released.
Tracks: "Casey Jones", "Hey Porter", "Legend Of John Henry's Hammer", "Wabash Cannonball", "City Of New Orleans", "Folsom Prison Blues", "Crystal Chandaliers And Burgundy", "Wreck Of The Old '97", "Waiting For A Train", "Orange Blossom Special", Texas '47", "Destination Victoria Station".

Most of these tracks were newly recorded and the album was released as a promotional item by CBS Special Products and sold only in the Victoria Station restaurant chain. The album would be re-issued by Bear Family Records of Germany a few years later.

1976

January
Tommy Cash, John's brother, becomes a regular on the road show. Around the same time Carl Perkins and Gordon Terry leave.

11-14 January
John acts as host for *200 Years Of Circus In America*. The show is taped at the Ringling Brothers Circus headquarters in St. Petersburg, Florida and is due to be broadcast on NBC-TV on 18 February.

16 January
Brown County Arena, Green Bay, Wisconsin.

17 January
P.E. Building, Rockford College, Rockford, Illinois.

18 January
Dane County Arena, Madison, Wisconsin.

21 January
Auditorium, Topeka, Kansas.

22 January
Hearnes Building, Columbia, Missouri.

23 January
Memorial Auditorium, Kansas City, Kansas.

24 January
Century II Arena, Wichita, Kansas.

25 January
Memorial Hall, Salina, Kansas.

26 January
Auditorium Theater, Oklahoma City, Oklahoma.

27 January

Gammage Auditorium, Arizona State University, Tempe, Arizona.

28 January
Coliseum, Amarillo, Texas.

30 January
Ector County Coliseum, Odessa, Texas.

31 January
University Gym, Portales, New Mexico.

February
Columbia release "Strawberry Cake"/"I Got Stripes" (Columbia 3-10279), two live tracks taken from the forthcoming album recorded in London in 1975.

1 February
Civic Center, El Paso, Texas.

2 February
Civic Auditorium, Albuquerque, Texas.

16 February
Cash makes a surprise appearance at a David Allan Coe concert at the Exit/In in Nashville. Together they perform "Cocaine Carolina", a track from the recent *John R. Cash* album.

28 February
Johnny Cash is nominated for his first gospel Grammy Award at the annual ceremony which is broadcast live by CBS from the Auditorium in Nashville, Tennessee. His album *Johnny Cash Sings Precious Memories* is nominated in the 'Best Gospel Performance (Other Than Soul Gospel)' category but is beaten by *No Shortage* (The Imperials). The eligibility period for this year's awards were 16 October 1974 – 15 October 1975.

Late-February
Johnny Cash, June Carter-Cash, The Carter Family and The Tennessee Three play a benefit concert at the Arizona State University in Tempe, Arizona for the American Freedom Train. The train was on

a 20,000 mile journey through 48 states celebrating the Bicentennial.

February-March
At the House of Cash Studios a back to basics sound is utilised on sessions for the *One Piece At A Time* recordings.

March
The live album *Strawberry Cake* (KC-34088) is released.
Tracks: "Big River", "Dialogue", "Doin' My Time", "Dialogue", "I Still Miss Someone", "Dialogue", "Dialogue", "I Got Stripes", "Dialogue", "Church In The Wildwood", "Lonesome Valley", "Dialogue", "Strawberry Cake", "Dialogue", "Rock Island Line", "Navajo", "Dialogue", "Destination Victoria Station", "The Fourth Man".

March
"One Piece At A Time"/"Go On Blues" (Columbia 3-10321) is released. An accompanying video is shot for *One Piece At A Time* and this video would be featured in most of Johnny Cash's concerts through the late-seventies and early eighties.

6 March
The live single "Strawberry Cake" starts its 7-week chart run, and will peak at #54.

10 March
John is honoured with a star on Hollywood Boulevard.

10-14 March
Circle Star Theatre, San Carlos, California.

18 March
Cash plays a benefit at the Middle Tennessee State University, Murfreesboro, Tennessee.

20 March
Johnny Cash Homecoming Day in Kingsland and Rison, Arkansas. The day began in Kingsland with various ceremonies and then John, June and John Carter-Cash travelled by train the 30-minute ride to Rison. Cash was awarded the Key to the City of Rison along with a plaque. A parade in the afternoon was followed by an hour-long concert in the evening.

30 March-3 April
Cash embarks on a European tour with the opening shows at the Hamburger Bors Club in Stockholm, Sweden.

3 April
The live recording *Strawberry Cake* makes its chart debut at #46. An eight-week run will see it go no higher than #33.

5 April
Scandinavium Hall, Gothenberg, Sweden.

During his time in Sweden he is presented with a platinum award for sales of over 130,000 copies of *Johnny Cash At San Quentin*. The award is presented by Jorgen Larsen, managing director of CBS.

6 April
Congress Hall, Hamburg, Germany

6 April
Cash appearance on the *Merv Griffith* TV Show is aired.

7 April
Kuppelsaal, Hannover, Germany.

8 April
Ludwigshafen, Germany.

9 April
Hallenstadion, Zurich, Sitzerland.

10 April
Champs-Elyse Theatre, Paris, France.

11 April
Ahoy Hall, Rotterdam.
24 April

Johnny Cash and June appear on *Hee-Haw*.

30 April
Ozark, Alabama.

May
One Piece At A Time (KC-34193) is released.
Tracks: "Let There Be Country", "One Piece At A Time", "In A Young Girl's Mind", "Mountain Lady", "Michigan City Howdy-Do", "Sold Out Of Flagpoles", "Committed To Parkview", "Daughter Of A Railroad Man", "Love Has Lost Again", "Go On Blues".

1 May
Arts Festival, Jackson, Mississippi.

7 May
Civic Auditorium, Bakersfield, California.

8 May
Civic Theater, San Diego, California.

9 May
Convention Center, Anaheim, California.

11 May
Sacramento, California.

12 May
Convention Center, Redding, California.

13 May
Coliseum, Portland, Oregon.

14 May
Billy Graham Crusade at the Arena, Seattle, Washington.

15 May
Memorial Arena, Victoria, British Columbia.

16 May
Queen Elizabeth Theatre, Kelowna, British Columbia.

17 May
Memorial Arena, Kamloops, British Columbia.

18 May
Stampede Corral, Calgary, Alberta.

20 May
Opera House, Spokane, Washington.

21 May
Civic Center Arena, Great Falls, Montana.

22 May
Civic Center, Billings, Montana.

29 May
The single "One Piece At A Time", which made its chart debut back in April reaches #1 and holds this position for two weeks. Its success is partly down to the accompanying video, but also the return to basics sound that was employed during the sessions. On the pop charts it climbs to #29.

31 May-17 June
Taping of four Johnny Cash Shows at the Grand Ole Opry House and Opryland in Nashville. The shows are produced by Joseph Cates and will feature Cash, June Carter-Cash, Carl Perkins, The Statler Brothers, The Carter Family and the Tennessee Three. These shows will run for four weeks between 29 August and 19 September.

12 June
A return to form sees Cash's latest album *One Piece At A Time* charting at #23. A 15 week spell on the chart followed during which it managed to hold the #2 spot for a couple of weeks in mid-July.

21-27 June
Front Row Theatre, Cleveland, Ohio.

28 June
Fair, Saratoga, New York.

GOOD OL' NEW JOHNNY CASH

"One Piece at a Time" is Johnny Cash's smash hit single. It's also the title of his new album that's just filled to the brim with the kind of great Johnny Cash songs and music that have made you love him all these years.

JOHNNY CASH AND THE TENNESSEE THREE ONE PIECE AT A TIME including Sold Out Of Flagpoles Michigan City Howdy Do Let There Be Country Love Has Lost Again Go On Blues

July

Cash records "I Wish I Was Crazy Again" and "There Ain't No Good Chain Gang" with Waylon Jennings. Both tracks, along with other material recorded during this period, will appear on the *I Would Like To See You Again* album.

July

"Sold Out Of Flagpoles"/"Mountain Lady" (Columbia 3-10381) released. This second single from the *One Piece At A Time* album reaches #29 in the charts.

3 July

"One Piece At A Time" gives Cash another British hit when it enters the singles chart. During a run of seven weeks the single peaks at #32.

4 July
John is Parade Marshall in Washington, D.C. during the bicentennial celebrations.

12-18 July
Music Tent, Warwick, Rhode Island.

20 July
Cattaraugus County Fairground, Little Valley, New York.

27 July-2 August
Most of this period is taken up with filming for John and June's appearance in the TV series *Little House On The Prairie* in Los Angeles.

9-15 August
Five performances at the Valley Forge Theatre, Devon, Pennsylvania.

16 August
Wolf Trap Theatre, Vienna, Virginia.

18 August
12,000 people attend two shows at the Iowa State Fair, Des Moines, Iowa.

19 August
State Fair, Milwaukee, Wisconsin.

22 August
Two performances at the Indiana State Fair, Indianapolis, Indiana, with the first a complete sell-out.

25-26 August
Ottawa Fair, Ottawa, Ontario.

28 August
Pacific National Exhibition, Vancouver, British Columbia.

29 August
Canadian National Exhibition, Toronto, Canada.

29 August
The first of the Johnny Cash TV Shows taped back in May and June is broadcast.

30 August
Illinois State Fair, Du Quoin, Illinois.

31 August
Ohio State Fair, Columbus, Ohio.

1 September
South Dakota Fair, Huron, South Dakota.

2 September
Civic Centre, Jamestown, North Dakota.

4 September
15,000 people attend a concert at the Nebraska State Fair, Lincoln, Nebraska.

5 September
Minnesota State Fair, St. Paul, Minnesota.

5, 12 & 19 September
The remaining three TV shows are broadcast on these three dates.

26 September
Kaintuck Territory, Benton, Kentucky.

28 September
Fair, Bloomsburg, Pennsylvania.

29 September
Cambria County War Memorial, Johnstown, Pennsylvania.

30 September
Beaver Falls, Ohio.

October
"It's All Over"/"Riding On The Cottonbelt" (Columbia 3-10424) released.

1 October
Civic Center, Charleston, Virginia.

2-3 October
WWVA Jamboree, Wheeling, West Virginia.

10-11 October
Grand Ole Opry, Nashville, Tennessee. John hosts the Country Music Association

Awards Show with Roy Clark. The show won the highest TV rating for the year and was attended by over 4,400. Waylon Jennings and Willie Nelson won two awards, for 'Duet Of The Year' and 'Single Of The Year' for their recording of "Good Hearted Woman".

16 October
John and June appear at a Super Rally for Youth For Christ at the Arrowhead Stadium, Kansas City.

17 October
Nearly 19,000 people attend the Tommy Barnett Crusade in Davenport, Iowa.

21 October
L.C.Walker Arena, Muskegon, Michigan.

22 October
Civic Center, Saginaw, Michigan.

23 October
Wings Stadium, Kalamazoo, Michigan.

24 October
John and June guest on the Billy Graham Crusade at the Stadium, Pontiac, Michigan.

November
"Old Time Feeling"/"Far Side Banks Of Jordan" (Columbia 3-10436) released. Both sides feature June Carter-Cash.

1-6 November
Taping for the forthcoming Christmas special, provisionally titled *Johnny Cash At Home*. Filming took place at the House Of Cash in Hendersonville, Bon Aqua, their farm in Hickman County and The Opry House in Nashville. Guests included Roy Clark, Tony Orlando, Merle Travis, Barbara Mandrell and Billy Graham.

10 November
City Auditorium, Beaumont, Texas.

11-14 November
Music Theater, Houston, Texas.

16 November
Johnny Cash and the Tennessee Three appear on the *Tony Orlando And Dawn Show*.

19 November
Felt Forum, New York City, New York.

20 November
Symphony Hall, Boston, Massachusetts.

21 November
Civic Center, Hartford, Connecticut.

24 November-3 December
Las Vegas Hilton, Las Vegas, Nevada.

November-December
The recent singles, "It's All Over" and "Old Time Feeling", both appear on the chart, with the latter being the most successful when, in early 1977, it climbs to #26.

1977

January
The House of Cash Studio changes its name and will now be known as Sound Spectrum Studios.

January
Keyboard player Larry McCoy leaves the Johnny Cash showband and is replaced by Earl Poole Ball.

January
"The Last Gunfighter Ballad"/"City Jail" (Columbia 3-10483) released. The a-side is the title track of Cash's forthcoming album.

14 January
San Francisco.

15 January
San Quentin & Folsom Prison.

16 January
John Denver TV Show.

21 January
Arena, Hershey, Pennsylvania.

22 January
War Memorial, Syracuse, New York.

23 January
Auditorium, Rochester, New York.

24 January
Broome County Arena, Binghamton, New York.

25 January
Auditorium, Kingston, Ontario.

26 January
Cornwall, Ontario.

27 January
High School Auditorium, Burlington, Vermont.

28 January
Civic Center, Augusta, Maine.

29 January
New Haven, Connecticut.

February
Records the concept album *The Rambler*.

February
The Last Gunfighter Ballad (KC-34314) is released.

Tracks: "I Will Dance With You", "Last Gunfighter Ballad", "Far Side Banks Of Jordan", "Ridin' On The Cottonbelt", "Give It Away", "You're So Close To Me", "City Jail", "Cindy, I Love You", "Ballad Of Barbara", "That Silver Haired Daddy Of Mine".

4 February
June Carter-Cash is presented with a Doctor of Humane Letters degree from the National University of San Diego. The presentation is held in front of 300 specially invited guests at The House of Cash in Hendersonville, Tennessee.

11 February
Greenville, South Carolina.

12 February
Columbia, South Carolina.

13 February
Savannah, Georgia.

14 February
Charleston, South Carolina.

15 February
Augusta, Georgia.

17 February
Fayetteville, North Carolina.

18 February
Hampton Roads, Virginia.

19 February
Wilmington, North Carolina.

20 February
A concert in Raleigh, North Carolina is cancelled.

22 February
An interview recorded backstage at Madison Square Garden in New York is first broadcast today. *Army Reserve Presents Country Cooking* was introduced by Lee Arnold, who talks to Cash about his

career and plays tracks from his *One Piece At A Time* album. Over the years Cash had recorded many interviews for the Army Reserve, and back in 1974/75 a similar-style show was recorded and broadcast with tracks from *The Junkie And The Juicehead*.

26 February
The title track of Cash's latest album enters the chart at #81 and goes on to peak at # 38 in April.

2 March
John along with Glen Campbell, Roger Miller and Mary Kay Place are all guests on the *John Denver-Thank God I'm A Country Boy* TV special broadcast this day.

5 March
Cash's latest album *The Last Gunfighter Ballad* charts at #45 and will eventually reach #29 during its seven-week run.

15 March
Atlanta, Georgia.

16 March
A show booked in Tallahassee, Florida is cancelled.

17 March
Lakeland, Florida.

18 March
Mobile, Alabama.

23 March
Johnny and June guest on the Billy Graham Crusade in Asheville, North Carolina.

25 March
Indiana State University, Terre Haute, Indiana.

26 March
Hammons Arena, SW Missouri State University, Springfield, Missouri.

27 March
Kiel Opera House, St. Louis, Missouri.

28 March
University of Dayton Arena, Dayton, Ohio.

29 March
High School Auditorium, Kokomo, Indiana.

April
Little House On The Prairie is shown on WRTV. In the long running TV show Cash guests as a con artist, Caleb Hodgekiss, posing as a preacher who believes the Lord helps those that help themselves. He takes this literally and helps himself to money and goods intended for the victims of a burned-out town.

15 April
Auditorium, Port Huron, Michigan.

16 April
University Gym, Central Michigan University, Mt. Pleasant, Michigan.

17 April
Civic Center, Lansing, Michigan.

18 April
I. M. A. Sports Arena, Flint, Michigan.

19 April
Auditorium, Grand Rapids, Michigan.

20 April
Gardens, Sault Ste. Marie, Ontario.

21 April
Lakeview Arena, Marquette, Michigan.

22 April
Wisconsin State University Field House, Stevens Point, Wisconsin.

23 April
University Arena, University of Wisconsin, Eau Claire, Wisconsin.

3-8 May
Music Fair, Westbury, New York.

15 May
A record crowd of 43,000 attend the Billy Graham Crusade held at the Notre Dame, South Bend, Indiana. During the show John performed "Why Me Lord" and, with June, "Far Side Banks Of Jordan".

16-17 May
Orpheum Theatre, Omaha, Nebraska.

18 May
Auditorium, Sioux Falls, South Dakota.

19 May
Auditorium, Sioux City, Iowa.

20 May
Auditorium, Cedar Rapids, Iowa.

21 May
4 Seasons Arena, Cedar Falls, Iowa.

22 May
A show scheduled at the Masonic Auditorium in Davenport, Iowa is cancelled due to John and June suffering from exhaustion.

31 May
St. Cloud, Minnesota.

1 June
Mankato, Minnesota.

2 June
Superior, Wisconsin.

3 June
University of North Dakota, Grand Forks, North Dakota.

4 June
Rochester, Minnesota.

5 June
Dallas, Texas.

30 June-6 July
Cash returns to the Sahara Tahoe, Stateline, Nevada for a short concert engagement.

July
"Lady"/"Hit The Road And Go" (Columbia 3-10587) released. This single, the first to be taken from the forthcoming *Rambler* album, does not make much impression on the chart, only reaching #46.

July
The Rambler (KC-34833) is released.
Tracks: "Hit The Road And Go", "Dialogue", "If It Wasn't For The Wabash River", "Dialogue", "Lady", "Dialogue", "After The Ball", "Dialogue", "No Earthly Good", "Dialogue", "A Wednesday Car", "Dialogue", "My Cowboy's Last Ride", "Dialogue", "Calilou", "Dialogue"

15 July
CBS place an advert for the new album in the music press:

"The Rambler is an entirely new kind of entertainment. It's a story. One that will make you laugh. And feel sad. And it's laced with some of the best music of Johnny Cash's career."

16 July
Brush Run Park, Richland, Ohio.

18 July
Concert Hall, Winnipeg, Manitoba, Canada.

19 July
Keystone Centre, Branden, Manitoba, Canada.

20 July
Centennial Theatre, Regina, Saskatchewan, Canada.

21 July
Coliseum, Edmonton, Canada.

23-25 July
Frontier Days, Cheyenne, Wyoming.

26 July
Rushmore Plaza, Rapid City, South Dakota.

30 July
Cash's latest release *The Rambler* opens its eight-week chart run when it debuts at #42.

5-6 August
Great Adventure, Lakewood, New Jersey

8-13 August
Melody Fair, Buffalo, New York.

16 August
Elvis Presley dies of a heart attack at his Graceland home in Memphis, Tennessee. The next day he was due to commence a nationwide tour starting in Portland, Maine. Mass hysteria follows the announcement, with crowds exceeding tens of thousands lining the sidewalks along Elvis Presley Boulevard. Thousands get the chance to view the body before a private burial ceremony.

A press release issued by Johnny Cash reads:
"June and I loved and admired Elvis Presley. We join his family friends and loved ones in mourning his death. He was the King of us all in country, rock, folk and rhythm and blues. I never knew an entertainer who had his personal magnetism and charisma. The women loved him and the men couldn't help watching him. His presence filled every room he walked in. He, of course, will never be forgotten and his influence will always be felt and reflected in the music world." - Johnny Cash

19 August
Illinois State Fair, Springfield, Illinois.

21 August
West Virginia Fair, Lewisburg, West Virginia.

25 August
Traverse City, Michigan.

25 August
Traverse City, Michigan.

26 August
Tulip Festival, Holland, Michigan.

28 August
Alpine Theatre, Troy, Wisconsin.

31 August
Pine Knob, Pontiac, Michigan.

1 September
New York State Fair, Syracuse, New York.

2 September
Jamestown, New York.

3 September
Canfield, Ohio.

15 September
Huntington, West Virginia.

17 September
Interstate Fair, York, Pennsylvania.

18 September
Wilkes-Barre, Pennsylvania.

19-20 September
Eastern State Expo, Springfield, Massachusetts.

26 September-2 October
Painters Mill Music Fair, Owing Mills, Maryland.

October
A second single from *The Rambler* is released. Like the previous single "After The Ball"/"Calilou" (Columbia 3-10623) it only makes it to the lower regions of the chart.

10 October
The annual CMA Awards Ceremony hosted by Johnny Cash is broadcast from the Opry House, Nashville, Tennessee. During the show Cash presented a Hall of Fame tribute to Merle Travis, who was the year's inductee.

14 October
The Johnny Cash Show tops the bill at the 19th CMA Awards Banquet at the Auditorium in Nashville.

15 October
CBS Records Show.
Auditorium, Nashville, Tennessee.

17-22 October
Taping for the CBS Christmas Special takes place in Nashville, Tennessee. Material for the Special had already been filmed in the Holy Land during a short visit when Cash wandered through Bethlehem's Church of the Nativity, Shepherd's Field and Galilee. Guests on the show included Roy Clark who performed "Rip It Up" and "The Great Pretender", Roy Orbison, The Statler Brothers, Jerry Lee Lewis, who sang "White Christmas", and Carl Perkins. Johnny Cash joined Perkins, Lewis and Orbison for a memorable tribute to the late Elvis Presley with "This Train Is Bound For Glory".

25 October
The second volume of Cash's greatest hits, *The Johnny Cash Portrait/His Greatest Hits Volume 2* achieves gold status.

3 November
Vienna, Austria.

4 November
Frankfurt, Germany.

13 November
Baton Rouge, Louisiana.

15 November
La Crosse, Wisconsin.

16 November
Green Bay, Wisconsin.

17 November
Madison.

18 November
Chicago, Illinois.

20 November
Shrine Auditorium, Peoria, Illinois.

Late November
The CBS television movie *Thaddeus Rose And Eddie* is filmed at locations including Floresville in Texas a small community near San Antonio. Local residents watch as a seemingly drunken Johnny Cash was driven up to the county courthouse by a law enforcement officer. There was no need for them to worry as the scene was repeated several times. The movie revolves around the attempts of Thaddeus "Sledge" Rose, played by Cash, to get out of his rut of drinking and women chasing by purchasing a citrus farm in the Rio Grande Valley of Texas. Shooting continues in Poth and Harlingen.

1978

14 January
Rapides Coliseum, Alexandria, Arkansas.

15 January
Pine Bluff Convention Centre, Pine Bluff, Arkansas.

16 January
John E. Tucker Coliseum, Russellville, Arkansas.

17 January
Memorial Hall, Joplin, Missouri.

18 January
Century II, Wichita, Kansas.

19 January
Gross Coliseum, Hays, Kansas.

20 January
Hearnes Multipurpose Building, Columbia, Missouri.

24 January
Cash, Jimmy Dean, Glen Campbell and Roy Clark appear on the *Kraft 75th Anniversary Special* aired by ABC-TV.

February
"I Would Like To See You Again"/"Lately" (Columbia 3-10681) released. The a-side is the title track of Cash's next album, to be released in April, and debuts on the chart at #74. It climbs to #12 during 13 weeks of chart action.

1-5 February
Billy Graham, Crusade, Las Vegas, Nevada.

13 February
Grady Gammage, Tempe, Arizona.

14 February
Civic Center, Yuma, Arizona.

15-19 February
Circle Star Theatre, San Carlos, California During the seven concerts they played to a total of 26,000 people.

24 February
Convention Center, Dallas, Texas.

24 February
Thaddeus Rose And Eddie is shown on TV.

March
Unissued Johnny Cash (BFX-15016) released.
Tracks: "Mama's Baby", "Fools Hall Of Fame", "Walkin' The Blues", "Cold Shoulder", "Viel Zu Spat (I Got Stripes)", "Wo Ist Zu Hause, mama (Five Feet High And Rising)", "Fable Of Willie Brown", "The Losing Kind", "So Do I", "Shamrock Doesn't Grow In California", "The Danger Zone", "I'll Be All Smiles Tonight".

This was the first release by re-issue specialists Bear Family Records of Germany. Over the next few years they would go on to release several more compilations of previously unissued material.

1 March
Jones Hall, Houston, Texas.

8 March
Civic Center, El Paso, Texas.

9 March
Civic Theater, Tucson, Arizona.

9 March
Behind Prison Walls, a one-hour special filmed inside Nashville's State Prison and featuring Cash, Linda Ronstadt, Roy Clark and Foster Brooks, is aired.

10 March
North Arizona University, Flagstaff, Arizona.

11 March
Convention Center, Anaheim, California.

12 March
Civic Theater, San Diego, California.

13 March
Santa Maria, California.

14 March
Selland Arena, Fresno, California.

15 March
Auditorium, Redding, California.

16 March
Huimboldt State Coliseum, Arcata, California.

30 March
Thibideaux, Louisiana.

31 March
Arkansas State University, Jonesboro, Arkansas.

April
I Would Like To See You Again (KC-35313) is released. The album includes Waylon Jennings on two tracks.
Tracks: "I Would Like To See You Again",

"Lately", "I Wish I Was Crazy Again", "Who's Gene Autry", "Hurt So Bad", "I Don't Think I Could Take You Back Again", "Abner Brown", "After Taxes", "There Ain't No Good Chain Gang", "That's The Way It Is", "I'm Alright Now".

9 April
Deutschlandhalle, Berlin, Germany.

10-11 April
The four concerts at the Ice Hall in Prague, Czechoslovakia draw crowds of 44,000. Recordings made at these concerts will be released on the album *Koncert V Praze (In Prague Live)*, although it is five years before they are issued. Rosanne Cash also appeared at this show.

13 April
CCH, Hamburg, Germany.

14 April
Munsterlandhalle, Munster, Germany.

15 April
Zurich, Switzerland.

17 April
Linz, Austria.

18 April
Sporthalle, Boblingen, Munich, Germany.

19 April
Deutsches Museum, Munich, Germany.

20 April
Sporthalle, Köln, Germany.

21 April
Philipshalle, Dusseldorf, Germany.

May
"There Ain't No Good Chain Gang"/"I Wish I Was Crazy Again" (Columbia 3-10742) released. Both these tracks are duets with Waylon Jennings and are lifted from the *I Would Like To See You Again* album.

5 May
Carowinds Park, Charlotte, North Carolina.

6 May
Charlottesville, Virginia.

11 May
Glen Sherley, who had written "Greystone Chapel", recorded by Cash during his 1968 Folsom Prison concert, died in Gonzales, California.

13 May
"I Would Like To See You Again" enters the charts at #50. It will remain on the chart until mid-August, reaching a high of #23.

14 May
In Memphis, Tennessee both John and June guest on the Billy Graham Crusade. The show is due to be broadcast on TV in June.

20 May
A double-header where Cash appears in Prince George Industrial Park, Petersburg, Virginia in the afternoon and in the evening at The Mosque, Richmond, Virginia.

21 May
Coliseum, Fort Wayne, Indiana.

23 May
International Ballroom, Conrad Hilton Hotel, Chicago, Illinois.

24 May
London Gardens, London, Ontario.

25 May
Memorial Auditorium, Kitchener, Ontario.

26 May
Memorial Centre, Peterborough, Ontario.

27 May
Memorial Gardens, North Bay, Ontario.

28 May
Sudbury Community Arena, Sudbury, Ontario.

June
The Johnny Cash/Kirk Douglas film, *A Gunfight,* receives its first TV transmission.

10 June
John receives the *Humanitarian Award* from the 14th Annual Citation Dinner hosted by the B'nai B'rith and Performing Arts Lodge in New York City.

July
In between touring Cash records tracks for the *Gone Girl* album. Material recorded includes the Jack Clement title track, "The Gambler", "A Song For The Life" written by Rodney Crowell and the Mick Jagger/Keith Richards song "No Expectations".

1 July
Convention Center, Niagara Falls, New York.

2 July
Trumbull County Fair, Cortland, Ohio.

7 July
A concert at the Middle Tennessee University, Murfreesboro, Tennessee with Waylon Jennings is cancelled and re-scheduled for October.

8 July
Lanierland Amusement Park, Cumming, Georgia.

8 July
"There Ain't No Good Chain Gang" reaches #2, where it will stay for a couple of weeks.

15-21 July
A week of concerts at the Sahara Tahoe, Lake Tahoe, Nevada.

24-29 July
Garden State Art Center, Woodbridge, New Jersey.

August
"Gone Girl"/"I'm Alright Now" (Columbia 3-10817) released. The a-side is the title track from his forthcoming release.

10 August
Fair, Ionia, Michigan.

11 August
Morris Civic Auditorium, South Bend, Indiana.

12 August
Wisconsin   State   Fair,   Milwaukee,
Wisconsin.

15 August
Ohio State Fair, Columbus, Ohio.

18-19 August
Executive Inn, Owensboro, Kentucky.

21-22 August
Temple University, Philadelphia,
Pennsylvania.

26 August
Wolf Trap, Vienna, Virginia.

27 August
Performing Arts Centre, Saratoga,
New York.

28 August
Nanuet, New York.

30 August
Jubilee Auditorium, Calgary, Edmonton,
Alberta.

31 August
Pacific National Exhibition, Vancouver,
British Columbia.

2 September
Nebraska State Fair, Lincoln, Nebraska.

3 September
Minnesota State Fair, St. Paul, Minnesota.

9 September
Following a couple of strong releases it is
surprising that *Gone Girl* only manages to
climb to #44 during its spell on the chart.

16-17 September
Western   Washington   Fair,   Puyallup,
Washington.

18 September
Opera House, Spokane, Washington.

19 September
Adams Fieldhouse, Missoula, Montana.

20 September
Civic Center Arena, Butte, Montana.

21 September
Civic Auditorium, Idaho Falls, Idaho.

22 September
Weber State College, Ogden, Utah.

23 September
Denver, Colorado.

1 October
King's Dominion, Richmond, Virginia.

9 October
Johnny Cash hosts the 12th annual Country
Music Association Awards Show, broadcast
live from the Grand Ole Opry House in
Nashville, Tennessee on the CBS-TV
network. The is the fifth time he has been
host or co-host of this prestigious event.
Dolly Parton wins Entertainer Of The Year
and Grandpa Jones is inducted into the Hall
Of Fame.

18 October
Johnny Cash and Waylon Jennings appear
at a four-hour concert held at the Middle
Tennessee   University,   Murfreesboro,
Tennessee. Cash opened the show with a
90-minute set and Waylon joined him for
"There Ain't No Good Chain Gang" and
"The Greatest Cowboy Of Them All".
Waylon Jennings's 45-minute set was
followed by 11 songs from Jessi Colter.

19 October
Tennessee   Technical   University,
Cookeville, Tennessee.

21-25 October
Christmas Special taping in Los Angeles,
California.

23 October
Mother Maybelle Carter, who was 69,

passes away. Her funeral is held on 25 October.

November
Gone Girl (KC-35646) is released. Tracks: "Gone Girl", "I Will Rock And Roll With You", "The Diplomat", "No Expectations", "It Comes And Goes", "It'll Be Her", "The Gambler", "Cajun Born", "You And Me", "A Song For The Life".

November
"It'll Be Her"/"It Comes And Goes" (Columbia 3-10855) is released. This second single from *Gone Girl* does worse than the first, peaking at #89 during a brief two-week chart run.

2-5 November
Concerts scheduled in Waco, Ft. Worth, Lubbock and Wichita Falls, all in Texas, are cancelled following the death of Mother Maybelle Carter. June's appearance on *Hollywood Squares* is also cancelled.

22 November
Cash, Bob Hope, Milton Berle and George Burns all appear on Steve Martin's first TV special aired on NBC-TV.

23-26 November
Sahara Tahoe Hotel, Lake Tahoe, Nevada.

December
"I Will Rock And Roll With You"/"A Song For The Life" (Columbia 3-10888) released. The b-side features Cash's daughter Rosanne.

6 December
Johnny Cash's Christmas Special, with guest stars Kris Kristofferson Rita Coolidge and Steve Martin, is televised. The closing song "Silent Night" was dedicated to the memory of Mother Maybelle Carter.

7 December
Kemper Arena, Kansas City, Missouri.

8 December
Sports Arena, Hutchinson, Kansas.

9 December
High School Auditorium, Manhattan, Kansas.

12 December
Cincinnati, Ohio.

23 December
John and June appear on the *Billy Graham Christmas Special*.

29-30 December
Orlando, Florida.

1979

January
This month saw the start of a series of recording sessions that would run through till June. The mammoth project was a gospel album and was a project very close to Cash's heart. Originally released on the Cachet label as a double album, it eventually gained a general release as a single album on Columbia.

8 January
Sara Carter, the only remaining original member of the legendary original Carter Family, passes away at her home in Lodi, California. She was 81 and had been suffering from heart problems for several months.

13 January
The third volume of *Greatest Hits* only manages two weeks on the chart. Meanwhile "I Will Rock And Roll With You", one of the strongest tracks from *Gone Girl,* sees an improvement on the previous releases when it climbs to #21 and remains on the chart for 13 weeks.

February
Johnny And June (BFX-15030) released.

Tracks: "The Baby Is Mine", "Cotton Pickin' Hands", "Close The Door Lightly", "That's What It's Like To Be Lonesome", "Thunderball", "One Too Many Mornings", "How Did You get Away From Me", "Adios Aloha", "Wer Kennt Den Weg (I Walk The Line)", "Ain't You Ashamed", "Smiling Bill McCall", "In Virginia".

As the title suggests this release included material by both Johnny Cash and June Carter-Cash.

1 February
St. Petersburg, Florida.

2 February
Ft. Myers, Florida.

4 February
Jacksonville, Florida.

5 February
Ft. Lauderdale, Florida.

16 February
Champaign, Illinois.

17 February
Madison, Wisconsin.

18 February
Peoria, Illinois.

19 February
A concert booked in Bloomington, Indiana was cancelled due to the weather.

20 February
Cedar Rapids, Iowa.

11 March
Cash starts a short UK tour with a show at the Centre, Brighton, England.

13-16 March
Wembley Conference Centre, London, England.

17 March
Birmingham, England.

18 March
Manchester, England.

20 March
Glasgow, Scotland.

21 March
Cash appears at a Church in Belfast, Ireland. Despite the tensions in the country both religions attended the show and sat on opposite sides of the church!

22 March
Stadium, Dublin, Ireland.

25 March
Billy Graham Crusade in Tampa, Florida.

April
At Hilltop Studios in Madison, Tennessee tracks are recorded by the B. C. Goodpasture Christian School Choir on which Cash will later overdub his vocals. The same month he starts work on his 25th anniversary album at Jack Clement Studios. Among the tracks recorded for this project is a new version of "Cocaine Blues". This track was recorded live at Folsom Prison back in 1968 but was originally recorded by Cash under the title "Transfusion Blues" and issued on his *Now There Was A Song* album.

9-12 April
Taping of the *Johnny Cash Spring Special*. Guests on the show include Waylon Jennings, Martin Mull, George Jones, June Carter-Cash, The Carter Family, The Tennessee Three, Earl Scruggs, Hank Williams Jnr. and Merle Kilgore.

16 April
Memorial Gardens, Sault St. Marie, Ontario.

17 April
Arena, Traverse City, Michigan.

18 April
Walker Arena, Muskegon, Michigan.

19 April
University of Michigan, Ann Arbor, Michigan.

20 April
Civic Centre, Saginaw, Michigan.

21 April
Wings Stadium, Kalamazoo, Michigan.

22 April
Civic Center, Lansing, Michigan.

May
"Ghost Riders In The Sky"/"I'm Gonna Sit On The Porch And Pick On My Old Guitar" (Columbia 3-10961) released. A return to form finds this single climbing to #2 and spending 16 weeks on the chart.

3 May
Bristol, Virginia.
This event featured only John, June and The Carter Family, with no other members of Cash's band appearing.

4 May
George R. Wallace Civic Center, Fitchburg, Massachusetts.

5 May
Symphony Hall, Boston, Massachusetts.

6 May
Civic Center, Portland Maine.

7 May
Aitken University Centre, Fredericton, New Brunswick.

8 May
Halifax Metro Center, Halifax, Nova Scotia.

9 May
Sydney Forum, North Sydney, Nova Scotia.

24-27 June
John & June appear at a Billy Graham Crusade in Nashville, Tennessee.

30 June-1 July
Longleat, England.

July
Tall Man (BFX-15033) released.
Tracks: "Tall Man", "Foolish Questions", "Pick A Bale O' Cotton", "I Tremble For You", "Besser So, Jenny Jo", "Kleine Rosemarie", "My Old Faded Rose", "Rodeo Hand", "Sound Of Laughter", "Hammers And Nails", "Engine 143", "On The Line".

July
"Waltz Across Texas"/"Jealous Loving Heart" (CS4-4501) released. This is an Ernest Tubb single with Cash appearing on the b-side only.

July
Jan Howard leaves The Johnny Cash Show.

8 July
Summerfest, Milwaukee, Wisconsin.

13 July
Playboy Club, Great Gorge, New Jersey.

14 July
Jamboree In The Hills, Wheeling, West Virginia.

15 July
Alpine Valley Music Theatre, Alpine Valley, Wisconsin.

Mid-July
John and June Carter-Cash joined a host of other country music stars for the taping of a TV special tribute to Mother Maybelle Carter. The special had the official title – probably the longest in the history of TV specials – *Lynn Anderson, Carter Family, Johnny Cash, Ray Charles, Larry Gatlin, Emmylou Harris, Waylon Jennings, Kris Kristofferson, Willie Nelson, Linda*

Ronstadt Tribute...The Unbroken Circle: A Country Celebration of Mother Maybelle Carter. Several of the artists taped their parts away from Nashville due to other commitments – Ronstadt and Harris were taped in Los Angeles, Kristofferson was filmed in Montana and Nelson's contribution was shot in Lake Tahoe. Cash, June, Helen and Anita Carter taped their parts outside the Opryland complex. Cash opened the show with memories of Mother Maybelle, remembering her as a tremendous musical influence and a good fishin' buddy!

27-29 July
Front Row Theatre, Cleveland, Ohio.

31 July-5 August
Ak-Sar-Ben Coliseum, Omaha, Nebraska.

August
Johnny Cash releases his 25th anniversary album *Silver* (JC-36086).
Tracks: "The L&N Don't Stop Here Anymore", "Lonesome To The Bone", "Bull Rider", "I'll Say It's True", "Ghost Riders In The Sky", "Cocaine Blues", "Muddy Waters", "West Canterbury Subdivision Blues", "Lately I Been Leanin' Towards The Blues", "I'm Gonna Sit On The Porch And Pick On My Old Guitar".

16 August
Cenung Fairgrounds, Elmira, New York.

17-18 August
Westchester Premier Theatre, Tarrytown, New York.

19 August
Waterloo Village, New Jersey.

20-25 August
South Shore Music Circus, Cohasset, Massachusetts.

26 August
Forum, Montreal, Quebec, Canada.

30 August
Fairgrounds, Mt. Pleasant, Iowa.

31 August
Du Quoin State Fair, Du Quoin, Illinois.

September
"I'll Say It's True"/"Cocaine Blues" (Columbia 1-11103) released. George Jones features on the a-side of this single. The single charts in October but only climbs to #42.

1 September
Canadian National Exhibition Fairgrounds, Toronto, Ontario.

2 September
King's Dominion Park, Doswell, Virginia.

8 September
Cash's 25th anniversary album *Silver* debuts at #30. Surprisingly, this album only manages to reach #28, with a stay of just 10 weeks.

17-19 September
LA County Fair, Pomona, California.

19 September
Radio interview on KLAC during which Cash talks about his life in Nashville, his son and his new album *Silver*.

21 September
Tri-State Fair, Amarillo, Texas.

22 September
Lanierland, Cumming, Georgia.

23 September
Holiday Beach, Douglas, Georgia.

27 September
Civic Center, Seattle, Washington.

28-29 September
Fair, Yakima, Washington.

30 September
Coliseum Arena, Portland, Oregon.

2 October
TV taping at the Ford Theater, Washington, DC in front of President Carter.

9 October
Truckers Convention, Chicago, Illinois.

11-12 October
Cachet Records Show at the Opry House, Nashville, Tennessee. This was a private function.

18 October
Cash receives the United Nations Humanitarian Award for his longstanding support for two children's homes in Jamaica and his work for the Youth For Christ Organisation. The ceremony is held at the Maxwell House Hotel in Nashville. Among those there for the presentation were John and June's children Rosey, Cindy, Kathy and John Carter. Rosanne could not attend as she was expecting her first child, while Carlene was on tour.

24 October
Five Seasons Center, Dubuque, Idaho.

25 October
Riverside Arena, Austin, Minnesota.

26 October
University Field House, Eau Claire, Wisconsin.

27 October
Brown County Arena, Green Bay, Wisconsin.

28 October
Lake View Arena, Marquette, Michigan.

2-4 November
Westbury Theater, Westbury, New York.

15 November
Civic Center, Huntington, West Virginia.

16 November
State Music Hall, Uniontown, Pennsylvania.

17 November
Eisenhower Auditorium, State College, Pennsylvania.

28 November-2 December
Music Theatre, San Carlos, California.

December
A Believer Sings The Truth (CL3-9001) is released. This double album was released on the Cachet label and later issued in the UK as a single album by CBS.
Tracks: "Wings In The Morning", "Gospel Boogie", "Over The Next Hill", "He's Alive", "I've Got Jesus In My Soul", "When He Comes", "I Was There When It Happened", "I'm A New Born Man", "There Are Strange Things Happening Everyday", "Children Go Where I Send Thee", "I'm Just An Old Chunk Of Coal", "Lay Me Down In Dixie", "Don't Take Everybody For Your Friend", "You'll Get Yours And I'll Get Mine", "Oh Come, Angel Band", "This Train Is Bound For Glory", "I'm Gonna Try To Be That Way", "What On Earth Will You Do (For Heaven's Sake)", "That's Enough", "Greatest Cowboy Of Them All".

December
At Nick Lowe's studio in London, Cash records the basic track for "Without Love".

5 December
The Johnny Cash Christmas Special is broadcast with special guests Andy Kaufman, Tom T. Hall and Anne Murray.

17 December
"I Wish I Was Crazy Again" starts a run of 12 weeks, including a couple of weeks at #22, the highest position it manages.

19 December
Century 21 Convention, Las Vegas, Nevada.

Late-1979
Johnny Cash Sings With B.C. Goodpasture Christian School (CHS 79) released.
Tracks: "Amazing Grace", "Sweet By And By", "When The Roll Is Called Up Yonder", "Precious Memories", "Old Rugged Cross", "Rock Of Ages", "American Trilogy", "Will The Circle Be Unbroken", "Daddy Sang Bass", "Everything Is Beautiful", "Gospel John", "Country Roads".

This album was recorded earlier in the year at Hilltop Studios, Madison, Tennessee with Cash's vocals overdubbed in Nashville at a later date.

Late-1979
Sessions begin for Cash's new album, to be titled *Rockabilly Blues*. The album is produced by Earl Ball with one track, "Without Love", produced by Nick Lowe and recorded at his London studio.

1980-1985

"Thank you for coming to our part of the show. We've got songs for you, lots of songs. I don't dance or tell jokes or wear my pants too tight like a lot of entertainers but I know a lot of songs. And I hope we've got some of your favourites. Some of these we've been singing for twenty-five years or more. Some are brand new, some are fairly new."

Johnny Cash on stage at the Wembley Country Music Festival 1981

1980

January

John, June and John Carter spend the early part of the month on vacation in England and Scotland and then travel to Rome and Egypt.

January

"Wings In The Morning"/"What On Earth Would You Do (For Heavens Sake)" (CCT-4506) released but fails to chart.

19 January

The gospel set *A Believer Sings The Truth* enters the chart at #45 and will peak two places higher during its six weeks on the chart. This is Cash's last chart entry for 15 months.

25-26 January

Sunrise Theatre, Ft. Lauderdale, Florida.

27 January

Robarts Arena, Sarasota, Florida.

29 January

Mississippi Coast Coliseum Convention Center, Biloxi, Mississippi.

30 January

Montgomery Civic Center Arena, Montgomery, Alabama.

31 January

John and June appear at a benefit show for the 100 Club of Nashville. Held at the Grand Ole Opry, other artists appearing were Waylon Jennings, Tammy Wynette, George Jones and Tommy Cash. The Club was formed to aid the families of police and firemen killed in the line of duty. Waylon Jennings opened the show followed by Tammy Wynette and George Jones, Tommy Cash and the Johnny Cash Show closed the evening, which was a sellout and raised over $35,000. An appearance for the *Good Morning America* programme is taped backstage during the benefit show.

February

Johnny Cash: The First 25 Years TV show is filmed. Celebrating his 25 years in the business, guests on the show include Kris Kristofferson, June Carter-Cash, Dolly Parton, Waylon Jennings, Tom T. Hall, Carl Perkins, Larry Gatlin and many more. Following the taping John and June held a party for 200 close friends.

February

"Bull Rider"/"Lonesome To The Bone" (Columbia 1-11237) released.

1 February

Von Braun Civic Center, Huntsville, Alabama.

2 February

Vandenburgh Convention Center, Evansville, Indiana.

3 February

Prairie Capital Center, Springfield, Illinois.

11 February

Good Morning America is broadcast.

14 February

John makes a guest appearance on the *Hank Williams: A Man And His Music* special being taped at the Grand Ole Opry.

19 February

Acker Gym, California State University, Chico, California.

20 February

Sacramento Community Convention Center, Sacramento, California.

21 February

During the afternoon Cash plays a show at the Soledad Prison in California followed by an evening show at the Bakersfield Civic Auditorium, Bakersfield, California.

22 February

Anaheim Convention Center, Anaheim, California.

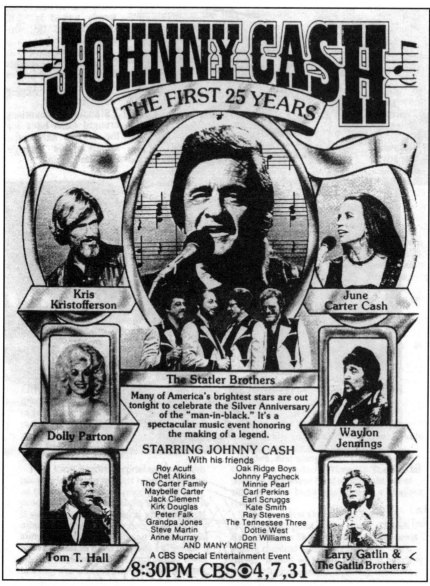

23 February
Claremont College, Bridges Auditorium, Claremont, California.

24 February
Gammage Auditorium, Arizona State University, Tempe, Arizona.

25 February
Community Center, Tucson, Arizona.

26 February
Civic Center, Yuma, Arizona.

27 February
John and June make a non-singing appearance at the annual Grammy Awards ceremony in Los Angeles.

March
Marshall Grant, the last remaining member

of the Tennessee Two, retires and multi-talented instrumentalist Marty Stuart joins the Johnny Cash Show Band. No longer known as Johnny Cash and The Tennessee Three, his new band will be called 'Johnny Cash And The Great Eighties Eight'. Personnel in the band are Bob Wootton (guitar), Marty Stuart (guitar), Joe Allen (bass). W. S. Holland (drums), Jerry Hensley (guitar), Earl Ball (piano), Jack Hale (horns) and Bob Lewin (horns). June Carter-Cash continues to tour with John.

2 March
Private party at the Hyatt Regency, Houston, Texas.

6-9 March
Holiday Star Theater, Merrillville, Indiana.

19 March
Civic Auditorium, Welch, Oklahoma.

20 March
Convention Hall, Wichita, Kansas.

21 March
Bicentennial Center, Salina, Kansas.

22 March
Memorial Hall, Kansas City, Missouri.

23 March
Civic Center, Des Moines, Iowa.

24 March
Corn Palace, Mitchell, South Dakota.

25 March
Sioux City Arena Theater, Sioux City, Iowa.

3 April
Dallas, Texas, Private Convention.

7 April
European tour opens in Hanover, Germany, where a TV show is also taped.

8 April
Olympiahalle, Munich, Germany.

9 April
Saarlandhalle, Saarbruecken, Germany.

10 April
Mozartsaal, Mannheim, Germany.

11 April
Jahrhunderthalle, Frankfurt, Germany.

12 April
Meistersingerhalle, Nuremburg, Germany.

13 April
Basel, Switzerland.

15 April
Halle Münsterland, Münster, Germany.

16 April
Eilenriedehalle, Hanover, Germany.

17 April
Westfalenhalle, Dortmund, Germany.

18 April
Deutschlandhalle, Berlin, Germany.

19 April
Stadthalle, Bremen, Germany.

19 April
After entering the chart at #88, "Bull Rider" will climb to #66 during a brief five weeks of chart action.

29 April
June Carter is honoured at the 11th Community Service Awards held at the Hillwood Country Club in Nashville. Presented by Dr. Nat Winston the award was to honour her community and charitable deeds over the past 12 months.

May
"Song Of The Patriot"/"She's A Goer" (Columbia 1-11283) is released. "Patriot"

features Marty Robbins and during a two month chart residency during June and July will climb to #54.

May
Another round of sessions gets underway with Earl Ball and Jack Clement producing.

1 May
Civic Centre Arena, Ottawa, Canada.

2 May
Onondaga County War Memorial Auditorium, Syracuse, New York.

3 May
Playboy Club, Great Gorge, New Jersey.

4 May
Wicomico Youth & Civic Center, Salisbury, Maryland.

7 May
CBS Affiliates Dinner, Los Angeles, California.

9-10 May
Resort International Hotel, Atlantic City, New Jersey.

24-26 May
Marriott, Gurnee, Illinois.

June
Rockabilly Blues (JC-36779) is released. Tracks: "Cold Lonesome Morning", "Without Love", "W-O-M-A-N", "Cowboy Who Started The Fight", "The Twentieth Century Is Almost Over", "Rockabilly Blues", "The Last Time", "She's A Goer", "It Ain't Nothing New Babe", "One Way Rider".

1 June
Meadowlands, New Jersey.

3 June
Wolftrap Theatre, Washington, DC.

8 June
The trade paper *Cashbox* includes a 36-page insert celebrating his silver anniversary.

14 June
Today is designated Johnny Cash Day in Hendersonville. Although John and June could not attend, the House of Cash was open all day.

27-28 June
Starlight Theatre, Indianapolis, Indiana.

29 June
Six Flags America Park, St. Louis, Missouri.

4 July
The Johnny Cash Silver Anniversary Special, produced by Ed Salamon and the Mutual Broadcasting System, is aired. During the broadcast Cash talks about his career and the show is interspersed with many of his greatest hits.

5 July
Cash plays a concert with the Dallas symphony in temperatures of 105^{0} at the Starfest Site, Dallas, Texas.

10 July
Grandstand, Geneva-On-The-Lake, Ohio.

11-13 July
Theatre-in-the-round, Framingham, Massachusetts.

18 July
KOA Campgrounds, Elkhart, Indiana. This show is advertised in local camping magazines and to see the show, and the Carter Family show the following day, the public had to book a site for the weekend at a cost of $40.

19 July
Dane County Memorial Coliseum, Madison, Wisconsin.

21 July
Rushmore Plaza, Rapid City, South Dakota.

22-24 July
Frontier Days, Cheyenne, Wyoming.

26 July
North Dakota State Fair, Minot, North Dakota.

27 July
Centennial Theatre, Regina, Saskatchewan, Canada

28 July
Manitoba Centennial Concert Hall, Winipeg, Manitoba, Canada

30 July-5 August
Los Angeles, California. These dates were scheduled for taping the *Alice* TV show but were cancelled when John was ill and unable to appear.

August
The latest issue of *Country Music Magazine* devotes most of its pages to John's silver anniversary and features his photo on the cover.

August
Taken from the *Rockabilly Blues* album "Cold Lonesome Morning"/"The Cowboy Who Started The Fight" (Columbia 1-11340) is released as a single. It charts at #88 and only manages to reach #53 during its eight week spell on the charts.

8-10 August
Promoters Fullmore hold a three-day country music festival at a disused airport in Portsmouth, England.

The full line-up for the event runs as follows:

Friday 8 August
Glen Campbell/Johnny Paycheck/Jeannie C. Riley/The Drifting Cowboys/Dee Dee Prestige.

Saturday 9 August
Nashville Superpickers/Tom T. Hall/Hank Williams Jnr./Leona Williams/Terri Hollowell

Sunday 10 August
Johnny Cash/June Carter-Cash/The Great Eighties-Eight/Hoyt Axton/Don King/Liz Howard/Johnny Tillotson/Billie Jo Spears.

Despite the line-up and the surrounding events the festival was a financial disaster. The promoters had hoped for an attendance of more than 100,00, but the total for the three days was only around 20,000. The good weather and the appearance of Johnny Cash, who gave an excellent show, on the final day drew the biggest crowd. Press reports following the event ran headlines like "Johnny Cash was there. Glen Campbell was there. Even Tom T. Hall was there. Only trouble was, the audience wasn't there." It was also reported that Cash offered a refund of part of his fee to help bail out the promoters.

11-13 August
London, England.
Filming *Muppets* TV Show.

16 August
Fairgrounds, Lewisburg, West Virginia.

17 August
Performing Arts Center, Saratoga Springs, New York.

19-20 August
Another selection of seasonal songs are recorded for release as *Classic Christmas* later in the year.

22 August
Fairgrounds, Imperial, Nebraska.

23 August
Fairgrounds, Sioux Falls, South Dakota.

24 August
Pacific National Exhibition Centre, Vancouver, British Columbia.

25 August
Oregon State Fair, Salem, Oregon.

26 August
Fairgrounds, Monroe,Washington.

28 August
Sunflower Exp., Topeka, Kansas.

29 August
Dallas, Texas.

30 August
Colorado State Fair, Pueblo, Colorado.

31 August
Minnesota State Fair, St. Paul, Minnesota.

September
Three tracks - "Six Gun Shooting", "Help Him Jesus" and "The Death Of Me" are recorded for inclusion on the Paul Kennerley-written concept album *The Legend Of Jesse James*. Plans were considered to take this album and Kennerley's previous project *White Mansions*, about the American Civil War, and produce it for the stage.

5 September
June Carter appears on the *Mike Douglas Show* while scheduled appearances on *Hollywood Squares* and Toni Tenille's Show are cancelled.

6 September
Fair, Spencer, Iowa.

7 September
Traverse County Fair, Wheaton, Minnesota.

10 September
Fair, Wooster, Ohio.

12-14 September
Oakdale Music Fair, Wallingford, Connecticut.

15 September
Poughkeepsie, New York.

16 September
Fair, Frederick, Maryland.

October
Classic Christmas (JC-36866) is released. Tracks: "Joy To The World", "Away In A Manger", "O Little Town Of Bethlehem", "Silent Night, Holy Night", "It Came Upon A Midnight Clear", "Hark, The Herald Angels Sing", "I Heard The Bells On Christmas Day", "O Come All Ye Faithful", "Little Gray Donkey", "The Christmas Guest".

6 October
Cash, along with Charles Colson, entertains 3,000 prisoners at the State Prison in Angola, Texas.

12 October
In an article headed *The Outlaw and the Rockabilly*, Johnny Cash interviews Waylon Jennings for *Country Music*

magazine. The magazine had wanted to interview Waylon but couldn't get hold of a number so they approached Cash who said "I'll get out my guns and go and find him. I want to ask him a few things myself." During the interview they talked about Waylon's early career, the record business, Willie Nelson and Kris Kristofferson.

13 October
At the Country Music Awards Show Cash is inducted into the Country Music Hall Of Fame. The presentation is made by Kenny Rogers and in the audience are members of his family and friends. During his acceptance speech Cash said "When I was a little boy, my mother was a great inspiration to me. She's here tonight. I remember in the cottonfields she would tell me to keep singing. I think the singing took us through the work in the cottonfields. She told me 'I think God has his hands on you and you'll be singing for the world someday'. We've had a lot of that dream realized. What with singing our songs all over this country, in Europe, the Orient, Australia, the Middle East, and to Czechoslovakia recently. I'm very grateful to all of you in Country Music. It was at times a struggle starting out and there was not always acceptance in the country music community in Nashville for a long-haired rockabilly from Memphis. But a lot of you welcomed us with open arms, a lot of you took us in as one of your own, and a lot of you did not know what to do with us.

For the past decade it's been a wonderful life. I'd like to say to all the new entertainers that are coming on the scene, to the young artists and singers, don't let yourself get caught in a bag because it's the stylists like Kenny Rogers and some of the great ones of our time…Waylon Jennings…that have made country music what it is…have built the excitement for us all to enjoy. It's given country music a great shot in the arm when the so-called rebels came along…people just doing it their own way.

I'd like to say this also, to all new

artists, that if you're concerned about competition, don't write me off yet!! cause my dad, Ray Cash, is sitting here tonight. he's 83 years old and if God lets me live that long, that's 35 more years that I'm gonna be out there singing country songs."

25 October
The Johnny Cash Show give two performances at the Carter Fold in Hiltons, Virginia.

30 October-1 November
Green Bay, Wisconsin.

November
The concept album *The Legend Of Jesse James* (A&M SP-3718) is released. Written by British songwriter Paul Kennerley, the album featured Levon Helm, Johnny Cash, Emmylou Harris, Charlie Daniels, Albert Lee, Rosanne Cash and Rodney Crowell. Cash appears on three tracks - "Six Gun Shooting", "Help Him Jesus" and "The Death Of Me". He also appears on the chorus of "One More Shot".

November
"Death Of Me"/"One More Shot" (A&M-2291) is released-with both tracks featuring Levon Helm. Taken from *The Legend Of*

Jesse James, the single fails to make any impression on the chart.

November
"The Last Time"/"Rockabilly Blues" (Columbia 1-11399) released. Surprisingly, this second strong release from *Rockabilly Blues* only reaches #85 on the charts.

2 November
LaCrosse Center, LaCrosse, Wisconsin.

6 November
Prison show in Angola, Louisiana.

14-16 November
Holiday Star Theatre, Merrillville, Indiana.

25-30 November
Casino, Lake Tahoe, California.

3 December
Astrodome, Houston, Texas.

3 December
Johnny Cash's 1980 Christmas Special is broadcast, featuring Mac Davis, Jeannie C. Riley and Larry Gatlin.

5 December
Nearly $40,000 is raised during a benefit concert in aid of the Port Richey and New Port Richey Police officers. The show is held at the Gulf High School Gym in Port Richey, Florida.

Late 1980
Running through to early 1981, material is recorded for the film *The Pride Of Jesse Hallam*. Both album and incidental film music are recorded. The movie, filmed entirely on location in Kentucky and Cincinatti, Ohio, tells the story of Jesse Hallam (Johnny Cash) a 45-year old Kentucky farmer who has to overcome his illiteracy after he is forced to leave his farm and move to Cincinatti when his daughter needs medical treatment. Embarrassed by his inability to read and write - he can't even fill in an application form - he attends school with his son and finally overcomes his problems. Several songs were featured in the movie, including John Prine's "Paradise", Billy Joe Shaver's "I'm Just An Old Chunk Of Coal", Cash's own "Movin' Up", and "Sweet Kentucky", composed by Alan Shapiro. Cash also sings a few lines of "Cripple Creek" unaccompanied. Although some of these tracks have been released on album, these film versions differ slightly and remain unissued.

1981

January
"Without Love"/"It Ain't Nothing New, Babe" (Columbia 1-11424) released.

7-10 January
Carlton, Minneapolis, Minnesota.

12-13 January
Youth For Christ TV taping in Toronto, Ontario.

19 January
TV taping with Merv Griffin and Dinah Shore in Los Angeles.

22 January
St. Lucie County Civic Center, Ft. Pierce, Florida.

23 January
Civic Center, Lakeland, Florida.

24 January
Sunrise Theatre, Ft. Lauderdale, Florida.

24 January
The *Muppet Show* starring Johnny Cash is broadcast. In the show Cash inspires Kermit to hold an old-fashioned hoedown. During the show he sings "Ghost Riders In The Sky" and a medley of his famous railroad songs. Unfortunately, Kermit has allowed radio station WHOG to broadcast live from the theatre and it can only mean trouble.

24 January
The Nick Lowe composition "Without Love" debuts at #89 at the start of a five week run that will see it go no higher than #78.

27-28 January
Police show, Nashville, Tennessee.

30 January
Ziegfield's Night Club, Tulsa, Oklahoma.

31 January
Hirsch Coliseum, Shreveport, Louisiana.

6 February
Caldwell Auditorium, Tyler, Texas.

7 February
Port Arthur Civic Center, Port Arthur, Texas.

8 February
Thibodaux Civic Center, Thibodaux, Louisiana.

12 February
Sumter, South Carolina.

13 February
Greenville Memorial Coliseum, Greenville, South Carolina.

14 February
Asheville Civic Center, Asheville, North Carolina.

22 February
Symphony Hall, Boston, Massachusetts.

23 February
Civic Auditorium, Albany, New York.

24 February
Civic Center, Springfield, Massachusetts.

26 February
Civic Center, Portland, Maine.

27 February
Memorial Auditorium, Burlington, Vermont.

28 February
Eastman Theatre, Rochester, New York.

March
During March Cash records with renowned Nashville producer Billy Sherrill. Even though Cash has been with CBS for 22 years and Sherrill has been producing CBS artists for 17 years this is the first time they have worked together. Material recorded during these sessions will appear on the album *The Baron*.

March
"The Baron"/"I Will Dance With You" (Columbia 11-60516) released.

1-4 March
A Home Box Office TV Special is taped at the Kennedy Center, Washington, DC.

3 March
CBS-TV premier the new movie *The Pride Of Jesse Hallam*.

3 March
The Mike Douglas Show is broadcast featuring special guest Johnny Cash.

7 March
Stanley Theatre, Pittsburgh, Pennsylvania.

8 March
Springer Auditorium, Cincinnati, Ohio.

9 March
Memorial Auditorium, Kitchener, Ontario.

10 March
London Gardens, London, Ontario.

11-12 March
Taping for the TV special *Country Comes Home* takes place over two days at the Opry House in Nashville. One segment of the show includes John, June and The Carter Family performing "Thinking Tonight Of My Blues Eyes" and going on to explain how this song evolved into three well-known country songs - "The Wild Side Of Life", "The Great Speckled Bird" and "It Wasn't God Who Made Honky Tonk Angels".

16-25 March
John and June film their Spring television special, to be titled *Johnny Cash And The Country Girls*, at the Grand Ole Opry in Nashville. It is planned to have nearly 30 female country guests on the show, including Emmylou Harris, Anne Murray and Rosanne Cash.

21 March
The Stars Salute..., is taped before a live audience at the Ford Theatre in Washington in front of President Ronald Reagan. It is scheduled for possible future broadcast.

21 March
"The Baron" begins its 15-week chart run #76. It works its way up the charts to a high of #10 at the end of May.

26 March
Civic Center, Danville, Illinois.

27 March
Civic Center, Decatur, Illinois.

28 March
Rockford Metro Center, Rockford, Illinois.

29 March
Five Seasons Center, Cedar Rapids, Iowa.

30 March
Civic Center, St. Joseph, Missouri.

April
Band member Marty Stuart records tracks for his solo album and Cash is on hand to provide vocals for some tracks.

10 April
A benefit show, with proceeds going to the Tennessee Institute of Learning Research, is held at the Volunteer State Community College in Gallatin, Tennessee. Also on the show are Larry Gatlin, The Gatlin Brothers, The Carter Family and Tom T. Hall.

11 April
Dallas Convention Center, Dallas, Texas.

14 April
John & June appear on a Gospel TV Show.

17 April
Cash's European tour opens with a show in Stockholm, Sweden.

18 April
Congresscentrum, Hamburg, Germany.

19 April
Both Carl Perkins and Jerry Lee Lewis appear at Cash's show at the Ahoy Hall in Rotterdam, Holland.

20 April
Wembley Arena, London, England.

22 April
Paris, France.

23 April
Sporthalle, Stuttgart, Germany.
The audience are surprised when Cash is joined on stage by fellow Sun artists Carl Perkins and Jerry Lee Lewis. In the sleevenotes of the resulting album Johnny Cash talked about how the reunion came about – "Carl's and Jerry Lee's appearance with me in Stuttgart, Germany on April 23, 1981 was a total surprise to the audience.

We had been appearing separately in various cities doing music festivals. And on the 23rd, they happened to have a night off. Midway into the first show in Stuttgart, June Carter caught my eye from the sidelines and gave me the message that Carl and Jerry Lee were there. At intermission, my producer Lou Robin brought us together backstage. I asked them to sing with me on the second half of the show." Among the tracks that did not make it onto the album *The Survivors* were "Matchbox" and "Rockabilly Fever" by Carl Perkins, "Boogie Woogie Medley" by Jerry Lee Lewis and "When The Saints Go Marching In" performed by the entire cast.

24 April
Jahunderhalle, Frankfurt, Germany.

25 April
Sporthalle, Cologne, Germany.

26 April
Hallenstadion, Zurich, Switzerland.

April-May
During this period Cash appeared on several TV shows, including *The Gatlin Brothers Special*, *Country Comes Home* and a re-run of the *Columbo* episode *Swan Song*. On 28 April the *Johnny Cash And The Country Girls* Special was also televised.

May
The Billy Sherrill-produced album *The Baron* (FC-37179) is released.
Tracks: "The Baron", "Mobile Bay", "The Hard Way", "A Ceiling, Four Walls And A Floor", "Hey, Hey Train", "The Reverend Mr Black-Lonesome Valley", "The Blues Keep Getting Bluer", "Chattanooga City Limits Sign", "Thanks To You", "Greatest Love Affair"

A full-page ad in the music press has a photo taken from the album cover and the line "Nobody can beat him... songs and stories as only Johnny can sing them"

15-17 May
Valley Forge Music Fair, Devon, Pennsylvania.

22 May
Ritz Theatre, Elizabeth, New Jersey.

23 May
Belmont Race Track, New York, New York.

24 May
Charleston Race Track, Wheeling, West Virginia.

25 May
Busch Gardens, Williamsburg, Virginia.

29 May
New Orleans, Louisiana.

30 May
Dallas TV Show Site, Dallas, Texas.

12 June
Waikiki Sheraton Hotel Ballroom, Honolulu, Hawaii.

15 June
An appearance on a TV show in Melbourne is taped before the Australian tour starts.

16 June
Johnny Cash undertakes his fourth tour of Australia with the opening show at the Entertainment Centre in Perth, Australia

17 June
Apollo Centre, Adelaide, Australia.

18 June
Melbourne, Australia.

19 June
Opera House, Sydney, Australia.

20 June
Canberra, Australia.

21 June
Opera House, Sydney, Australia.

23 June
Festival Hall, Brisbane, Australia.

June/July
Jerry Lee Lewis undergoes emergency surgery on a perforated stomach. Doctors only give him a 50/50 chance of surviving. During his spell in hospital he is visited by Cash.

July
The second single from the album *The*

Baron is released – "Mobile Bay"/"The Hard Way" (Columbia 18-02189).

4 July
Following the success of the single "The Baron" the album of the same name debuts at #29. A chart run of 12 weeks will see it hit a high of #24.

10 July
Amphitheatre, Poplar Creek, Illinois.

11 July
Opry House, Nashville, Indiana.

25 July
"Mobile Bay" enters the chart at #83 and will reach #60 during a spell of five weeks on the chart.

31 July
Johnny Cash makes his second appearance of the year on *The Mike Douglas Show*.

5 August
Fairgrounds, Casopolis, Michigan.

7 August
Fairgrounds, Monticello, Iowa.

8 August
Fairgrounds, Monroe, Michigan.

11 August
Jubilee Auditorium, Calgary, Alberta.

12-13 August
Nightclub, Edmonton, Alberta.

15 August
S. Fallsbrook, New York.

16 August
Music Park, Salem, Ohio.

20 August
Fairgrounds, Alexandria, Minnesota.

21 August
Fairgrounds, New Ulm, Minnesota.

22 August
Fairgrounds, Princeton, Illinois.

23 August
State Park Speedway, Wausau, Wisconsin.

24 August
Billy Graham Crusade in Calgary, Alberta.

27 August
Cash appears at a Hank Snow-sponsored benefit at the Opry House, Nashville, Tennessee.

28 August
Chautauqua Theatre, Jamestown, New York.

29 August
Fairgrounds, Wellington, Ohio.

30 August
Wolftrap Park, Washington, DC.

5 September
State Fairgrounds, Lincoln, Nebraska.

6 September
State Fairgrounds, Huron, South Dakota.

13 September
Fairgrounds, Montpelier, Ohio.

17 September
Fairgrounds, York, Pennsylvania.

18 September
Fairgrounds, Cape Girardeau, Missouri.

19 September
High School Gymnasium, Dwight, Illinois.

1 October
Performing Arts Center, Milwaukee, Wisconsin.

2-3 October
Mill Run Theatre, Niles, Illinois.

6 October
Records "The General Lee" for inclusion on the *Dukes Of Hazzard* album. A popular TV series, *The Dukes Of Hazard* featured the voice of Waylon Jennings as narrator and 'The General Lee' was the car featured in the series. Jennings also sang the theme song "Good Ole Boys (Theme From Dukes Of Hazzard)".

12 October
The Cash troupe travel to Scotland, where the next six days are scheduled for taping scenes for the 1981 Christmas Special. On this first day, despite biting winds, filming takes place at Falkland Palace in Fife. Cash was filmed singing "Footprints In The Sand" for the show and later in the day recorded "Greensleeves" as a duet with Andy Williams.

13 October
Filming continues in Kinghorn, Elie and St. Monans. The day began with scenes filmed around the Fife coast, beginning at Pettycur and onto Anstruther and St. Monans, where 29 children from the local primary school were at the Parish Church providing background music. Filming in St. Monans was due to start at 2pm but technical problems meant that filming did not finish until 7pm.

14-16 October
More filming takes place for the Christmas Special.

17 October
The concert at the Playhouse in Edinburgh is filmed for use in the Christmas Special.

18 October
Apollo, Manchester, England.

19 October
City Hall, Sheffield, England.

20 October
Albert Hall, London, England.

21 October
Coliseum, St. Austell, Cornwall.

22 October
Arts Centre, Poole, Dorset.

23-24 October
Diamond Cabaret Club, Caerphilly.

4 November
Five Flags Center, Dubuque, Iowa.

5 November
Mayop Civic Auditorium, Rochester, Minnesota.

6-7 November
Carlton West, Green Bay, Wisconsin.

9 November
Civic Center, Grand Rapids, Michigan.

10 November
McMorran Memorial Auditorium, Port Huron, Michigan.

15 November
John and June appear at the Billy Graham Crusade in Houston, Texas.

24 November
John is honoured with the *Pride Of Tennessee Award* for his promotion of a statewide campaign against adult illiteracy. The recent movie *Pride Of Jesse Hallam* was the basis for the award, which was established by Governor Lamar Alexander.

December
"Chattanooga City Limit Sign"/"Reverend Mr. Black" (Columbia 18-02669) released.

December
"Mr. Garfield"/"I'm A One Woman Man" (E-47254) released. This Merle Kilgore single featured Johnny Cash on the a-side.

1 December
Utah State University, Ogden, Utah.

2 December
Long Beach, California.

4-6 December
Music Fair, Westbury, Long Island, New York

7 December
Poughkeepsie, New York.

9 & 10 December
Christmas In Scotland is broadcast on CBS. Andy Williams, June Carter-Cash, John Carter-Cash and Carlene Carter all guest on the show. Songs featured in the show include "Ring Of Fire", "Footprints In The Sand", "The Reverend Mr Black", "Keep On The Sunnyside" and "Man Gave Names To All The Animals".

23 December
While the Cash family are sitting down to enjoy their evening meal, three armed intruders break into their Montego Bay home. John and his guests were all locked in a cellar and over $35,000 worth of items were stolen during the robbery. Luckily all were unharmed during the ordeal, which police believe was carried out by a gang of terrorists.

24 December
A Johnny Cash Christmas Show is recorded and broadcast from Hendersonville. The show includes interviews and songs.

31 December
Billy Bobs, Ft. Worth, Texas.

1982

9 January
Following a recommendation from the Hendersonville Chamber of Commerce, the City Commission dedicate Highway 31, known locally as Gallatin Road, as the *Johnny Cash Parkway*. A ceremony is held in the parking lot at The House Of Cash.

13-16 January
Carlton, Minneapolis, Minnesota.

19 January
Jerry Lee Lewis TV show in Nashville.

21 January
Barbara Mandrell TV show in Nashville.

22 January
Arlington Theatre, Santa Barbara, California.

23 January
Convention Center, Anaheim, California.

23 January
Cash's latest single, "Chattanooga City Limit Sign", registers on the charts at #84 and in a brief five-week spell will rise to #71.

24 January
Fox Theatre, San Diego, California.

25-26 January
Bridges Auditorium, Claremont, California.

27 January
Fresno Convention Arena, Fresno, California.

27 January
Is There A Family In The House?, a 3-hour television special aimed at strengthening the American family, is broadcast in the Milwaukee area. Produced by Youth For Christ, this show is packed with musical variety, entertainers and nationally known entertainers including Johnny Cash. The programme features dramatic re-enactments of real-life stories about teenage alcoholics, drug addicts and gangs. John and June talk about their previous failed marriages and the secret for keeping their marriage alive, and the entertainers on the show include Dionne Warwick, B. J. Thomas, Amy Grant and Roy Clark. Regional director for Youth For Christ,

THE QUESTION ECHOES IN HOME AFTER HOME AS
FAMILIES SILENTLY CRY FOR HELP...

**IS THERE
A FAMILY
IN THE HOUSE?**

A dramatic, penetrating, yet hopeful look, deep inside
the pain and tragedy of the American family.

STARRING JOHNNY AND JUNE CASH
BOB HOPE • RICH LITTLE • DIONNE WARWICK
ROY CLARK • CHERYL LADD • STEVE ALLEN • B.J. THOMAS
ANDY GRIFFITH • DENNIS WEAVER • HOWARD K. SMITH
BILLY GRAHAM • WILLIAM SHATNER • EDDIE ALBERT
DEBBY BOONE • GEORGE KENNEDY

Richard Epps said "This program can have a real impact on the community," and went on to say "A lot of programs have talked about the various problems in today's families. What we're trying to do is show that someone cares, that someone is doing something about it."

28 January
Sacramento Community Convention Center Theatre, Sacramento, California.

29 January
Redding Civic Auditorium, Redding, California. During this show Cash was honoured by the American Legion Clearlake Konocti Post No. 437 when they made him a paid-up lifetime member.

30-31 January
Circle Star, San Carlos, California.

February
At JMI Studios, with Jack Clement back in the producer's chair, Cash records tracks for The Adventures Of Johnny Cash album.

11 February
University Of Missouri, Rollo, Missouri.

12 February
Memorial Auditorium, Joplin, Missouri.

13 February
Century II Arena, Wichita, Kansas.

14 February
University of Oklahoma, Norman, Oklahoma.

15 February
Bicentennial Center, Salina, Kansas.

16 February
Warrensburg, Missouri.

17 February
Rockford, Illinois.

18 February
Dane County Coliseum, Madison, Wisconsin.

In Stuttgart the previous April Johnny Cash was joined on stage by Carl Perkins and Jerry Lee Lewis, and that legendary combination appeared together again at this concert in Madison. A crowd approaching 4,000 watched as Carl Perkins opened the show with a 30-minute set including "Matchbox", "Honey Don't" and "Blue Suede Shoes", followed by the Johnny Cash Show. Jerry Lee Lewis, still recovering from recent stomach surgery, worked through his greatest hits and the show concluded with all three performing a selection of gospel material including "Old Time Religion", "I Saw The Light" and "Peace In The Valley". The Wisconsin State Journal proclaimed "It was loose, spontaneous and truly a testimonial. To the Creator, by the creators."

19 February
A show scheduled at the Hullman Auditorium, Terre Haute, Indiana is cancelled due to bad weather.

20 February
Masonic Auditorium, Davenport, Iowa.

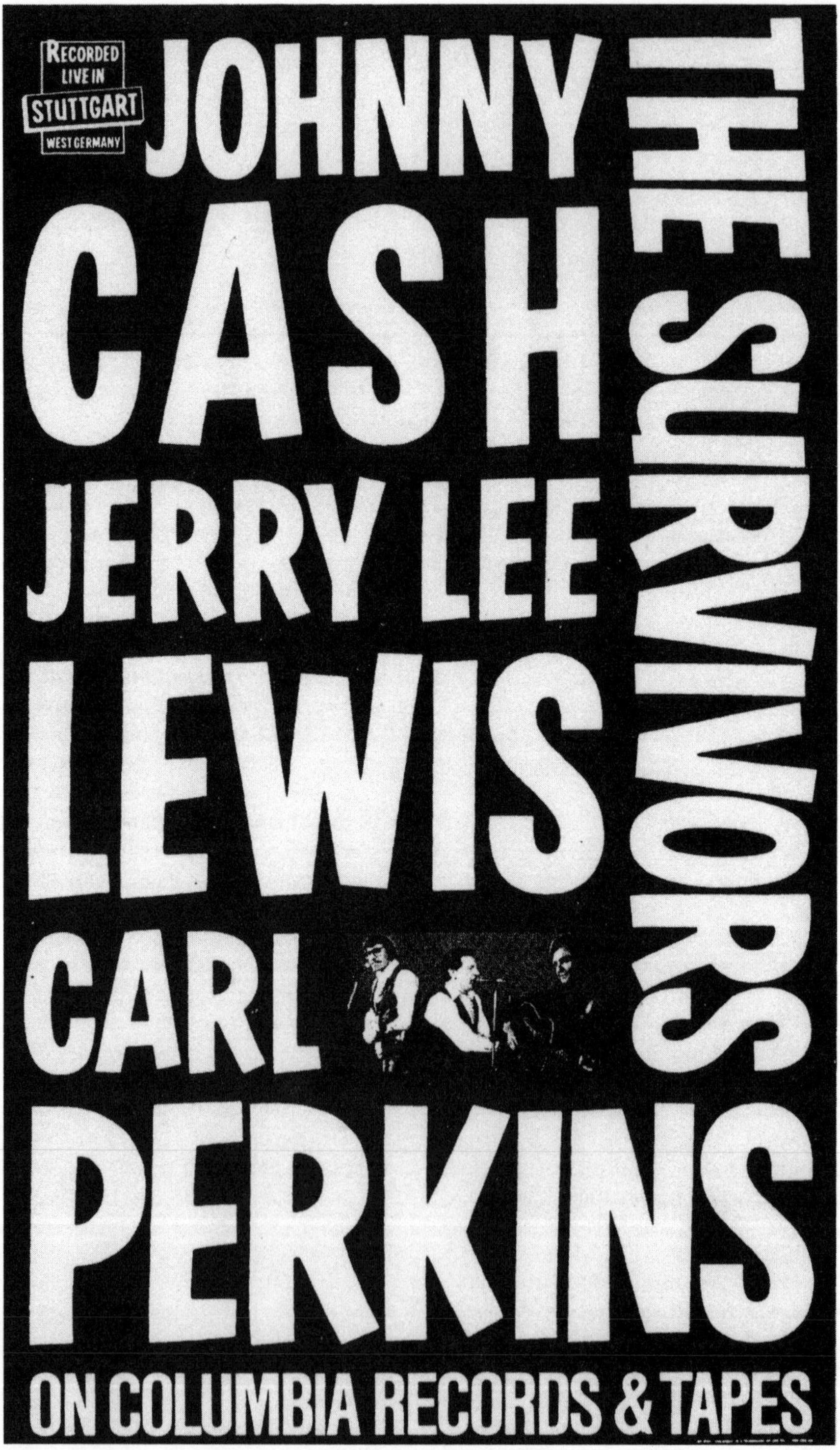
RECORDED
LIVE IN
STUTTGART
WEST GERMANY
JOHNNY
CASH
JERRY LEE
LEWIS
CARL
PERKINS
THE SURVIVORS
ON COLUMBIA RECORDS & TAPES

21 February
Civic Center, Des Moines, Iowa.

5 March
Sunrise Theatre, Ft. Lauderdale, Florida.

6 March
Tupperware Convention Center, Orlando, Florida.

8 March
Municipal Auditorium, West Palm Beach, Florida.

9 March
Bay Front Center, St. Petersburg, Florida.

10 March
Tallahassee-Leon Civic Center, Tallahassee, Florida.

11 March
Lake City Community College Gym, Lake City, Florida.

22-27 March
Johnny Cash is in Texas filming scenes for the TV special *Johnny Cash: Cowboy Heroes*. Filming takes place at the Alamo and other historic sites. During this period he plays two concerts in Kerrville, Texas (25 March) and Jackson, Tennessee (27 March).

April
An extensive marketing campaign that includes in-store merchandising and television advertising is developed by Epic Records for the release of the *Dukes Of Hazzard* LP, drawn from the popular TV series featuring John Schneider, Tom Wopat and Catherine Bach. The initial single is "The General Lee"/"Duelin' Dukes" (ZS5-02803) and features Cash on the a-side. The album also includes material by Schneider, Wopat and Doug Kershaw.

April
The Survivors (FC-37961) is released. Recorded back in April 1981 the album

features Cash and special guests Carl Perkins and Jerry Lee Lewis.
Tracks: "Get Rhythm", "I Forgot To

Remember To Forget", "Goin' Down The Road Feelin' Bad", "That Silver Haired Daddy Of Mine", "Matchbox", "I'll Fly Away", "Whole Lotta Shakin' Goin' On", "Rockin' My Life Away", "Blue Suede Shoes", "Peace In The Valley", "Will The Circle Be Unbroken", "I Saw The Light"

10 April
Country Comes Home is broadcast on CBS Channel 2. Hosted by Glen Campbell the show includes a guest list that reads like a Who's Who of country music - Roy Acuff, Chet Atkins, Roy Clark, Crystal Gayle, Kris Kristofferson, Loretta Lynn, Jimmy C. Newman, Hank Thompson, Mel Tillis, Don Williams, Boxcar Willie and Johnny Cash.

17 April
Johnny Cash hosts *Saturday Night Live* with Elton John as his special guest.

17 April
Helped by the TV series *Dukes Of Hazzard* and the subsequent album, Cash's latest single, "The General Lee", debuts at #62 and will eventually rise to #26 during its 12-week run.

18 April
Twenty Five Years Of Jerry Lee...A Celebration is broadcast on the Home Box

Office Channel. Joining Jerry Lee Lewis to celebrate are Johnny Cash, Carl Perkins, Charlie Rich, Mickey Gilley, The Oakridge Boys and Dottie West. The show is broadcast three more times during April (21, 23 & 27).

24 April
Fair, Fordyce, Arkansas.

24 April
The Johnny Cash, Carl Perkins and Jerry Lee Lewis live album *The Survivors* debuts at #29. It will reach #21 during a 13-week chart residency. It would be nearly three years before he had an album in the charts again.

29 April
Erie, Pennsylvania.

30 April
Catholic Youth Hall, Scranton, Pennsylvania.

1 May
Capitol, Theater, Williamsport, Pennsylvania.

2 May
Masonic Hall, Altoona, Pennsylvania.

6 May
Johnny Cash: Cowboy Heroes is broadcast on CBS. The special includes guest appearances by Glen Campbell, The Oakridge Boys and John Anderson. Songs featured on the show include "Remember The Alamo", "El Paso", "Bobbie Sue", "The General Lee", "A Cowboy's Prayer" and "Don't Take Your Guns To Town".

8 May
Casper Events Center, Casper, Wyoming.

9 May
Yellowstone Metra, Billings, Montana.

10 May
Civic Center, Helena, Montana.

11 May
Four Seasons Arena, Great Falls, Montana.

12 May
Sportsplex-Arena, Lethbridge, Alberta.

14 May
Saskatchewan Centennial Auditorium, Saskatoon, Saskatchewan.

15 May
Saskatchewan Centre Of The Arts, Regina, Saskatchewan.

17 May
Manitoba Centennial Concert Hall, Winnipeg, Manitoba.

5-6 June
Worlds of Fun Park, Kansas City, Missouri.

11 June
Milledgeville, Georgia.

13 June
Billy Graham Crusade, New Orleans, Louisiana.

19-20 June
Kennedy Center, Washington, DC, taping a Home Box Office TV Special.

21 June
Pitman, New Jersey.

23-25 June
Oakdale Music Theater, Wallingford, Connecticut.

26-27 June
South Shore Music Circus, Cohasset, Massachusetts.

July
"Georgia On A Fast Train"/"Sing A Song" (Columbia 18-03058) released. Both tracks

are from the forthcoming Jack Clement-produced album *The Adventures Of Johnny Cash*.

4 July
Knoxville World's Fair, Knoxville Coliseum, Knoxville, Tennessee

18 July
Cash performs "It Comes And Goes" on *Pop Goes The Country*.

August-December
Marty Stuart, multi-talented instrumentalist and member of Johnny Cash's showband, produces a series of gospel sessions. The material recorded will find a release on the album *Believe In Him*.

7 August
Georgia On A Fast Train enters the chart at the start of its 8-week run. It will eventually peak at #55.

21 August
Along with John Prine, Steeve Goodman and Rodney Crowell, Cash appears on an HBO Special from Washington.

September
Adventures Of Johnny Cash (FC-38094) is released.
Tracks: "Georgia On A Fast Train", "John's", "Fair Weather Friends", "Paradise", "We Must Believe In Magic", "Only Love", "Good Old American Guest", "I'll Cross Over Jordan", "Sing A Song", "Ain't Gonna Hobo No More".

3 September
Cash performs two songs on the Jerry Lee Lewis telethon taped at Mud Island in Memphis.

4 September
Fair, Van Buren, Michigan.

5 September
Fair, Van Wert, Ohio.

6 September
City Fair, La Porte, Indiana.

10 September
Ball State University, Muncie, Indiana.

11 September
Little Nashville Opry House, Nashville, Indiana.

12 September
Braden Auditorium, Normal, Illinois

15-16 September
Melody Fair, N. Tonawanda, New York

21 September-15 October
Cash films the CBS-TV movie *Murder In Coweta County*. Set in Georgia in 1948, the movie is based on the true story of Sheriff Lamar Potts who puts away the most powerful and ruthless land baron in the county, who is suspected of killing a sharecropper. As far back as 1975 Cash had read Margaret Ann Barnes' novel *Murder In Coweta County* and submitted the idea for a movie to the heads of various networks, who turned it down. In the end CBS agreed to produce the film at a cost of nearly $3 million. The tagline for the movie read: "'The Kingdom,' a backwoods dynasty of moonshine and murder. This is the story of the man who ran it, and the man who crushed it". During filming in Griffin, Georgia an attempt was made on Johnny Cash's life when the brake hose was cut on a 1948 Ford that Cash was due to drive. Days later sugar was poured into the petrol tanks of two more cars.

3 October
Cash performs at a Billy Graham Crusade in Charlotte, North Carolina.

21 October
Texas Dance Hall, San Antonio, Texas.

23 October
Magic Mountain, Valencia, California.

THE MAGICAL SOUNDS OF CHRISTMAS!

JOHNNY CASH

A MERRY MEMPHIS CHRISTMAS

Join the holiday fun and excitement in the rock 'n rollin', bluesy, country soul city where the Johnny Cash legend and career began!

Guest Stars:
June Carter Cash and The Mighty Clouds of Joy
Special Guests: Rosanne Cash, Crystal Gayle and Eddie Rabbitt
A CBS SPECIAL PRESENTATION

9PM

24 October
Fairgrounds, Phoenix, Arizona.

2 November
Cash opens an eleven date tour of Germany with a concert in Nuremberg.

3 November
Berlin, Germany.

4 November
Hannover, Germany.

5 November
Dusseldorf, Germany.

6 November
Kassel, Germany.

7 November
Kiel, Germany.

8 November
Münster, Germany.

10 November
Frankfurt, Germany.

11 November
Manheim, Germany.

12 November
Augsburg, Germany.

13 November
Karlsruhe, Germany.

18-24 November
Johnny Cash's 1982 Christmas Special *A Merry Memphis Christmas* is taped. Filmed in and around Memphis, the show includes guest appearances by June Carter-Cash, Rosanne Cash, Crystal Gayle, Eddie Rabbitt, the gospel group Mighty Clouds Of Joy and Jack Clement.

December
"Fair Weather Friends"/"Ain't Gonna Hobo No More" (Columbia 38-03317) released. Despite being another strong single from *The Adventures Of Johnny Cash*, it fails to chart.

3-5 December
Music Center, Valley Forge, Pennsylvania.

7 December
The Christmas special *A Merry Memphis Christmas* is broadcast on CBS-TV.

9 December
Police benefit in Nashville, Tennessee.

14 December
Indianapolis, Indiana.

17 December
Houston, Texas.

18 December
Oklahoma City, Oklahoma.

19 December
Billy Bob's, Fort Worth, Texas .

1983

Early-1983
Material recorded during Cash's April 1978 European tour is finally released on *Koncert V Praze (In Prague Live)* (SUP-1113.3278ZD).
Tracks: "Ring Of Fire", "Folsom Prison Blues", "I Still Miss Someone", "Big River", "I Ride An Old Paint", "Streets Of Laredo", "Sunday Morning Coming Down", "I Walk The Line", "Last Date", "City Of New Orleans", "Hey Porter", "Wreck Of The Old '97", "Casey Jones", "Orange Blossom Special", "Wabash Cannonball".

January
"We Must Believe In Magic"/"I'll Cross Over Jordan Some Day" (Columbia 38-03524) is released. The single only spends two weeks on the chart, reaching #84.

13-14 January
Seattle Music Hall, Seattle, Washington.

15 January
Capitol Theatre, Yakima, Washington.

16 January
Spokane Opera House, Spokane, Washington.

18 January
Sports Centre, Victoria, British Columbia.

19 January
Orpheum Theatre, Vancouver, British Columbia.

20 January
Armory, Salem, Oregon.

21 January
Performing Arts Centre, Eugene, Oregon.

22 January
Civic Auditorium, Portland, Oregon.

5 February
Poughkeepsie, New York.

6 February
Syracuse, New York.

8 February
Civic Center, Augusta, Maine.

9 February
Civic Center, Wooster, Massachusetts.

11 February
Burlington, Vermont.

12 February
Montreal, Canada.

13 February
Eastman Theatre, Rochester, New York.

14 February
Hamilton Place, Hamilton, Ontario.

15 February
Cash attends a Youth For Christ benefit in Toronto, Ontario.
15 February

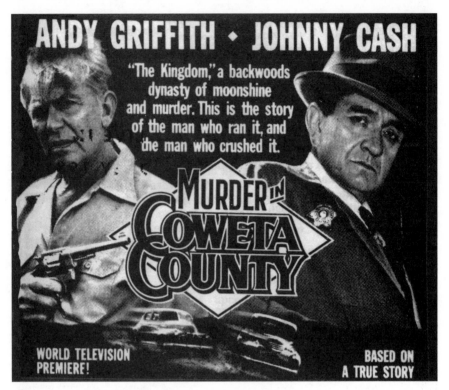

Murder In Coweta County, starring Andy Griffith and Johnny Cash, receives its first TV transmission.

2 March
Strawberry Festival, Hillsbough County Fair, Plant City, Florida.

4 March
Ft. Lauderdale, Florida.

5 March
Civic Center, Fort Myers, Florida.

6 March
Ft. Pierce, Florida.

7 March
Daytona Beach, Florida.

11-12 March
Club, Green Bay, Wisconsin.

25 March
Mansfield, Ohio.

26 March
Washington, D.C.

31 March
Cindy Cash marries Johnny Cash's guitarist Marty Stuart.

April
During sessions at Magnolia Studios in North Hollywood, Cash records "Johnny 99" and "Highway Patrolman", two tracks from the pen of 'the Boss' Bruce Springsteen. Among the musicians on hand are those that formed the nucleus of Elvis's touring band in the seventies - James Burton, Glen D. Hardin and Jerry Scheff.

16 April
Cash appears on a TV show in Augsburg, Germany the day before his European tour starts.

17 April
European tour kicks off with a concert at the Deutsches Museum, Munich, Germany.

18 April
Rheingold Halle, Mainz, Germany.

19-20 April
Congresszentrum, Hamburg, Germany.

21 April
Sporthalle, Cologne, Germany.

22 April
Karl Diem Halle, Wurzburg, Germany.

23 April
Freitzeithalle, Hof, Germany.

25 April
European tour closes with two shows at the Sports Arena in Budapest, Hungary.

4-7 May
Club, Minneapolis, Minnesota.

8 May
Watertown, South Dakota.

9 May
Benefit show at the Rosebud Indian Reservation, South Dakota.

13 May
Peoria, Illinois.

14 May
Joliet, Indiana.

25 May
Durham, Ontario.

26 May
Hamilton Place, Hamilton, Ontario.

28 May
North Hudson, New York.

18 June
Benefit show in La Ronge, Saskatchewan.

19 June
Prince Albert, Saskatchewan.

21 June
Medicine Hat, Alberta.

22 June
Jubilee Auditorium, Calgary, Alberta.

23 June
Edmonton, Alberta.

24 June
Grand Prairie, Alberta.

25 June
Prince George, British Columbia.

26 June
Kamloops, British Columbia.

1-4 July
Lake Tahoe, Nevada.

7-12 July
A Japanese film crew spends time in Vancouver, British Columbia filming scenes for the film *Kairei*, which is financed by the Billy Graham Organisation. Translated into English, *Adrift At Sea* is the story of three Japanese fishermen who were shipwrecked and captured by Indians at Cape Flattery. Johnny Cash plays the role of John McLoughlin, the head of Fort Vancouver, who bought the Japanese from the Indian tribe and sent them to England after converting them to Christianity. Although Cash speaks no Japanese his lines will be dubbed into Japanese in the finished film.

14 July
Fair, Seymour, Wisconsin.

15 July
Fair, Logansport, Indiana.

16 July
Music ParkCummins, Georgia.

22-24 July
Music Theatre, Hyannis, Massachusetts.

30 July
Canadian National Exhibition, Toronto, Ontario.

31 July
State Fair, Salem, Oregon.

1 August
Chicago, Illinois.

9 August
Fair, Paso Robles, California.

11 August
Fair, Costa Mesa, California.

13 August
Fair, Elma, Washington.

14 August
Fair, Vancouver, Washington.

16 August
Fair, Eugene, Oregon.

17 August
Fair, Grants Pass, Oregon.

18 August
Fair, Linden, Washington.

20 August
Sullivan Arena, Anchorage, Alaska.

21 August
A show scheduled at the Baseball Park, Fairbanks, Alaska had to be cancelled following two days of torrential rain which left the field under water.

September
Johnny 99 (FC-38696) is released with a cover photo of John taken on the set of his recent movie *Murder In Coweta County*. The album includes the two Bruce Springsteen tracks that Cash recorded earlier in the year.

Tracks: "Highway Patrolman", "That's The Truth", "God Bless Robert E. Lee", "New Cut Road", "Johnny 99", "Ballad Of The Ark", "Joshua Gone Barbados", "Girl From The Canyon", "Brand New Dance", "I'm Ragged But I'm Right"

"I'm Ragged But I'm Right"/"Brand New Dance" (Columbia 38-04068) is the first single to be lifted from the album. June Carter-Cash appears on the b-side.

16 September
Fair, Albuquerque, New Mexico.

17 September
Auditorium, Wichita Falls, Texas.

18 September
State Fair, Des Moines, Iowa.

21 September
Omaha, Nebraska.

28 September
Private party at the Fountainbleau Hotel, Miami Beach, Florida.

17-21 October
Filming takes place at the Carter Fold in Maces Spring, Virginia for the 1983 Christmas Special. June Carter was quoted as saying "We're trying to remember what Christmas was like when we were young, the love that this valley generates." Also

there for the filming are Merle Haggard, The McLain Family Band, John Carter-Cash, Ricky Skaggs and Janette Carter. Among the songs performed and scheduled for the show are "I'm Ragged But I'm Right", "Brand New Dance", "Christmas Times A-Comin" and "I Wonder How The Old Folks Are At Home".

1 October
"I'm Ragged But I'm Right" peaks at #75 during a four-week spell.

1-2 October
Holiday Star Theatre, Merrilville, Indiana.

5 October
Toronto, Canada.

8 October
Las Vegas, Nevada.

23 October
Billy Graham Crusade, Oklahoma City, Oklahoma.

24 October
Barbara Walters TV interview.

28 October
Lahti, Finland.

30 October
Ruhstorf, Germany.

31 October
Vienna, Austria.

3 November
Norrkoping, Sweden
During this show Cash performs "Johnny 99", "Highway Patrolman", "Over There" and "Old Rugged Cross".

4 November
Drammen, Norway.

5 November
Stuttgart, Germany.

6 November
Zurich, Switzerland.

7 November
Freiburg, Germany.

9 November
Antwerp, Belgium.

10 November
Nottingham, England.

11 November
Odeon, Birmingham, England.

12 November
Hammersmith Odeon, London, England.

November
Plans had been made to play a series of concerts in the Soviet Union during Cash's European tour. Shows were due to be played in Leningrad and Moscow, but following the downing of a Korean airliner the shows were cancelled.

22 November
Cash undergoes surgery for an ulcer at Nashville's Baptist Hospital.

December
The Bruce Springsteen composition "Johnny 99", the title track of Cash's latest album, is backed with "New Cut Road" and released as a single (Columbia 38-04227).

3 December
Johnny Cash's 1983 Christmas Special is broadcast, featuring Ricky Scaggs, Merle Haggard and The Carter Family.

4-6 December
London, Ontario.

6 December
The Barbara Walters Special *Modern Day Legends* is broadcast on ABC-TV. Guests on the show include Johnny Cash and Walter Cronkite. Cash's part was filmed in November at his home in Hendersonville.

8 December
Battle Creek, Michigan.

9 December
Washington, D.C.

14 December
Johnny Cash and Mayor Richard Fulton trade swings at a golden spike during the 'construction kick-off' ceremony at the site of Nashville's Baptist Hospital's new $12 million wellness center.

1984

February
"That's The Truth"/"Joshua Gone Barbados" (Columbia 38-04428) is the third single to be lifted from *Johnny 99*.

February
Nashville Now is broadcast featuring Johnny Cash, Tom T. Hall and Dan Seals.

25 March
Kansas City, Kansas.

27-28 March
Des Moines, Iowa.

29 March
Burlington, Iowa.

30 March
Iowa City, Iowa.

1 April
Jones Country Music Park, Colmesneil, Texas.
Johnny Cash and George Jones appear at the opening of Jones Park. During the show they perform their new duet "I Got Stripes".

2 April
Celebrity Playhouse, Houston, Texas.

April
Cash makes his second appearance of the year on Ralph Emery's *Nashville Now*. The show also includes Rosanne Cash, Tom T. Hall, Rhonda Ingle and The Judds.

2-6 April
The Ralph Emery Show is broadcast each day and features guest Johnny Cash. The programs were taped earlier in the year and are sponsored by Red Man Chewing Tobacco. During the show Cash mentions that he is planning an album of Hank Williams gospel songs. This project never materialises.

4 April
Boca Raton, Florida.

6 April
Lake City, Florida.

12 April
Cash records "Chicken In Black". One of the worst records he ever recorded, it is also one of his last for CBS before his contract expires.

25 April
Sun City West Sun Dome Center for Performing Arts, Phoenix, Arizona.

26-27 April
Luther Burbank Center for the Arts, Santa Rosa, California.

28 April
College of the Desert, Palm Springs, California.

29 April
Convention Center, Anaheim, California. Also appearing on the show are Carl Perkins and Steve Goodman.

1 May
Civic Auditorium, Bakersfield, California.

2 May
Arlington Theater, Santa Barbara, California.

4 May
Bridges Auditorium, Claremont Men's College, Claremont, California.

10 May
Kellog Center, Battle Creek, Michigan.

12 May
Broadway Theater, Pitman, New Jersey.

12 May
In a chart run of five weeks, "That's The Truth" will only reach #84.

19 May
Little Nashville Opry, Little Nashville, Indiana.

23 May
Cash tapes his segment for the Bob Hope 81st birthday celebration in New Orleans. He performs his forthcoming single "Chicken In Black".

24 May
World's Fair, New Orleans, Louisiana.

27 May
City-In-The-Square, Kitchener, Ontario.

June
Issue #58 of the UK music magazine *Record Collector* runs a six-page overview of Cash's career, including a detailed UK discography with current mint values for singles and albums.

June
"Chicken In Black"/"The Battle Of Nashville" (Columbia 38-04513) released. Both tracks are produced by Billy Sherrill.

19-21 June
London, Ontario.

23 June
Race Track, Charleston, West Virginia.

25-27 June
Cash shoots the video for the "Chicken In Black" single. Scenes are filmed in Downtown Nashville at the corner of Fourth and Charlotte, the Citizens Bank and inside the Ryman Auditorium. Footage was also filmed outside a train car in Springfield. The three days of work gave employment to 70 local residents. The director of the video, Arnold Levine, had worked on videos for Bruce Springsteen, Neil Diamond and Meatloaf as well as two for Cash which featured on a TV Special. For this video Cash dressed in an outrageous blue and yellow mock superman outfit and looked out-of-character, but managed to maintain a sense of humour during filming.

29-30 June
Premier Entertainment Center, Sterling Heights, Michigan.

3 July
Brookfield High School, Brookfield, Illinois.

4 July
Iowa Fair, Cedar Rapids, Iowa.

14 July
"Chicken In Black" debuts at #72 on the charts. During a run of 11 weeks it will climb to #45. Possibly helped by the accompanying video, this is Cash's highest chart position for two years, not bad considering it was one of his worst records!

4-24 July
Filming for the TV movie *The Baron And The Kid* takes place. Scenes are filmed mainly in and around Nashville, although additional footage is shot in Las Vegas.

11 August
Festival, Soo Pass Ranch, Detroit Lakes, Minnesota.

26 August
Kitsap County Fair, Bremerton, Washington.

28 August
Antelope Valley Fair, Lancaster, California.

29 August
State Fair, Sacramento, California.

30 August
Saddlerack, San Jose, California.

31 August
Kittitas Fair and Rodeo, Ellensburg, Washington.

6 September
Nebraska State Fair, Lincoln, Nebraska.

8 September
Cannon Dam at Mark Twain Reservoir, Palmyra, Missouri.

9 September
Rodeo Arena, St. Tite, Quebec.

12 September
County Fair, Allegan, Michigan.

13 September
La Crosse, Wisconsin.

14 September
Clay County Fair, Spencer, Idaho.

15 September
Civic Arena, St. Joseph, Missouri.

16 September
Kansas State Fair, Hutchinson, Kansas.

21 September
Chateau De Ville, Framingham, Massachusetts.

22 September
West Point Academy, West Point, New York.

23 September
Hockey Arena, Watertown, New York.

26-29 September
Carlton Dinner Theatre, Bloomington, Minnesota.

30 September
Acme Boot Co., Dallas, Texas.
Private function.

6-7 October
Wheeling Jamboree, Wheeling, West Virginia.

28 October
State Fair, Phoenix, Arizona.

31 October
Cash's UK and European tour opens at the Apollo Theatre, Oxford, England.

1 November
St. Davids, Cardiff, Wales.

3 November
Ice Arena, Helsinki, Finland.

4 November
Scandanavium, Gothenburg, Sweden. At this show Cash performs his latest single "Chicken In Black" and also "Rock 'n' Roll Ruby".

5 November
Fairfield Hall, Croydon, England.

6 November
Royal Centre, Nottingham, England.

7 November
City Hall, Sheffield, England.

8 November
Guild Hall, Preston, England.

9 November
Capitol Theatre, Aberdeen, Scotland.

11 November
Apollo Theatre, Glasgow, Scotland.

12-16 November
Montreux, Switzerland.
Following the UK tour Johnny Cash, June Carter-Cash and the the band fly out to Montreux, Switzerland to begin taping their CBS Christmas Special. Guests on the show include Waylon Jennings, Willie Nelson, Kris Kristofferson, June Carter-Cash, Toni Wine, Connie Nelson and Jessi Colter. They stay at the Montreux Palace Hotel during rehearsals and filming. Piano player Earl Ball suggested the show be called *Recovery Christmas*, as everybody was healthy and clear-eyed, while Cash offered *One Christmas At A Time*, but it was the producer who came up with *Christmas On The Road*. It was during the taping of this special that the Highwayman idea was formed.

21 November
The Baron And The Kid is shown on television. *TV Guide* advertise the film with the line 'A gambler plays for the biggest stakes of his life… his son'.

27-29 November
Hamilton Place, Hamilton, Ontario.

30 November
Cash appears on the *Tommy Hunter TV Show* in Toronto, Ontario.

December
Music City News publish the first part of an exclusing interview between Marty Stuart and Johnny Cash.

December
Christmas On The Road is broadcast with the promotional line "Four legendary country music giants celebrate together in an extraordinary holiday event. Set in the Swiss Alps! Plus fabulous music videos. All wrapped up with that warm down-home feeling."

December
Johnny Cash joins Willie Nelson, Dolly Parton, Brenda Lee and Kris Kristofferson

for a show at the Tennessee Performing Arts Center in Nashville. The show is taped for broadcast early in 1985.

1 December
Harrisburg, Pennsylvania.

14 December
Johnny Cash presents an inspirational talk, *The World Of Johnny Cash*, and performs some songs at Austin Christmas '84, presented by the Texas Research Society on Alcoholism.

Late 1984
Cash is joined by Willie Nelson, Waylon Jennings and Kris Kristofferson for a series of recordings that will be issued under the collective title *The Highwaymen*. These sessions, produced by Chips Moman, are a direct result of the four artists working together on Cash's Christmas Special, filmed in Switzerland back in November.

19 December
Cash hosts *Nashville Now* with special guests Grandpa Jones and Riders In The Sky.

1985

January
Music City News continues its exclusive interview between Marty Stuart and Johnny Cash that started back in the December 1984 issue.

17 January
Veteran's Memorial Coliseum, San Rafael, California.

18 January
El Camino College, Redondo, California.

19 January
Civic Center, San Diego, California.

22 January
Nanaimo, British Columbia.

23 January
Vancouver, British Columbia.

24 January
Seattle, Washington.

25 January
Eugene, Oregon.

26 January
Portland, Oregon.

27 January
Spokane, Washington.

February-June
Cash is signed to play the role of John Brown in the ABC mini-series *North And South*. Based on John Jakes' best selling novel, the cast also includes Lesley-Anne Down, Morgan Fairchild, Robert Mitchum and Patrick Swayze. Filming takes place in Southern California; Charleston, South Carolina; St. Francisville, Louisiana; Natchez, Mississippi and Reader, Arkansas.

1 February
South Florida Fair, West Palm Beach, Florida.

2 February
Civic Center, Lakeland, Florida.

3 February
Ruth Eckert Hall, Clearwater, Florida.

7 February
Johnny Cash and Waylon Jennings appear on *Late Night with David Letterman* and *Saturday Night Live*.

8-10 February
Johnny Cash and Waylon Jennings play three sold-out shows at Radio City Music Hall in New York.

15 February
Cash performs "I Came To Believe" on *Grand Ole Opry Gospel Time*.

19 February
War Memorial Arena, Johnstown, Pennsylvania.

20 February
A concert in Newcastle, Pennsylvania is cancelled.

21 February
Embassy Theater, Fort Wayne, Indiana.

22 February
McMorran Place, Port Huron, Michigan.

23 February
Paramount Arts Center, Aurora, Illinois.

24 February
Toledo Masonic Auditorium, Toledo, Ohio.

March
"Three Bells"/"They Killed Him" (Columbia 38-04740) released. Both of these tracks were recorded around the same period as both *Rainbow* and the first *Highwayman* album and, although not issued on either album, they may have been considered for inclusion. The a-side was based on a French tune and was a hit back in 1959 for The Browns.

13 March
Kleinhans Music Hall, Buffalo, New York.

14 March
Temple Civic Center, Rochester, New York.

15 March
Broone County Arena, Binghampton, New York.

16 March
Lowes Theater, Worcester, Massachusetts.

17 March
Proctors Theater, Schenectady, New York.

19 March
Stanley Theater, Utica, New York.

20 March
Flynn Theater, Burlington, Vermont.

21 March
Mid-Hudson Civic Center, Poughkeepsie, New York.

23 March
Handler High School Auditorium, Winchester, Virginia.

27 March
John appears on *Entertainment Tonight*.

29 March
Billy Bobs, Fort Worth, Texas.

30 March
Bankers Convention, New Orleans, Louisiana.

2 April
A benefit concert in Montego Bay, Jamaica raises over $20,000 for Montego Bay's SOS Childrens Village and the Cornwall Regional Hospital's Children's Ward.

6-8 April
Opera House, Cork, Ireland.

9 April
Bournemouth, England.

10 April
Southport, England.

12 April
Berlin, Germany.

13 April
Frankfurt, Germany.

14 April
Zurich, Switzerland.

23 April
The show taped back in December 1984 at the Tennessee Performing Arts Center in Nashville is broadcast under the title *The Winning Hand*.

May
"Crazy Old Soldier"/"It Ain't Gonna Worry My Mind" (Columbia 38-4860) released. This Ray Charles single features Cash on the a-side.

May
Highwayman (FC-40056) is released.
Tracks: "Highwayman", "The Last Cowboy Song", "Jim I Wore A Tie Today", "Big River", "Committed To Parkview", "Desperadoes Waiting For A Train", "Deportee", "Welfare Line", "Against The Wind", "The Twentieth Century Is Almost Over".

"Highwayman"/"The Human Condition" (Columbia 38-04881) is the first single lifted from the album. The a-side features Cash with Waylon Jennings, Willie Nelson and Kris Kristofferson while the b-side is just Cash and Nelson and did not appear on the album.

18 May
"Highwayman" debuts on the charts at #60 and will stay for 20 weeks.

26 May
Bob Wootton was unable to play at a concert in Toronto, Canada due to a family emergency and Cash called Waylon Jennings to see if he knew of a replacement. Jennings offered to fly up and stand in for Wootton, which he did.

26-28 May
Roy Thompson Hall, Toronto, Canada.

29 May
Travels to Australia.

1 June
Highwayman becomes Cash's first chart album for nearly three years when it debuts at #51. During an incredible chart run of 62 weeks the album spends 19 weeks in the top 10, with a week at the summit.

4-9 June
Twin Towns Night Club, Tweedheads, New South Wales.

11 June
Sydney, New South Wales.

12 June
Camberra

14 June
Showground, Launceston, Tasmania.

15 June
Melbourne, Victoria.

16 June
Rockhampton, Queensland.

17 June
Townsville, Queensland.

During his series of concerts in Australia CBS Records presented Cash with an original oil painting, in recognition of 10 million dollars worth of record and tape sales in Australia. The presentation was made by international product manager John Sackson, marketing manager Chris Moss, publicity and international relations manager Viv Hudson and managing director Denis Handlin.

July
Cash, Kris Kristofferson, Waylon Jennings and Willie Nelson sign with CBS for a remake of the John Ford classic *Stagecoach*. Filming is set to take place in Arizona and Mexico.

4 July
South Park Meadows, Austin, Texas
Johnny Cash plays a one hour show at the annual Willie Nelson Picnic and also appears with fellow Highwaymen Willie Nelson, Waylon Jennings and Kris Kristofferson. This was the first time they had recreated the characters from their album *Highwayman*.

5 July
Cash appears with Waylon Jennings and Jessi Colter at Brookfield Zoo, Chicago, Illinois.

7 July
Chastain Park, Atlanta, Georgia.

26 July
Fair, Janesville, Wisconsin.

27 July
Fair, Tomah, Wisconsin.

28 July
John & June appear in Anaheim, California with Billy Graham.

August
"I Will Dance With You"/"Too Bad For Love" (7-28979) released. This Karen Brooks single includes Cash on the a-side.

1-2 August
Hampton Beach, New Hampshire.

3 August
Bloomfield, Connecticut.

6 August
Beaverbrook Arena, St. Johns, New Brunswick. Prince Charles came to the show with his naval training group.

8 August
Sportflex, Dartmouth, Nova Scotia.

9 August
Summer Theatre, Hyannis, Massachusetts.

10 August
Summer Theater, Cohasset, Massachusetts.

11 August
Summer Theater, Warwick, Rhode Island.

16 August
Fair, Escanaba, Michigan.

17 August
Fair, Green Bay, Wisconsin.

17 August
"Highwayman" gives Cash his first #1 single since "One Piece At A Time" hit the top spot back in 1976.

19 August
June Carter-Cash hosts *Nashville Now* with guest stars Merle Haggard, Rosey Carter and other Carter Family members. Johnny Cash makes a surprise appearance at the end of the show.

August
The second single by The Highwaymen is released – "Desperadoes Waiting For A Train"/"The Twentieth Century Is Almost Over" (Columbia 38-005594).

September
Johnny Cash records in Memphis for the first time since July 1958. He joins Carl Perkins, Jerry Lee Lewis and Roy Orbison for a series of recording sessions at the famous Sun Studio and American Sound, both in Memphis. Among the musicians and vocalists present for the session are Marty Stuart, John Fogerty and British rocker Dave Edmunds. Producer Chips Moman, who had been responsible for countless hits at American, including Elvis's "Suspicious Minds" and "In The Ghetto", oversees the sessions. Two of Cash's previous producers, Sam Phillips and Jack Clement, are also present to lend their vocal skills to the John Fogerty track "Big Train From Memphis". A television crew are on hand to film the historic event and both "Home Of The Blues", a solo performance by Cash, and a jam on "Maybelline" by all four artists are featured in the TV documentary, but do not appear on the album. During the sessions Carl Perkins turned to Marty Stuart, who had just signed with Columbia, and said "I heard you just got signed to Columbia. Well, you're going to need something," and handed Stuart one of his Fender Stratocaster guitars as a gift. After the sessions finished a euphoric Moman commented "It was the highlight of my career. I've never worked in a situation that meant more to me. I couldn't believe when I woke up this morning that it was reality, not a dream."

September
Most of the month is taken up with the filming of *The Last Days Of Frank And Jesse James*. Cash plays Frank while Kris Kristofferson plays Jesse. The supporting cast includes Waylon Jennings, Ed Bruce and David Allan Coe. Most of the scenes were filmed in and around Nashville. During the movie Cash is clad in western gear from the collection of the late John Wayne.

14 September
"Desperadoes Waiting For A Train" joins "Highwayman" on the chart. While not repeating the success of the first single, "Desperadoes" does reach #15 during a run of 18 weeks.

14-15 September
St. Louis, Missouri.

22 September
The Highwaymen play a show during Farm Aid in Champaign, Illinois.

30 September - 5 October
The 10th Anniversary Johnny Cash Christmas Special is taped in Nashville. Appearing with Cash at the Grand Ole Opry were June Carter-Cash, Helen and Anita Carter, Rosanne Cash, Jerry Lee Lewis and Larry Gatlin.

October
Rainbow (FC-39951) is released.
Tracks: "I'm Leaving Now", "Here Comes That Rainbow Again", "They're All The Same", "Easy Street", "Have You Ever Seen The Rain", "You Beat All I Ever Saw", "Unwed Fathers", "Love Me Like You Used To", "Casey's Last Ride", "Borderline (A Musical Whodunnit)"

An album titled *In Living Color*, produced by Billy Sherrill, was originally scheduled to follow the *Johnny 99* album and may have included tracks like "Out Among The Stars", "I Drove Her Out of My Mind", "Rock and Roll Shoes", "My Elusive Dreams" and the recent single "Chicken In Black" but for unknown reasons the album never materialised, even though CBS in Europe had allocated a catalogue number to it - CBS 26147. *Rainbow* became Cash's next album and it is strange that the titles share a similar theme.

4 October
Columbus, Ohio.

5 October
Lampe, Missouri.

14 October
The Highwaymen appear at the Country Music Association Awards Ceremony in Nashville, Tennessee.

18 October
Paramount Theater, Asbury Park, New Jersey.

19 October
Sussex County Civic Center, Sparta, New Jersey.

20 October
National Horse Show, Landover, Maryland.

24 October
Memphis, Tennessee.

26 October
Salina, Kansas.

November
The video for the song "Highwayman" by Johnny Cash, Waylon Jennings, Willie Nelson and Kris Kristofferson is awarded a gold medal in the country & western category at the International Film and Television Festival held in New York.

16 November
Carter Fold, Hiltons, Virginia.

22 November
Lowell, Massachusetts.

23 November
Canada Trust Depositors Convention Center, Ottawa, Ontario.

30 November
Club, Detroit, Michigan.

1 December
Civic Center, Saginaw, Michigan.

4-7 December
Carlton Dinner Theater, Bloomington, Minnesota.

7 December
The *10th Anniversary Johnny Cash Christmas Special* is broadcast with special guests Rosanne Cash, June Carter-Cash, Jerry Lee Lewis and Larry Gatlin.

ALL NEW!

10 years a Christmas TV tradition... 30 years a country legend and rock 'n roll giant...Tonight— early Memphis days, his biggest hits, all-time great moments. A Cash family holiday celebration!

Guest stars:
JUNE CARTER CASH
JOHN CARTER CASH
LARRY GATLIN

Special guest stars:
ROSANNE CASH,
JERRY LEE LEWIS

THE 10TH ANNIVERSARY
CHRISTMAS JOHNNY CASH SPECIAL

A CBS Special Presentation
9PM CBS◉4,7,31

away following a long illness aged 88. A retired Arkansas sharecropper, he is survived by his wife Carrie, whom he married in 1920, and six children. The funeral is held on 26 December in Hendersonville.

31 December
Sheraton Convention Center, Valley Forge, Pennsylvania.

13 December
Carlton Dinner Theater, Green Bay, Wisconsin.

14 December
Rialto Square Theater, Joliet, Illinois.

23 December
Ray Cash, Johnny Cash's father, passes

1986-1993

"We were singing together every night and got to sounding really good. Willie and I talked about doing a duet album together, but I told him I didn't want to stand in line with everyone else who wanted to do a duet with him. So Kris, Waylon and all of us started talking about doin' this thing *together*."

Johnny Cash from the Highwaymen tour brochure 1992

1986

January
"I'm Leaving Now"/"Easy Street" (Columbia 38-05672) are released as a single. These are the only tracks lifted from *Rainbow* for releases in this format.

Early January
The cast and crew arrive in Arizona and Mexico for a 24-day shooting schedule for the TV-movie *Stagecoach*. Based on the Ernest Haycox short story *Stage to Lordsburg*, and originally filmed by John Ford back in 1939 with John Wayne playing the Ringo Kid, this version was directed by Ted Post, who had previously worked on the Clint Eastwood movies *Hang 'em High* and *Magnum Force*. Johnny Cash played the role of US Marshall Curly Wilcox and the part of the Ringo Kid went to Kris Kristofferson. Willie Nelson played Doc Holliday, a dentist, Waylon Jennings a cheating gambler called Hatfield and there were parts for John Schneider, Mary Crosby, Elizabeth Ashley and Anthony Newley.

10 February
The Record Industry Association of America award a gold disc to the album *The Highwaymen*.

25 February
It had been ten years since Cash was last up for a Grammy Award. At the ceremony, broadcast live by CBS from the Shrine Auditorium in Los Angeles and covering the eligibility period 1 October 1984 – 30 September 1985, the track "Highwayman" by Johnny Cash, Willie Nelson, Waylon Jennings & Kris Kristofferson was nominated for the 'Best Country Performance By A Duo Or Group With Vocal' award. Although it was beaten by the Judds with "Why Not Me" the song did win the 'Best Country Song (Songwriter's Award)' for Jimmy Webb. Cash's daughter Rosanne was nominated and won 'Best Country Vocal Performance, Female' for "I Don't Know Why You Don't Want Me".

5 March
Civic Center, Grand Rapids, Michigan.

7 March
Premier Theater, Detroit, Michigan.

8 March
Rialto Theater, Joliet, Illinois.

9 March
Civic Center, Rockford, Illinois.

22 March
Mid-South Coliseum, Memphis, Tennessee.

29 March
Southport, England.

30 March
Carlisle, England.

31 March
Country Music Festival, Wembley Arena, London. This show is filmed by BBC Television and broadcast as part of their *Sing Country* series later in the year.

2 April
Belfast, Ireland.

3 April
Newport, Wales.

4 April
Stavanger, Norway.

5 April
Frankfurt, Germany.

6 April
Zurich, Switzerland.

9-10 April
Munich, Germany.

11 April
Ipswich, England.

12 April
Birmingham, England.

18 April
Owensboro, Kentucky.

23 April
Barre, Vermont.

24 April
Concord, New Hampshire.

25 April
Lyndon State Alumni College Gym, Lyndonville, Vermont.

26 April
Civic Auditorium, Trenton, New Jersey.

May
The Johnny Cash and Waylon Jennings duet album *Heroes* (FC-40347) is released, featuring a cover shot taken on the set of *Stagecoach*.
Tracks: "Folks Out On The Road", "I'm Never Gonna Roam Again", "American By Birth", "Field Of Diamonds", "Heroes", "Even Cowgirls Get The Blues", "Love Is The Way", "The Ballad Of Forty Dollars", "I'll Always Love You (In My Own Crazy Way)", "One Too Many Mornings".

"Even Cowgirls Get The Blues"/ "American By Birth" (Columbia 38-05896) make up the first single to be issued from the album.

May
Class Of '55 (America/Smash A/S-830-002-39951) is released featuring the material recorded back in September 1985 by Cash, Carl Perkins, Jerry Lee Lewis and Roy Orbison.
Tracks: "Birth Of Rock And Roll", "Sixteen Candles", "Class Of '55", "Waymore Blues", "We Remember The King", "Coming Home", "Rock And Roll (Fais-Do-Do)", "Keep My Motor Running", "I Will Rock And Roll With You", "Big Train From Memphis".

May
Believe In Him (WR-8333) released.
Tracks: "Believe In Him", "Another Wide River To Cross", "God Ain't No Stained Glass Window", "Over There", "Old Rugged Cross", "My Children Walk In Truth", "You're Driftin' Away", "Belshazah", "Half A Mile A Day", "One Of These Days I'm Gonna Sit Down And Have A Little Talk With Paul".

This material, recorded back in 1982 and produced by Marty Stuart, finally gets a release. Jessi Colter (Mrs Waylon Jennings) sings a duet with John on "Old Rugged Cross".

1-3 May
Carlton Dinner Theatre, Bloomington, Minnesota.

4 May
Bemidji State University, Bemidji, Minnesota.

12 May
Ice Rink, Red Deer, Alberta.

13 May
Performing Arts Centre, Calgary, Alberta.

14 May
A show booked at the Ice Rink, Kimberley, British Columbia is cancelled due to a snowstorm and the entire show were trapped in Calgary.

15-16 May
Orpheum Theater, Vancouver, British Columbia.

17 May
The Waylon Jennings and Johnny Cash single "Even Cowgirls Get The Blues" debuts at #70 at the start of its 11-week run. On 5 July the single will reach its highest position of #35.

24 May
New Orleans, Louisiana.

31 May
On The Strand, Galveston, Texas.

June
Johnny Cash makes a surprise appearance at the annual Fan Fair held in Nashville. Cash joined Carl Perkins and Jerry Lee Lewis to perform "I'll Fly Away" and they appear at the Mercury/Polygram stand to promote their Memphis Homecoming album *Class Of '55*.

June
Two singles taken from the *Class of '55* album are released – "Class Of '55"/"We Remember The King" (888-142-7) and

"Rock And Roll (Fais Do Do)"/"Birth Of Rock And Roll" (884-760-7).

June
The Tom T. Hall composition "Ballad Of Forty Dollars" is backed with "Field Of Diamonds" (Columbia 38-06287) and released as the new single.

June
Cash's novel on the apostle Paul, *Man In White*, is published.

1 June
Morgan City, Louisiana.

11 June
'The Johnny Cash & June Carter-Cash Breakfast' during which John sings "Man In White" and "A Backstage Pass".

12 June
Private party, Conrad Towers, Chicago, Illinois.

13 June
A concert scheduled in Canton, Ohio is cancelled.

14 June
Waterloo Village, Stanhope, New Jersey.

16 June
Washington, DC.

17 June
Keene, New Hampshire.

18 June
Berlin, New Hampshire.

19 June
Castleton, Vermont.

21 June
Camden County Fair, Camdenton, Missouri.

21 June
Heroes, Cash's album with Waylon

Jennings, enters the chart at #51. The same day the Memphis homecoming album *Class Of '55* debuts four places lower. Both albums register on the charts through to October.

28 June
Executive Inn, Owensboro, Kentucky.

1-4 July
Taping *Statue Of Liberty TV Show* in New York.

7 July
Johnny Cash was honored with the Shalom Peace Award from the Jewish National Fund at a testimonial dinner/celebrity roast held at the Peabody Hotel in Memphis. Executive director of the JNF, Marcia Werbin, said "Johnny Cash was selected for this honor for his contributions and efforts to promote peace through music." The event centered around a tribute roast to Cash by his friends and colleagues including Waylon Jennings, June Carter-Cash, Tony Joe White, producers Chips Moman and Sam Phillips, Jeannie C. Riley and Jessi Colter. Proceeds from the event go towards projects in Israel.

17 July
Centennial Theater, Winnipeg, Manitoba.

17-18 July
USA Today prints articles concerning Columbia Records' decision not to renew Johnny Cash's contract. Cash had released a steady string of hit singles and over 30 albums during his 28 years with the label. Rick Blackburn, head of Columbia/Nashville, was quoted as saying "This is the hardest decision that I've ever had to make in my life." The label gave no official reason for the decision.

18 July
Fairgrounds, Regina, Saskatchewan.

19-20 July
Frontier Days, Cheyenne, Wyoming.

22-23 July
Christian Booksellers Convention in Washington, DC.

1-7 August
Harrah's Casino, Lake Tahoe, Nevada.

18 August
Fairgrounds, Gray, Tennessee.

21-22 August
Luther Burbank Center, Santa Rosa, California.

23 August
Fairgrounds, Kennewick, Washington.

25 August
Fairgrounds, Salem, Oregon.

27 August
Bellingham, Washington.

28 August
Vancouver, British Columbia.

30 August
Fairgrounds, Elkhorn, Wisconsin.

31 August
Fairgrounds, Sheboygan, Wisconsin.

September
Cash records his first material for his new label Mercury at JMI Studios.

September
"Rock And Roll (Fais Do Do)"/ "Sixteen Candles" (888-934-7) released. This third release from *Class Of '55* is the second to feature the track "Rock And Roll (Fais Do Do)" while the b-side is handled by Jerry Lee Lewis and does not feature Cash.

12 September
Forum, Los Angeles, California. Also on the show are The Gatlins and John Schneider.

14 September
High School Stadium, Corona, California.

18 September
Tommy Hunter TV show, Toronto, Ontario.

19 September
Place des Arts, Montreal, Quebec.

27 September
County Fairground, Hillsdale, Michigan.

27 September
Cash is a special guest on *Hee Haw*. Also on the show are Roy Clark, Loretta Lynn and Kathy Mattea.

Late-September
Cash signs copies of his *Man In White* book at several bookstores in Nashville.

4 October
Music Park, Calhoun, Georgia.

22 October
Opry Convention, Nashville, Tennessee.

23 October
Cash gives a lecture in Fargo, North Dakota.

24 October
University of North Dakota, Grand Forks, North Dakota.

25 October
Norwegian Festival, Minot, North Dakota.

26 October
Civic Center, Jamestown, North Dakota.

November
Following his earlier appearance on *Hee Haw* back in September Cash is guest on two more shows during November. Along with regular Roy Clark other guests include Dwight Yoakam and The Gatlin Brothers.

1 November
While the *Heroes* album drops out of the chart *Class Of '55* remains for a further six weeks.

1 November
Clearwater, Florida.

2 November
Tupperware Auditorium, Kissimmee, Florida.

4 November
Performing Arts Hall, Sarasota, Florida.

8-9 November
Billy Graham Crusade, Tallahassee, Florida.

10 November
Joan Rivers TV Show.

12-17 November
Caesars Palace, Las Vegas, Nevada.

21 November
Back in October 1968 *Johnny Cash At Folsom Prison* was certified gold by the RIAA (Record Industry Association of America). Eighteen years on the album is certified double platinum. Both *Johnny Cash At San Quentin* and *Johnny Cash's Greatest Hits* also achieve double platinum status on this day.

22 November
Executive Inn, Paducah, Kentucky.

December
"Better Class Of Loser"/"Take The Long Way Home" (MCA-52989) released. The a-side of this John Schneider single features both Cash and Waylon Jennings.

December
Cash re-records a selection of his greatest hits at Gospel Country Network Studio and Berry Hill Sound.

18 December
Johnny Cash headlines a Toys For Tots benefit show at Nashville's Grand Ole Opry

House. Other guests included Tom T. Hall, Kathy Mattea, Larry Boone and the Carter Family.

Late December
"The Man In White"/"The Man In White" (EZRA-227) released. The same song featured on both sides of this single with a version in stereo on the a-side and mono on the reverse. Although exact dates cannot be confirmed, a video was filmed to promote the single. Produced by Jimmy R. Snow, filming took place at Gospel County Network, Taylors Hill, the Executive Plaza, The Parthenon and Woodlawn Cemetary, all in Nashville, with additional footage shot at the Executive Inn in Paducah, Kentucky.

1987

Early January
It is announced in Memphis that Johnny Cash, Waylon Jennings and other performers will combine patriotism and pickin' in a series of rallies and concerts in 10 cities during May and June to raise money for veterans groups. *The Johnny Cash Freedom Train* will run from Memorial Day to Flag Day and is being organised by W. S. Holland. Profits from the ticket sales will go to veterans groups or causes supported by them. Cash said of the event "It's good to be able to wave the flag again, I come from a long line of flag wavers."

3 January
Johnny Cash tapes an appearance on *Austin City Limits* with June Carter-Cash, Helen and Anita Carter, Tommy Cash and Carlene Carter. Nearly three hours of material were taped, to be edited down to one hour for the broadcast.

7 January
Johnny Cash is a special guest on *Crook And Chase* where he talks about his forthcoming debut album on Mercury.

16 January
Fort Myers, Florida.

17 January
Ft. Lauderdale, Florida.

29 January
Salt Lake City, Utah.

30 January
Cupertino, California.

31 January
Salinas, California.

4 February
Boise, Idaho.

5 February
Portland, Oregon.

6 February
Medford, Oregon.

7 February
Scottsdale, Arizona.

24 February
Although the recent album *Class Of '55* was not nominated for any awards, *Interviews From The The Class Of '55 Recording Sessions* featuring Johnny Cash, Carl Perkins, Jerry Lee Lewis, Roy Orbison, Sam Phillips, Rick Nelson and Chips Moman did win the 'Best Spoken Word Or Non-Musical Recording' category at the annual Grammy Awards, broadcast live by CBS from the Shrine Auditorium in Los Angeles. The awards covered the eligibility period 1 October 1985 – 30 September 1986.

26 February
Civic Center, Des Moines, Iowa.

27 February
Century II Arena, Wichita, Kansas.

28 February-1 March
Denver, Colorado.

Early March
Several days were reserved for filming although this was later cancelled.

March
Mercury release "The Night Hank Williams Came To Town"/"I'd Rather Have You" (Mercury 888-459-7), Cash's first single for his new label. The a-side also features Waylon Jennings. Despite being a strong single it only manages to climb to #43 during an 11-week chart residency.

3 March
Orlando, Florida.

11 March
Green Bay, Wisconsin.

12 March
Coliseum, Madison, Wisconsin.

13 March
Duluth, Minnesota.

14 March
Thunder Bay, Ontario.

19-20 March
Naval Base, Guantanemo Bay, Cuba.

27 March
Saenger Theatre, Pensacola, Florida.

28 March
Ocean Opry, Panama City, Florida.

1-4 April
Carlton, Bloomington, Minnesota.

April
Johnny Cash Is Coming To Town (M/P-832.031) is released. This is Cash's first album for his new label Mercury Records. Tracks: "The Big Light", "Ballad Of Barbara", "I'd Rather Have You", "Let Him Roll", "The Night Hank Williams Came To Town", "Sixteen Tons", "Letters From Home", "W. Lee O'Daniel (And The Light Crust Doughboys)", "Heavy Metal (Don't

Mean Rock And Roll To Me)", "My Ship Will Sail".

April
Kris Kristofferson and Johnny Cash duet on Dylan's "Masters Of War" at the Bottom Line in New York.

18 April
Executive Inn, Owensboro, Kentucky.

23 April
Cash appears on *Nashville Now*, introduced by Ralph Emery. Also on the show are June Carter-Cash, The Carter Family and Tommy Cash. He promotes his new album and performs "The Big Light" and "The Night Hank Williams Came To Town". During the show he is presented with three double-platinum awards by Columbia executive Rick Blackburn, for *Johnny Cash At Folsom Prison, Johnny Cash At San Quentin* and *Greatest Hits*.

24 April
Grand Opera House, Wilmington, Delaware.

25 April
Paramount Theater, Asbury Park, New Jersey.

2 May
Billy Graham Crusade, Columbia, South Carolina.

9 May
Lansing, Michigan.

10 May
Grand Rapids, Michigan.

14 May
Oxnard, California.

15 May
Sports Arena, Los Angeles, California.

16 May
Johnny Cash Is Coming To Town debuts at #57. This first album on his new label will remain on the chart for 26 weeks and will peak at #36. It is his first solo chart album for nearly six years.

16 May
A concert scheduled in Council Bluffs, Idaho is cancelled when Cash is hospitalised with exhaustion.

30 May-14 June
Scheduled Freedom Train Dates are postponed due to lack of sponsorship. Concerts/rallies were scheduled in the following cities:

Memphis, Tennessee (30 May)
Birmingham, Alabama (31 May)
Atlanta, Georgia (3 June)
Knoxville, Tennessee (5 June)
Louisville, Kentucky (6 June)
Cincinatti, Ohio (7 June)
Charleston, South Carolina (10 June)
Pittsburgh, Pennsylvania (12 June)
Washington, DC (13 June)
Baltimore, Maryland (14 June)

Only the Baltimore show takes place.

3-4 June
The third annual 'jail-a-thon' takes place at Hendersonville High School where a special jail cell was erected complete with telephone. Offenders were brought in by members of the Hendersonville Police Department who were then assigned to raise bail money from pledges from family and friends. Johnny Cash was charged with 'wearing white socks with basic black' and was incarcerated on the 4 June. Following several hours making calls to Gene Autry, Kris Kristofferson and Ricky Scaggs, Cash raised $18,400 and was released – only after several people called to pledge money to keep him in! June Carter-Cash was subsequently jailed for 'overdressing'.

June
Johnny Cash and the Carter Family appear at the Mercury/Polygram Stand at the annual Fan Fair celebrations in Nashville.

13 June
North Platte, Nebraska.

14 June
The only Freedom Train date takes place in Baltimore, Maryland.

25 June
Auditorium, Sudbury, Ontario.

26 June
Auditorium, Kitchener, Ontario.

27 June
Ontario Place, Toronto, Ontario.

28 June
Hamilton Place, Hamilton, Ontario.

30 June
Bayshore Community Center, Owen Sound, Ontario.

July
The Merle Travis composition "Sixteen Tons" is paired with "Ballad Of Barbara" for single release (Mercury 888-719-7).

4 July
Johnny Cash joins the Boston Pops for a concert broadcast live. He performs "The Battle Of New Orleans", "Paul Revere", recites "The Gettysburg Address" and ends with "The Battle Hymn Of The Republic".

17-23 July
South Shore Room, Harrah's, Lake Tahoe, Nevada.

7 August
Festival, Detroit Lakes, Minnesota.

9 August
Fair, Enumclaw, Washington.

10 August
Fair, Vancouver, Washington.

11 August
Fair, Roseburg, Oregon.

14 August
Meadowbrook Theater, Detroit, Michigan.

16 August
Ponderosa Park, Salem, Ohio.

22 August
Cash opens his European tour with a concert in Gdansk, Poland.

25 August
Ostend, Belgium.

26 August
Oslo, Norway.

27 August
Kristiansand, Norway.

28 August
Copenhagen, Denmark.

29 August
Moellis, Switzerland.

30 August
Peterborough, England.
Cash, Kris Kristofferson, Hoyt Axton, Billie Jo Spears and The Nitty Gritty Dirt Band headline the Peterborough Country Music Festival.

Sometime during their time in England Cash, Kristofferson and Spears guest on the BBC-TV Wogan Show introduced by Derek Jameson. During the show Cash performs "The Night Hank Williams Came To Town" and "Will The Circle Be Unbroken".

31 August
The Carter Family only appear in London, England.

1 September
South Shields, Newcastle, England.

2 September
Rotterdam, Holland.

9 September
Private party, Atlantic City, New Jersey.

10 September
Wilkes-Barre, Pennsylvania.

12 September
Cash returns to Council Bluffs, Idaho for a show to make up for the one cancelled back in May.

18 September
Johnny Cash is special guest on *Nashville Now*. Other guests include Johnny Rodriguez, Stella Parton and Waylon Jennings.

19 September
Benefit in Hendersonville, Tennessee.

25 September
Little Nashville, Indiana.

26 September
Centerville, Missouri.

27 September
Lima, Ohio.

October
Two more tracks from the ...*Coming To Town* album are issued: "Let Him Roll"/"My Ship Will Sail" (Mercury 888-838-7).

1 October
Sydney, Nova Scotia. Conway Twitty appears on this and the following two shows.

2 October
Halifax, Nova Scotia.

3 October
Moncton, New Brunswick.

9 October
E. J. Thomas Hall, University of Akron, Akron, Ohio.

10 October
Heinz Hall for Performing Arts, Pittsburgh, Pennsylvania.

19 October
Aspin Hotel, Pasippany, New Jersey.

20 October
Clemens Performing Art Center, Elmira, New York.

21 October
Memorial Centre, Kingston, Ontario.

22 October
Flynn Theater, Burlington, Vermont.

23 October
Proctors Theater, Schenectady, New York.

24 October
Landmark Theater, Syracuse, New York.

25 October
Rajah Masonic Temple, Reading, Pennsylvania.

28 October
Stanley Theater, Utica, New York.

30 October
The Auditorium, Bangor, Maine. Steven King joins show for the evening.

31 October
Symphony Hall, Springfield, Massachusetts.

5 November
Memorial Hall, Dayton, Ohio.

6 November
Paramount Arts Center, Aurora, Illinois.

7 November
Masonic Temple, Davenport, Iowa.

8 November
Jr. High School Auditorium, Quincy, Illinois.

14 November
The Arena, Grand Prairie, Alberta.

15 November
The Red Barn, Edmonton, Alberta.

16 November
Jubilee Auditorium, Calgary, Alberta.

18 November
TNN (The Nashville Network) broadcast the 1974 special *Ridin' The Rails*.

19 November
Civic Center, Lloydminster, Alberta.

20 November
Centennial Auditorium, Saskatoon, Saskatchewan.

21 November
Cypress Center, Medicine Hat, Alberta.

22 November
Center for the Arts, Regina, Saskatchewan.

23 November
Pantages Playhouse, Winnipeg, Manitoba.

December
"W. Lee O'Daniel (And The Light Crust Dough Boys)"/"Letters From Home" (Mercury 888-010-7) released.

5 December
Cameron Indoor Stadium, Duke University, Durham, North Carolina.

7 December
Municipal Auditorium, San Antonio, Texas.

12 December
"Let Him Roll" had failed to chart, but the third single taken from the *Johnny Cash Is Coming To Town* album, "W. Lee O'Daniel (And The Light Crust Dough Boys)" spends 5 weeks on the chart and peaks at #72.

1988

13 January
Seaside, Oregon.

14 January
Yakima, Washington.

15 January
Bremerton, Washington.

16 January
Marsee Auditorium, El Camino College, Torrance, California.

17 January
McCallum Theatre, Palm Springs, California.

19 January
Orange County Performing Arts Center, Costa Mesa, California.

20 January
Convention Center, Tucson, Arizona.

22-23 January
Showroom, Riverside Resort Hotel, Laughlin, Nevada.

24 January
Flint Center for the Performing Arts, Cupertino, California.

29 January
Cape Girardeau, Missouri.

30 January
Louisville, Kentucky.

31 January
The Philadelphia Inquirer prints an article about a forthcoming mini-tour of three mid-American college campuses starring Johnny Cash, June Carter-Cash, Waylon Jennings and Jessi Colter. With ticket prices at just $9.50 the tour is dubbed the *Affordable Art* tour. "In going back to basics, we are bringing a more intimate, simple show with little flash and flair, less lighting, less sophisticated sound and instrumentation," Cash said. "We will do the songs the fans want to hear, but we'll do them without the high-tech schmaltz that has been the trend lately." The tour is due to stop at the Universities of Oklahoma, Missouri and Illinois.

5 February
Charleston, South Carolina.

6 February
Cornerstone Presbyterian Church, Columbia, South Carolina.

13 February
Rosanne Cash's recording of "Tennessee Flat Top Box", taken from her album *King's Record Shop*, hits the top spot on the country chart. Rosanne had recorded it partly because her husband Rodney Crowell had reminded her of it. She assumed the song was in the public domain "because I'd known it all my life" she said. Her dad bought space in *Billboard* magazine publishing a letter to his daughter. It read "Rosanne, a lot of people have made such a big deal out of the fact that you didn't know that I wrote 'Tennessee Flat Top Box' when you recorded it. I'm glad you didn't. It tells me still another nice thing about you. You have always been your own person – even when you were five years old. You never took me

for granted. I think you always loved me almost as much as I love you. If that's possible. But you had your own dreams, your own goals, your own hopes and cares. I could never put into words how much it meant to me that you recorded my song. Your own 'My Old Man' is one of my life's greatest joys, but your success with 'Tennessee Flat Top Box' is one of my life's greatest fulfillments. I love you. Dad.

20 February
Dallas, Texas.

21 February
The *Affordable Art* tour opens at the University of Oklahoma. Only Bob Wootton, W. S. Holland and Jim Soldi from Cash's band were at the show, along with a couple of musicians from Waylon's touring band.

23 February
The tour continues with a show at the University of Missouri in Columbia.

24 February
The last date of the short *Affordable Art* tour is held at the University of Illinois in Champaign. The audience are treated to an appearance by Brooke Shields, who performs a song she had written with a friend.

27 February
Mowhawk Performance Center, North Adams, Massachusetts.

28 February
Bayville, New Jersey.

9 March
Civic Center, Bismarck, North Dakota.

10 March
Civic Arena, Aberdeen, South Dakota.

11 March
Municipal Auditorium, Sioux City, Iowa.

12 March
Coliseum, Sioux Falls, South Dakota.

13 March
Corn Palace, Mitchell, South Dakota.

15 March
Bicentennial Center, Salina, Kansas.

16 March
Civic Auditorium, Dodge City, Kansas.

17-19 March
Three dates in Kansas in Ottawa, Emporia and Independence are cancelled when Cash is taken ill with bronchitis.

22 March
The Country Music Hall of Fame in Nashville's Music Row opens *The Johnny Cash Exhibit*. Cash opened the exhibition with one of the 'biggest parties ever' . The star-studded guest list included Emmylou Harris, Chet Atkins, Waylon Jennings, Jessi Colter, Lynn Anderson, Sam Phillips and Bill Monroe. It wasn't only American artists who were there – British pop hit maker and commedienne Tracy Ullman also turned up. All the Cash family turned up to celebrate the event, which was so packed you could hardly see the exhibits, prompting Cash to say "I really haven't seen it yet, myself. I hope to".

The largest biographical salute in the Hall of Fame's history, it cost around $70,000 and would stay open through 1990. Besides the 1200 square feet of the Briley Gallery, an additional theatre covering 800 square foot was redesigned for this exhibit. It was expected to attract more than one million visitors over the next two years. Hall of Fame Director Bill Ivey said of the exhibit "This collection provides unprecedented documentation of country music's most distinguished career. It is extraordinarily rich due to Cash's unusual level of co-operation and interest and the availability of his extensive personal archives."

A press release from the Hall of Fame described the exhibit: Structured in seven sections plus the special gallery housing a 'signature collection', the exhibit traces the artist's life and career from his Arkansas birth in 1932 through his emergence as a popular music icon appealing to urban and rural audiences, young and old, domestically and around the world. The visitor sees the breadth of a diverse career and is provided an intimate glimpse of the artist's personal and family life. Alongside the recording and performing history, the exhibit traces Cash's film, television and literary career from the 1950's through his contemporary status as a legend in popular culture. At Cash's suggestion, the exhibit is presented through the use of uniform black, white and silver graphics, which lend a dramatic look distinct from other museum exhibits. Through the use of sound and video recordings and direct quotes in Cash's own handwriting in the exhibit text, the visitor receives the closest possible visit with an American hero.

The following is a brief description of each section of the exhibit, based on the press release:

ROOTS: Reviews his early life in the rural south, military service and early efforts at songwriting and performing. Artifacts include his Air Force uniform, service record, school report cards, family Bible, photos of family, home and young Cash himself.

ROCKABILLY: Looks at his move to Memphis, professional debut and early hits. Displayed are Cash's white jacket, musical instruments used by Cash, Luther and Marshall and early television clips including "Big River" and "I Walk The Line".

BALLADEER: This section looks at his emergence as an American troubadour and an insight into his expanded popularity with young, urban audiences. It also covers his early concept albums, the appearance at the Newport Festival and his friendship with Bob Dylan. On show are the steel bars used during performances of "John Henry's Hammer", song manuscripts and photos from the period.

STARDOM: Focuses on his concerts and, to a lesser extent, his recordings. It traces the development of his audiences domestically and internationally. Artifacts include a logbook documenting some of his successful recording sessions, prison garb presented to inmates to commemorate his historic prison concerts, tour books and photos including his marriage to June Carter. Other memorabilia looks at his concerts through press headlines.

SCREEN: This section is divided into two parts covering television and film. On show are cue cards from his ABC-TV Shows, the hat, shirt and gun worn by Cash in *A Gunfight*, the dress June Carter-Cash wore when she played the part of Mary Magdalene in The *Gospel Road* and call-sheets and scripts from films and TV shows. On screen clips from various shows are available.

LEGEND: Covering his career from 1969 through 1988 it outlines his success in various media including publishing. On show is the Man in Black outfit and a selection of tour jackets and also the Grammy Award Cash won for his sleeve-notes to Dylan's *Nashville Skyline* album. The section also looks at his religious mission through the first edition of his autobiography *Man In Black* and the recently published novel about the life of St. Paul, *Man In White*, a personal letter from President Jimmy Carter commending him for humanitarian service and photos of his many performances at Billy Graham crusades.

OFF STAGE: Is a look at his private life and his relationship with his family and friends. Hobbies and personal interests are covered with displays of fishing tackle and a selection of photos with friends like Waylon Jennings and the late Johnny Horton.

SIGNATURE COLLECTION: The special gallery leads the visitor on a personal video tour of Cash's home and a private commentary on many of his personal items on display including an Indian belt, fine art, books, his collection of Roman coins, antique furniture and other special items.

April
Classic Cash (M/P-834-526-1) is released. Tracks: "Get Rhythm", "Tennessee Flat-Top Box", "Long Black Veil", "A Thing Called Love", "I Still Miss Someone", "Cry, Cry, Cry", "Blue Train", "Sunday Morning Coming Down", "Five Feet High

And Rising", "Peace In The Valley", "Don't Take Your Guns To Town", "Home Of The Blues", "Guess Things Happen That Way", "I Got Stripes", "I Walk The Line", "Ring Of Fire", "Ballad Of Ira Hayes", "Ways Of A Woman In Love", "Folsom Prison Blues", "Suppertime"
This album of re-recordings was originally released in Europe during his April tour and later made available at the Country Music Hall Of Fame *Johnny Cash Exhibit*. It was eventually given a general release in the States.

7-9 April
Replacement dates for the cancelled March shows in Kansas with two sold-out shows at the Municipal Auditorium in Ottawa on 7 April followed by shows in Emporia and the Memorial Hall in Independence.

20 April
Concert promoters Jeffrey & Howard Kruger present Johnny Cash's European tour. The opening night is at the ICC, Berlin, Germany.

21 April
Meistersingerhalle, Nurnberg, Germany.

23 April
Tennis Bar, Bad Homburg, Germany.

24 April
Jahrhunderthalle, Frankfurt, Germany.

25 April
Eberthalle, Ludwigshafen, Germany.

26 April
Philipshalle, Dusseldorf, Germany.

27 April
CCH, Hamburg, Germany.

28 April
Deutsches Museum, Munich, Germany.

30 April
Coliseum, St. Austell, Cornwall, England.

May
"Get Rhythm"/"Cry, Cry, Cry" (Mercury 870-237-7), both from the *Classic Cash* album of re-recordings, released.

1 May
Corn Exchange, Cambridge, England.

2 May
Bournemouth International Centre, Bournemouth, England.

3 May
De Montfort Hall, Leicester, England.

4 May
Two shows at the Ritz Theatre, Lincoln, England.

6 May
Opera House, Blackpool, England.

7 May
Apollo Theatre, Manchester, England.

8 May
Sands Centre, Carlisle, England.

10 May
Cliffs Pavilion, Southend, England.

11 May
Centre, Brighton, England.

12 May
Royal Albert Hall, London, England
Glen Campbell is a special guest at the Brighton and London dates. They each play their own set and appear on stage together for a selection of hits.

28 May
Executive Inn, Paducah, Kentucky.

30 May
Busch Gardens, Williamsburg, Virginia.

17 June
Benefit concert on the Cayman Islands.

23 June
Cash appears on TNN's *Nashville Now* hosted by Ralph Emery.

24 June
Holiday Inn Entertainment And Convention Center, Stevens Point, Wisconsin.

25 June
Private party at Grays Lake, Illinois.

27 June
Larry Gatlin is a guest at a concert in Cincinnati, Ohio.

22 July
During a concert tour Bob Dylan takes time out to visit *The Johnny Cash Exhibit* at the Country Music Hall of Fame.

4 July
County Fair, Del Mar, California.

5-6 July
County Fair, Pleasanton, California.

7 July
Luther Burbank Center, Santa Rosa, California.

8 July
Coos Bay, Oregon.

9 July
Vancouver, British Columbia.

10 July
Kelona, British Columbia.

11 July
Trail, British Columbia.

15 July
Fair, Waukesha, Wisconsin.

16 July
Fair, Seymour, Wisconsin.

18 July
Private function at Old Hickory, Tennessee.

29 July
La Ronde Park, Montreal, Quebec.

30 July
Agora Park, Quebec City, Quebec.

31 July
Low, Quebec.

August
While in Canada Cash films his portions of the Davy Crockett series for Disney.

5 August
Cash appears on *Nashville Now*. Also appearing on the show are David Lynn Jones and David Cooksey.

6 August
Easton, Pennsylvania.

7 August
Lido Beach, New York.

8 August
Private Party, Hilton, Chicago, Illinois.

16 August
Chehaus, Wisconsin.

17 August
Fair, Grants Pass, Oregon.

19 August
Fair, Scott's Bluff, Nebraska.

20 August
Fair, Grand Island, Nebraska.

26 August
Ritz Cafe, New York City.

27 August
Hampton, New Hampshire.

28 August
Webster, Massachusetts.

September
"That Old Wheel"/"Tennessee Flat Top Box" (Mercury 870-688-7) released. The a-side featured Hank Williams Jnr and is from the forthcoming album *Water From The Wells Of Home*, while the b-side is taken from *Classic Cash*.

September
Cash starts recording the entire New King James version of the New Testament for release by the Thomas Nelson Organization on fourteen cassettes. Sessions will continue, on and off, for the rest of the year and conclude in late summer 1989.

3 September
Colorado State Fair, Pueblo, Colorado.

4 September
Speedway, Peterborough, Ontario.

11 September
Holiday Star Theater, Merrillville, Indiana.

17 September
Balloon Festival, Airport, Statesville, North Carolina.

24 September
Grand Cayman Islands.

24 September
"That Old Wheel" debuts at #77 for a 20-week run that will see it climb to #21.

1 October
Johnny and June Carter-Cash appear on *Hee Haw*.

21 October
Auditorium, White Plains, New York.

22 October
Cash performs at a benefit show for Shalom et Benedictus, a drug and alcohol treatment community for adolescents and their families. The show is held at the Handley High School Auditorium in Winchester, Virginia. Before the show both John and June speak a few words at a reception given in their honor. John was presented with a plaque and told that the day had been declared 'Johnny Cash Day.'

23 October
Cowboy Hall Of Fame Club, Bayville, New Jersey.

25 October
At the Faith Assembly of God Church in Kernersville, North Carolina Cash lent a hand to his sister Joanne Cash-Yates's dream of recording a live video of Christian music at the church. He appearerd on a portion of the 16-song set with the backup of a 28-voice church choir.

26 October
Highpoint, North Carolina.

28 October
New Brunswick, New Jersey.

29 October
Park Theater, Union City, New Jersey.

30 October
Paramount Theater, Middleton, New York.

November
Water From The Wells Of Home (M/P-834-778-1) is released.
Tracks: "Ballad Of A Teenage Queen", "As Long As I Live", "Where Did We Go Right", "Last Of The Drifters", "Call Me The Breeze", "That Old Wheel", "Sweeter Than The Flowers", "A Croft In Clachan (The Ballad Of Rob MacDunn)", "New Moon Over Jamaica", "Water From The Wells Of Home".

The album features a host of guest artists including Rosanne Cash, Hank Williams Jr., Waylon Jennings, Emmylou Harris, John Carter-Cash and ex-Beatle Paul McCartney.

2 November
TV show in Madrid, Spain.

3 November
The second European tour of the year opens at the Austria Center, Vienna, Austria.

4 November
Donauhalle, Regensburg, Germany.

5 November
Parkhalle, Iserlohn, Germany.

6 November
Beethovenhalle, Bonn, Germany.

7 November
Horsens, Denmark.

10 November
Ulster Hall, Belfast, Northern Ireland.

11 November
Two shows at the Olympia Theatre, Dublin, Ireland.

12 November
Another show in Dublin, Ireland. During his time in Ireland, Cash appears on the *Late, Late Show*.

18 November
Brady Theater, Tulsa, Oklahoma.

19 November
Otoe Bingo Parlor, Redrock, Oklahoma.

20 November
The Disney Television Production of *Davy Crockett* premieres on NBC. Tim Dunigan and Johnny Cash play the parts of the young and old Crockett respectively in an episode called *Rainbow In The Thunder*. Tim Dunigan had previously been seen in the series *The A-Team*. Samantha Eggar and David Hemmings, who also directs the show, star in the series. In this episode Cash, as the middle-aged Crockett, reminisces about his young days in the Tennessee Volunteers and then the program flashbacks to that period with Tim Dunigan playing the part. Cash appears in two more episodes - *Guardian Spirit* and *A Natural Man*.

24-26 November
Riverside Hotel, Laughlin, Nevada.

26 November
Hee Haw, featuring Johnny Cash, June Carter-Cash and Holly Dunn is broadcast.

17 December
Water From The Wells Of Home debuts at #57.

19-24 December
A few days before Christmas Cash is admitted to Baptist Hospital in Nashville where he undergoes open heart surgery. Following the double bypass operation he is hit with a serious bout of pneumonia and put on a life support system. By Christmas Eve the news comes through that he is out of the woods and slowly recovering. Ironically, Waylon Jennings had the same

operation a few days before and was in a room not far from Cash. Both Cash and Jennings receive special awards from Baptist Hospital for their strength and courage exhibited during their operations. A billboard size Christmas and Get-Well greeting card to Cash and Jennings signed by over 4,000 people from the Kansas area was delivered to Nashville and installed outside the hospital. Radio station KFDI's Johnny Western, a long-time friend of Cash's, prompted the idea when he heard that both Cash and Jennings were in the same hospital.

1989

7 January
Water From The Wells Of Home had spent the last two weeks of 1988 in the chart and would spend a further 19 weeks on the chart peaking at # 48.

February
"Ballad Of A Teenage Queen"/"Get Rhythm" (Mercury 872-420-7) released. Like the previous single this combines material from Cash's two recent albums *Classic Cash* and *Water From The Wells Of Home*.

22 February
"Will The Circle Be Unbroken" *(from Will The Circle Be Unbroken, Vol. 2)* featuring Johnny Cash, Roy Acuff, Ricky Skaggs, Levon Helm and Emmylou Harris, is nominated in the 'Best Country Vocal Collaboration' category at the Grammy Awards ceremony covering the period 1 October 1988 – 30 September 1989 and broadcast live by CBS from the Shrine Auditorium in Los Angeles. The award goes to "There's A Tear In My Beer" by Hank Williams Jnr. & Hank Williams Snr..

25 February
The single "Ballad Of A Teenage Queen" reaches #45 during its 9-week chart spell.

March
During the early part of March the Highwaymen record tracks for their second album. Recordings take place at Emerald Sound in Nashville. One track, "Yabba Dabba Do", possible a Waylon Jennings track, is not used on the album and remains unissued.

10 March
Embassy Theater, Fort Wayne, Indiana.

11 March
Community College, Jackson, Mississippi.

20 March
Guthrie Theatre, Minneapolis, Minnesota.

22 March
Civic Center, Des Moines, Iowa.

30 March
At a ceremony attended by 300 music stars and business moguls Cash is honoured with the renamed Johnny Cash Americanism Award from the B'nai B'rith's Anti-Defamation League. He receives the honour from Dick Asher, President of Polygram Records, who said "He's a living expression of the rich tradition of brotherhood in America". During the banquet at the Doubletree Hotel in Nashville he listened to a parade of speakers laud him for his humanitariianism.

"Despite the words of his song 'I Walk The Line', there are important lines that Johnny Cash doesn't walk, but crosses over – the lines of race, religion and ethnicity that are used too often to keep us apart, to separate us." (Jane Eskind)

"You sparked something in me. It was tolerance. And that's what I love about you." (Rosanne Cash)

"Johnny Cash cares. Johnny Cash dares. Johnny Cash gives a damn." (Guy Clark)

"Johnny's known worldwide as The Man in

Black, but we know he has a heart of gold."
(Connie Bradley)

6 April
Kirby Center, Wilkes-Barre, Pennsylvania.

7 April
Count Basie Theater, Redbank, New Jersey.

8 April
Aspen Manor, Parsippinay, New Jersey.

14 April
Maryland Theater, Hagerstown, Maryland.

15 April
Warners Theater, Torrington, Connecticut.

21 April
September's Place, Springfield, Pennsylvania.

26 April
Cork, Ireland.

28 April
Castlebar, Ireland.

29 April
Dundrum, Northern Ireland.

1 May
Omagh, Northern Ireland.

3 May
Paris, France.

5 May
Sonderborg, Denmark.

6 May
Country Festival, Zug, Switzerland.

8 May
Two shows in Cambridge, England.

9 May
Nottingham, England.

11 May
Glasgow, Scotland.

13 May
Royal Albert Hall, London, England.

15 May
Paignton, Devon, England.

15 May
Cash is interviewd by Southern Television.

16 May
St. Austell, Cornwall, England.

7 June
Cash appears on the BBC-2 TV show *The Late Show*.

21 June
At the American Cancer Society Jail-A-Thon held in Hendersonville Cash is arrested by Sgt. Josh Graves. Cash called Willie Nelson who pledged $1,000 for his release. At the end of the day the event had raised $20,000.

July
"Ragged Old Flag"/"I'm Leaving Now" (Columbia 38-69067) released. This was a re-issue of "Ragged Old Flag" and was released following the Supreme Court flag burning ruling.

July
"The Last Of The Drifters"/"Water From The Wells Of Home" (Mercury 874-562-7) released. Tom T. Hall and John Carter-Cash feature on the a - and b-sides respectively.

4 July
Fairgrounds, Greely, Colorado.

5-6 July
Fairgrounds, Pleasanton, California.

8 July
Sands, Las Vegas, Nevada.

15 July
Theatre In The Round, North Tonawanda, New York.

19 July
Humphreys Outdoor Theater, San Diego, California.

19 July
June Carter-Cash receives the 'Virginian Of The Year' Award at Virginia Beach, Virginia.

20 July
Orange County Fair, Costa Mesa, California.

28 July
Fairgrounds, Mt. Vernon, Ohio.

29 July
Front Row Theater, Cleveland, Ohio.

1 August
Fairgrounds, Santa Rosa, California.

2 August
Fairgrounds, Turlock, California.

3 August
Football Stadium, Shasta, California.

5 August
Johnny Cash is among 12 other recipients of the Golden Boot Award. Presented by the Motion Picture and Television Fund to actors and other entertainers who have left their mark on the western genre. Robert Duvall, Robert Mitchum, Angie Dickinson, Casey Tibbs and Vera Miles were among the other recipients.

8-9 August
Fairgrounds, San Mateo, California.

11 August
Fairgrounds, Paso Robles, California.

12 August
Ramona Bowl, Hemet, California.

18 August
Regal, Minnesota has the honour of being the smallest place Johnny Cash has ever played. The farm town, consisting of two bars, a church and a baseball field only has a population of around 45 people, although a crowd approaching 5000 people, mostly

from out of town, attended the show. The show was billed as 'Cornstalk '89'.

19 August
Fairgrounds, Beaver Dam, Wisconsin.

1 September
Johnny Cash makes his second guest appearance on *Crook And Chase*.

2 September
State Fair, Lincoln, Nebraska.

30 September
Opry, Little Nashville, Indiana.

5 October
The *All Star Gospel TV Show*, in Birmingham, Alabama is cancelled.

20 October
Capitol Theater, Concord, New Hampshire.

21 October
Garde Arb Center, New London, Connecticut.

23 October
Performing Arts Center, Stamford, Connecticut.

25 October
Zeiterion Theater, New Bedford, Massachusetts.

27 October
Performing Arts Center, Elmira, New York.

28 October
Ritz Theater, New York City.

November
TNN (The Nashville Network) broadcast their *Inside Look At Johnny Cash* special introduced by Ralph Emery.

11 November
High School, Arnold, Missouri.

14 November
Fair, Ocala, Florida.

17 November
Capitol Theater, Williamsport, Pennsylvania.

18 November
Berkeley Performing Arts Center, Lenox, Massachusetts.

5 December
An Inside Look with Ralph Emery is taped/broadcast by The Nashville Network.

9 December
Cash appears on *Nashville Now* introduced by Ralph Emery. During the show he performs "Cats In The Cradle", "Farmers Almanac", "Big River", and "If I Were A Carpenter".

Late 1989-1992
Although new material will still be released over the next few years, including work with the Highwaymen, Cash is actually out of contract and with no label lends his hand to a number of other artists' recordings. This period will see him guesting on records by Martin Delray, Razzy Bailey, Sandy Kelly, One Bad Pig, Mark O, Connor, John Schneider and the Irish rock group U2.

1990

January
Cash enters his 35th year in the music business.

January
"Cats In The Cradle"/"I Love You, Love You" (Mercury 875-626-7) both taken from the forthcoming *Boom Chicka Boom* album are released. "Cats In The Cradle" was originally a number 1 hit for its writer, Harry Chapin, back in 1974.

January
"Silver Stallion"/"American Remains" (Columbia 38-73233) released. Both tracks are taken from the forthcoming album *Highwaymen II*.

8 January
Filming of the *Mother Maybelle's Carter Scratch* video is completed. The video pays homage to her influential guitar technique and filming took place in Texas. Her daughters Helen, Anita and June, along with grandchildren David Jones, Rosey Carter and Lorrie Bennett, all appear in the video. Johnny Cash is also filmed for the video which is due to be released in the Spring.

12-13 January
McCallum Theater, Palm Desert, California.

19 January
Barbara Mann Performing Arts Center, Ft. Myers, Florida.

20 January
Van Wezel Hall, Sarasota, Florida.

22 January
Private party in West Palm Beach, Florida.

25 January
San Carlos, California.

27 January
Coral Ridge Presbyterian Church, Ft. Lauderdale, Florida.

February
Highwayman II (C-45240) is released.
Tracks: "Silver Stallion", "Born And Raised In Black And White", "Two Stories Wide", "We're All In Your Corner Tonight", "American Remains", "Anthem '84", "Angels Love Badmen", "Songs That Make A Difference", "Living Legends", "Texas".

15-24 February
Concert appearances scheduled in Naples, Florida; Tampa, Florida; San Bernardino, California; Phoenix, Arizona and Redondo

Beach, California are cancelled following recent surgery.

March

Boom Chicka Boom (M/P-834-526-1) is released.
Tracks: "A Backstage Pass", "Cats In The Cradle", "Farmer's Almanac", "Don't Go Near The Water", "Family Bible", "Harley", "I Love You, Love You", "Hidden Shame", "Monteagle Mountain", "That's One You Owe Me".
When issued in Europe it included an additional track – "Veterans Day".

3 March
"Silver Stallion" debuts at #70 and will reach #25 during a chart run of 14 weeks.

3 March
Following the release of their second collaboration The Highwaymen undertake their first tour. John plays the entire tour with a broken jaw thinking, and being told by dentists, that the pain was from work performed a few days before the tour!

The opening show was at the Houston Livestock Show and Rodeo and it broke all attendance records with ticket sales reaching 55,983.

5 March
Civic Center, Peoria, Illinois.

6 March
Rosemont Horizon, Chicago, Illinois.

7 March
Palace, Detroit, Michigan.

7 March
A Salute To Ralph Emery is broadcast, featuring Johnny Cash and Barbara Mandrell.

9 March
Metropolitan Center, Minneapolis, Minnesota.

10 March
Hilton Coliseum, Iowa State University, Ames, Iowa.

12 March
Capitol Center, Landover, Maryland.

13 March
Centrum, Worcester, Massachusetts.

14 March
Nassau Coliseum, Uniondale, New York
This show is filmed and later released on video.

15 March
Convention Center, Niagara Falls, New York.

16 March
Coliseum, Cleveland, Ohio.

17 March
Breslin Center, East Lansing, Michigan.

17 March
Highwayman II debuts at #62 at the start of a 46-week run that would see it reach a high of #4.

22 March-7 April
Johnny Cash's UK and European tour is cancelled when he is hospitalised for follow-up dental surgery. The tour was scheduled to take in the following cities:

Leewardin, Holland (22 March)
Alphen aan den Ryn, Holland (23 March)
Minehead, England (24 March)
Dartford, England (26 March)
Bucharest, Romania (28 March)
Bayreuth, Germany (29 March)
Berlin, Germany (30 March)
Bremerhaven, Germany (31 March)
Doncaster, England (2 April)
London, England (3 April)
Dublin, Ireland (4 April)
Cork, Ireland (5 April)
Reykjavik, Iceland (7 April).

There were also two dates scheduled in June at the Geiselwind Truckfestival in Germany.

April
"Farmers Almanac"/"I Shall Be Free" (Mercury 876-428-7) released. The a-side is taken from *Boom Chicka Boom* while the b-side is a track from the same sessions that did not make the final album selection.

27 April
Paramount Theater, Denver, Colorado.

May-June
Replacement dates for the recent cancelled tour of the UK and Europe have to be cancelled again due to health problems. The scheduled dates were:

Dublin, Ireland (22 May)
Cork, Ireland (23 May)
Doncaster, England (24 May)
Liverpool, England (26 May)
Dartford, England (28 May)
Bremerhaven, Germany (29 May)
Berlin, Germany (30 May)
Bayreuth, Germany (31 May)
Alphen aan den Ryn, Holland (1 June)
Heerenveen, Holland (2 June)
London, England (4 June)
Reykjavik, Iceland (7-8 June)

June
"Born And Raised In Black And White"/"Texas" (Columbia 38-73381) released. This is the second single lifted from the *Highwaymen II* album and the b-side features Willie Nelson only. It fails to gain any chart action.

3 June
The Carter Family and Johnny Cash are both inducted into the National Broadcasters Hall of Fame. The ceremony takes place at the Berkley Carterette Hotel in Asbury Park, New Jersey.

21 June
Country Club, the UK country music program, broadcasts an interview with Cash.

22 June
Rialto Theater, Joliet, Illinois.

23 June
Fair, Beloit, Wisconsin.

29 June
Queens, New York.

30 June
Dartmouth University, Hanover, New Hampshire.

4 July
The Highwaymen appear at the Willie Nelson Picnic in Austin, Texas.

12 July
Auditorium, Thunder Bay, Ontario.

13-14 July
Fairground, Hinkley, Minnesota.

20 July
Sudbury, Ontario.

21 July
Ontario Place, Toronto, Ontario.

24 July
Fairgrounds, Chippewa Falls, Wisconsin.

26 July
Zoo, Cincinatti, Ohio.

27 July
Theater, Glenside, Pennsylvania.

28 July
Paramount Theatre, Asbury Park, New Jersey.

2 August
New Haven, Connecticut.

3 August
Fairgrounds, Cumberland, Maryland.

4 August
Hotel, Catskill, New York.

10 August
Hershey Park, Pennsylvania.

11 August
Executive Inn, Owensboro, Kentucky.

13 August
Johnny Cash, John Carter-Cash, Marty Stuart, June Carter-Cash and Carlene Carter all appear on Ralph Emery's *Nashville Now*.

17 August
Fairground, Lewisburg, West Virginia.

18 August
Fairground, Adrian, Michigan.

21 August
Fairground, Ventura, California.

23 August
County Fair, Kennewick, Washington.

24 August
Fairground, Boise, Idaho.

25 August
Fairgrounds, Klamath Falls, Oregon.

25 August
Highwayman II is joined in the chart, albeit for three weeks only, by their first collaboration *Highwayman*.

27 August
State Fair, Monroe, Washington

28 August
Fairground, Salem, Oregon.

29 August
Red Lion Inn, Pendleton, Oregon.

September
"Goin' By The Book"/"Beans For Breakfast" (Mercury 878-292-7) released.

Both sides of this single are from the forthcoming *Mystery Of Life* album.

September
During the late-seventies Bear Family Records had released a series of albums that featured previously unissued material. During the following years they released several comprehensive box sets on different artists. These sets, which normally ran to 5-6 CDs, included large format booklets full of information, discographical information and many previously unseen pictures. Turning their attention to Johnny Cash they issued the 5-CD set *The Man In Black 1954-1959* (BCD-15517). With over 140 tracks, many previously unreleased, this set traced his career from his days at Sun Records through to his first recordings for Columbia. The final CD was a fly-on-the-wall look at a recording session with multiple takes of many songs.

1 & 3 September
Knotts Berry Farm, Anaheim, California.

9 September
The Highwaymen tour for the second time this year. The tour opens with a concert in Little Rock, Arkansas.

10 September
Dallas, Texas.

11 September
Houston, Texas.

13 September
New Mexico State University, Las Cruces, New Mexico.

14 September
Denver, Colorado.

15 September
Salt Lake City, Utah.

17 September
Tucson, Arizona.

18 September
Phoenix, Arizona.

19 September
San Diego, California.

20 September
Motor Speedway, Bakersfield, California.

21 September
Universal Amphitheater, Los Angeles, California.

22 September
Costa Mesa, California.

22 September
Probably helped by the accompanying video "Goin' By The Book" manages to chart, albeit only at #70. This will be Cash's last chart single.

27 September
Arco Arena, Sacramento, California.

28 September
Pavilion, Concord, California.

29 September
Amphitheater, Mountain View, California.

October
Country Music People, the UK magazine, features Cash on the cover and inside in a three page article.

1 October
Universal Amphitheater, Los Angeles, California.

2 October
Fresno, California.

4-9 October
The Highwaymen close their tour with a series of shows at the Mirage Hotel, Las Vegas, Nevada.

11 October
Lake Perris Fair, Hemet, California.

12 October
Fairground, Fresno, California.

18 October
Following the cancelled tours earlier in the

year Cash undertakes his 35th Anniversary tour with an opening show at the Empire, Liverpool, England.

19 October
The Dome, Doncaster, England.

20 October
Newport Centre, Newport, Wales.

22 October
Fairfield Hall, Croydon, England.

23 October
Bournemouth International Centre, Bournemouth, England.

24 October
The National Club, Kilburn, London, England.

26 October
Rijnstreekhal, Alphen aan den Ryn, Holland.

27 October
Thialf Sporthal, Heerenveen, Holland.

29 October
Olympia Theatre, Dublin, Northern Ireland.

1 November
Belfast, Ireland.

2 November
Cavan, Ireland.

3 November
Galway, Ireland.

22 November
Johnny Cash, Jim Stafford, Williams & Ree and Margo Smith all appear on *Nashville Now* introduced by Ralph Emery.

5 December
Quincy Jones, Johnny Cash, Billy Joel and Aretha Franklin tape a two-hour CBS Special.

1991

25 January
Celebrity Theater, Phoenix, Arizona.

26 January
Celebrity Theater, Anaheim, California.

February
Martin Delray films the video for his new release *Get Rhythm*, which features Johnny Cash and is filmed in Nashville by Pollaro Media.

February
The Mystery Of Life (M/P-834-051-2) is released.
Tracks: "The Greatest Cowboy Of Them All", "I'm An Easy Rider", "The Mystery Of Life", "Hey Porter", "Beans For Breakfast", "Goin' By The Book", "Wanted Man", "I'll Go Somewhere And Sing My Songs Again", "The Hobo Song", "Angel And The Badman".

The title track is paired with "I'm An Easy Rider" (Mercury 878-968-7) and released as a single.

8-9 February
Riverside Resort, Laughlin, Nevada.

11 February
Civic Auditorium, Salinas, California.

12 February
Redding, California.

13 February
Fox Theater, Hanford, California.

14 February
Private Party in San Diego, California.

15 February
Billy Bobs, Fort Worth, Texas.

16 February
Clearwater, Florida.

18 February
Civic Performing Arts Center, Melbourne, Florida.

19 February
St. Lucie Performing Arts Center, Ft. Pierce, Florida.

20 February
At the annual Grammy Awards ceremony broadcast live from Radio City Music Hall in New York Johnny Cash was honoured with the 'Living Legends Award.'

21 February
The 14-cassette *Spoken Word New Testament* that Cash recorded back in the late eighties is awarded the *Sweepstakes Angel Award* as album of the year at the 14th Annual International Angel Awards held in Beverley Hills, California. The awards are presented by Excellence In Media to honour productions of outstanding moral, spiritual and social impact. The judges, made up of producers and business, civic and religious leaders, awarded the project a top mark of 10 and Mary Dorr, President of Excellence In Media, said "The judges couldn't stop raving about it."

24 February
Johnny Cash appears at the *Operation Desert Star* benefit organised to raise money for families of servicemen and women serving in the Persian Gulf.

28 February
Club, Kitchener, Ontario.

1 March
Proctor Theater, Schenectady, New York.

2 March
Syracuse, New York.

11 March
Carrie Cash, Johnny Cash's mother, passes away. She was 86 and died at her home in Hendersonville.

15 March
Stanley Performing Arts Centre, Utica, New York.

16 March
Broome County Arena, Binghamton, New York.

20 March
At Reba McEntire's request Johnny Cash speaks during the service held for the eight band members and two pilots killed in an air crash on 16 March. He opened his speech by singing the song "Jim, I Wore A Tie Today" and when it came time to say the name in the song Cash replaced it with the name of each band member – "Jim, Chris, Kirk, Joey, Paula, Terry, Tony and Mike, I wore a tie today." He ended his part of the service with a rendition of the Hank Williams recitation "Negro Funeral".

28 March
Cash's UK and European tour opens with a show at the Palace Theatre, Manchester, England.

30 March
Cash plays a show at the Wembley Country Music Festival in London.

2 April
Capitol Theatre, Aberdeen, Scotland.

3 April
Royal Concert Hall, Glasgow, Scotland. Sandy Kelly joins Cash on stage to sing their recent duet "Woodcarver".

5 April
Arnheim, Holland.

6 April
Messehalle, Frankfurt, Germany.

7 April
Festival, Zurich, Switzerland.

10 April
Graz, Austria.

11 April
HCC, Hamburg, Germany.

12 April
Turku, Finland.

13 April
Lakeside Country Club, Camberley, England.

15 April
Colston Hall, Bristol, England.

19 April
Luther Burbank Center, Santa Rosa, California.

20 April
El Camino College, Torrance, California.

27 April
Fox Theater, St. Louis, Missouri.

4 May
Private party in San Diego, California.

5-25 May
Highwaymen tour of Australia and New Zealand including dates at the Athletic Park in Wellington (11 May), Auckland, New Zealand (12 May), Brisbane (15-16 May) The Entertainment Centre in Sydney (18-19 May) and Melbourne, Adelaide (22-23 May).

13-18 June
The Highwaymen play the Mirage Hotel, Las Vegas. The *Highwaymen Live* is shown on the Disney Channel on the 16 & 26 June.

22 June
Milwaukee, Wisconsin.

4 July
Ponderosa Park, Salem, Ohio.

5 July
Ft. Laramie, Ohio.

6 July
Oyster Bay, New York.

2 August
Music 91, Squamish, British Columbia.

5 August
Clark County Fair, Vancouver, Washington.

6 August
Douglas County Fair, Roseburg, Oregon.

7 August
Rodeo Grounds, Sisters, Oregon.

8 August
Fair, Yreka, California.

9 August
Plumas County Fair, Quincy, California.

10 August
California Mid State Fair, Paso Robles, California.

13 August
N. W. Washington Fair, Lyndon, Washington.

21 August
Summerfest, Auburn Hills, Minnesota.

23 August
State Fair, Minneapolis, Minnesota. Also appearing on the show are Willie Nelson and his band.

24 August
Cubby Bear Club, Chicago, Illinois.

28 August
Cash and Willie Nelson play to an audience of 12,000 at the Central Wisconsin State Fair, Marshfield, Wisconsin. The capacaity at this venue had been reduced drastically since Cash set an attendance record of 21,332 back in 1969. Willie Nelson had also set a record at this venue with 10 appearances.

30 August
Private party in Winston-Salem, North Carolina.

31 August
Private party in Charlotte, North Carolina.

September
Bear Family Records issue *The Man In Black, 1959-1962* (BCD-15562) and *Come Along And Ride This Train* (BCD-15563). The first set carried on from where the earlier release finished and, again, featured 5 CDs, a comprehensive booklet and many previously unissued tracks. The second collected seven of Cash's concept albums - *Ride This Train, Blood, Sweat And Tears, Ballads Of The True West, Bitter Tears, America-A 200 Year Salute, From Sea To Shining Sea* and *The Rambler*. Only three unreleased tracks found their way onto this release.

9 September
Fair, London, Ontario.

10 September
Fair, Allegan, Michigan.

16 September
Benefit show at Loews L'Enfant Plaza Hotel, Washington D.C..

17 September
War Memorial Auditorium, Johnstown, Pennsylvania.

20 September
Capitol Celebrity Theater, Davenport, Idaho.

24 September
The Purple Onion, Oshawa, Ontario.

25 September
Roadie's Roadhouse, Mississauga, Ontario.

26 September
Lulu's Roadhouse, Kitchener, Ontario.

28 September
Opry, Little Nashville, Indiana.

8-10 October
Fair, Topsfield, Massachusetts.

11 October
Hutchins Hall, University of Maine, Orono, Maine.

12 October
Warner Theater, Torrington, Connecticut.

16 October
Rome, Georgia.

19 October
Norskfest, Minot, North Dakota.

21 October
Yorktown, Saskatchewan.

22 October
Saskatoon, Saskatchewan.

23 October
Regina, Saskatchewan.

25 October
Calgary, Alberta.

26 October
Edmonton, Alberta.

28 October
Northern Lights Palace, Helfort, Saskatchewan.

8 November
Two shows at the Fairfield Hall, Croydon T. R. Dallas is the support act for the tour but on this opening show Roy Orbison's son Wesley makes a special appearance and he will also appear at the German concerts. The UK dates on this tour are promoted by Roundabout Theatrical Productions Ltd.

9 November
Guildhall, Portsmouth.

12 November
Berlin, Germany.

13 November
Nurenburg, Germany.

14 November
Ludwigshafen, Germany.

16 November
Dresden, Germany.

18 November
City Hall, Sheffield, England.

19 November
De Montfort Hall, Leicester, England.

20 November
Pavilions, Plymouth, England.

22 November
International Centre, Harrogate, England.

23 November
Two shows at the Derngate, Northampton, England.

25 November
St. David's Hall, Cardiff, Wales.

30 November
The Highwaymen perform two benefit shows for the BASS Tickets Foundation at the 3,000 seater Paramount Theatre in Oakland, California.

1 December
The Highwaymen play a hospital benefit in San Bernardino, California.

3 December
The Highwaymen appear at the Universal Amphitheater, Los Angeles, California.

5-10 December
The Highwaymen play a series of concerts at the Mirage Hotel, Las Vegas, Nevada. A show from this engagement is recorded and broadcast at a later date.

1992

15 January
Neil Young, Keith Richards, Jeff Beck, Jimmy Page, John Fogerty and Robbie Robertson were all gathered at the the Waldorf-Astoria Hotel in New York when Johnny Cash was inducted into the Rock And Roll Hall Of Fame.

16 January
Cash tapes an appearance on the U.S. kids TV show *Sesame Street* for broadcast at a later date.

17-18 January
King's Court Showroom, Trump's Castle, Atlantic City, New Jersey.

13 February
Fair, Tampa, Florida.

14 February
Private party in Orlando, Florida.

15 February
McComb Center, Mt. Clemens, Michigan.

16 February
A short Highwaymen tour opens at the Livestock Show, Houston Texas.

18 February
Atlanta, Georgia.

20 February
West Palm Beach, Florida.

21 February
The Highwaymen close their short tour with a date in Orlando, Florida.

29 February
Coral Ridge Church, Ft. Lauderdale, Florida.

5 March
Sun Dome, Phoenix, Arizona.

6-7 March
Riverside Hotel, Laughlin, Nevada.

9-10 March
Crazy Horse Club, Santa Ana, California.

1 April
The Highwaymen (Johnny Cash, Willie Nelson, Waylon Jennings and Kris Kristofferson) undertake their first tour of the UK and Europe with dates promoted by Marshall Arts Ltd.

The set list for this tour is taken from the following song list: "Mystery Train", "Highwayman", "Mamas Don't Let Your Babies Grow Up To Be Cowboys", "Good Hearted Woman", "Good Ole Boys", "There Ain't No Good Chain Gang", "Folsom Prison Blues", "Blue Eyes Crying In The Rain", "Help Me Make It Through The Night", "Sunday Morning Coming Down", "Ring Of Fire", "Loving Her Was Easier", "Best Of All Possible Worlds", "Desperadoes Waiting For A Train", "Are You Sure Hank Done It This Way", "Always On My Mind", "Me And Bobby McGee", "Trouble Man", "Get Rhythm", "Johnny Lobo", "They Killed Him", "Crazy", "Ghost Riders In The Sky", "Don't Take Your Guns To Town", "I've Always Been Crazy", "Night Life", "Long Black Veil", "Dreaming My Dreams", "Angel Flying Too Close To The Ground", "Yabba Dabba Doo", "Big River", "Orange Blossom Special", "Why Me Lord", "Luckenbach, Texas", "On The Road Again".

The tour opens with a concert at the Typhoon Arena, Turku, Finland.

2 April
Valbyhallen, Copenhagen, Denmark.

3 April
The Globen, Stockholm, Sweden.

6 April
The Spektrum, Oslo, Norway.

10 April
Wembley Arena, London, England.

11 April
The N.E.C., Birmingham, England.

12 April
Sheffield Arena, Sheffield, England.

13 April
Exhibition Centre, Aberdeen, Scotland.
This show is filmed for television broadcast later in the year.

15 April
The Point, Dublin, Ireland.

16 April
King's Hall, Belfast, Northern Ireland.

18 April
Forest Nationale, Brussels, Belgium.

20 April
Ahoy, Rotterdam, Holland.

21 April
Sportshalle, Hamburg, Germany.

22 April
Deutschlandhalle, Berlin, Germany.

23 April
Festhalle, Frankfurt, Germany.

25 April
Olympiahalle, Munich, Germany.

26 April
The Highwaymen tour closes at the Hallenstadion, Zurich, Switzerland.

1 May
Earlier in the year a Californian property developer had announced a $35 million project to be called Cash Country. An entire Johnny Cash theme park with a 2,500 seater theatre was planned for a 140-acre site on Country Music Boulevard in Branson, Missouri. Work was halted before completion and the contractors filed bankruptcy petitions against the developers. Despite the hopes and rumours of new financing, the project was never completed and in November the project was sold to new owners. Although Johnny Cash had no financial involvement in the project he stayed in Branson throughout May waiting to see what would happen. Although he never gave a live performance he did appear on the Larry King radio program broadcast live from the unfinished theatre and to an audience of a few fans who were allowed in. Cash planned to perform shows at the new Wayne Newton Theater in Branson starting in June 1993.

16 & 23 May
Two episodes of the the Disney television production of *Davy Crockett* starring Johnny Cash and Tim Dunigan are televised on London Weekend Television. *Guardian Spirit* is shown on the 16 May while *A Natural Man* is televised on the 23 May.

25 May
The Highwaymen's appearance at the Mirage Hotel in Las Vegas taped in June

1991 is broadcast on TNN (The Nashville Network).

18 June
Winnipeg, Ontario.

19 June
Hamilton, Ontario.

20 June
Poughkeepsie, New York.

22 June
Alexandria, Virginia.

24 June
Stockton, California.

27-28 June
Alameda Country Fair, Pleasanton, California.

30 June
Santa Maria, California.

1 July
San Raphael, California.

4 July
Catskill, New York.

11 July
A show scheduled in Charlottsville, Virginia is postponed until 17 October.

August
John, along with daughter Rosanne and grand-daughter Carrie, visits *Sesame Street* and tapes two segments for the show. John performs "Don't Take Your 1's To Town" (sung to "Don't Take Your Guns To Town") and "Tall Tales".

7 August
Coach House Club, San Juan Capistrano, California.

10 August
The Strand Club, Redondo Beach, California.

12-16 August
Desert Inn Hotel, Las Vegas, Nevada.

17 August
Stadium, Joliet, Illinois. This date and the following five shows are Highwaymen dates.

18 August
Rochester, Michigan.

19 August
State Fair, Columbus, Ohio.

20 August
Roberts Stadium, Evansville, Indiana.

22 August
Atlantic City, New Jersey.

23 August
Garden State Arts Center, Holmdel, New Jersey.

30 August
Oslo, Norway.

12 September
Little Nashville, Indiana.

19 September
Capital Civic Center, Manitowoc, Wisconsin.

23 September
Tower Theater, Fresno, California.

25 September
John and June join Billy Graham for a crusade that draws a crowd of over 40,000 at Portland, Oregon.

26 September
Kelseyville, California.

27 September
Oceanside Amphitheater, Oceanside, California.

3 October
Hillsdale County Fair, Hillsdale, Michigan.

15 October
The day before he is due to appear at the Bob Dylan Celebrations in New York Cash performs Dylan's "Blowing In The Wind" on the *David Letterman Show*.

16 October
Madison Square Garden, New York, NY. Along with June Carter-Cash he performs "It Ain't Be Babe" at the Bob Dylan 30th Anniversary Celebrations and joins Ron Wood, George Harrison, Roger McGuinn, Tom Petty, Neil Young for the finale.

17 October
Performing Arts Center, Charlottesville, Virginia.

20 October
Auditorium, Santa Fe, New Mexico.

21 October
Farmington, New Mexico.

23 October
Colorado Springs, Colorado.

24 October
Harrah's, Lake Tahoe, Nevada.

25 October
Paramount Theater, Denver, Colorado.

30 October
Chicago, Illinois.

31 October
James Rickman Auditorium, Arnold, Missouri.

5 November
Toad's Place, New Haven, Connecticut.

6 November
North Shore Music Theatre, Beverly, Massachusetts.

7 November
Garde Arts Center, New London, Connecticut.

8 November
Auditorium, Carney's Point, New Jersey.

10 November
Arts Centrer, North Bay, Ontario.

11 November
Hockey Arena, Rouyn-Norand, Quebec.

12 November
Hockey Arena, Timmons, Ontario.

14 November
Theatre, Sault Ste. Marie, Ontario.

December
Bob Wootton returns to the Johnny Cash band and Dave Roe joins as the new bass player. They replace Kerry Marx and Steve Logan.

8-9 December
TV Show in Vienna.

11 December
Maryland Theatre, Hagerstown, Maryland.

12 December
Dover, Delaware.

13 December
Olean, New York.

16 December
The Ritz, New York, NY. Mark Collie makes a guest appearance at this show.

17 December
Center For The Arts, Stamford, Connecticut.

18 December
State Theater, Easton, Pennsylvania.

19 December
Keswick Theatre, Glenside, Pennsylvania.

1993

16 January
Johnny Cash makes his first guest appearance in the series *Dr Quinn, Medicine Woman*. An hour-long Western family adventure series produced by the Sullivan Company and CBS Entertainment Productions, *Dr Quinn, Medicine Woman* is built around the life and exploits of Dr Michaela (Mike) Quinn, a woman doctor who moves from the civilised world of Boston to the rough frontier town of 1860's Colorado Springs to open her own medical practice. The series explores issues including gun control, environmental pollution, battling disease and liberating oppressed frontier women. The show is steeped in family values and an understanding of the spirit and strength that helped to shape America.

Johnny Cash plays Kid Cole in an episode entitled *Law Of The Land*, the story of a starving orphaned immigrant who takes desperate action to feed his family and steals a cow. Instead of taking pity on the lad the people take action to have him hanged and Michaela has to step in and hire Cole to oversee a fair trial.

30 January
Kurhalle, Vienna, Austria.

1 February
Frankfurt, Germany.

2 February
Hof, Germany.
Kris Kristofferson appears on this date and some of the other shows.

3 February
Dresden, Germany.

4 February
Bremerhaven, Germany.

6 February
Butlins Southcoast World, Bognor Regis, West Sussex, England. Two appearances, at a country music weekend festival, were Cash's only dates in England during his European tour.

7 February
Tralee, Ireland.

8 February
Late afternoon John records with rock group U2 for their *Zooropa* album.

In the evening during a concert at the Olympia in Dublin, Cash invites Bono and U2 to join him on stage.

10 February
Limerick, Ireland.

11 February
TV taping in Dublin, Ireland.

12 February
Carrickmacross, Ireland.

13 February
Waterford, Ireland.

14 February
Castlebar, Ireland.

27 February
Rhythm Cafe, Santa Ana, California. It was on this day that Cash met Rick Rubin for the first time.

28 February
McCallum Theater, Palm Springs, California.

1 March
John and June celebrate their 25th wedding anniversary.

5-6 March
Trump's Castle, Atlantic City, New Jersey.

Early-March
Cash is signed up by Eric Herbst, owner of Better Place Publishing Inc., to sing "The Ballad Of The Two-Cookie Kid" for a new book and audio cassette package for children to be released later in the year. This was Herbst's second coup - previously he had signed blues legend B. B. King to sing and play guitar on "The Rainy Day Blues". Herbst was quoted as saying "For many people Johnny Cash is the real roots of country music."

19 March
Long Island Music Festival, Westbury, New York.

20 March
Devon Theater, Valley Forge, Pennsylvania.

21 March
State Theater, Uniontown, Pennsylvania.

25 March
Alfred University, Hornell, New York.

26 March
Mansfield University, Mansfield, Pennsylvania.

27 March
Brantford Civic Center, Brantford, Ontario.

28 March
Massey Hall, Toronto, Ontario.

8 April
The Highwaymen start another tour with
the opening concert in Halifax, Nova Scotia

9 April
Augusta, Maine.

10 April
Albany, New York.

13 April
Capitol Center, Landover, Maryland.

14 April
Coliseum, Cleveland, Ohio.

15 April
Kellog Center, Battle Creek, Michigan.

16 April
Erwin J. Nutter Center, Wright State
University, Dayton, Ohio.

17 April
Detroit, Michigan.

18 April
Trump Taj Mahal, Atlantic City, New
Jersey .

19 April
Under the heading *Unchained Melodies* the
paper *USA Today* prints a report about
2,800 never before released tapes that were
discovered at a Nashville auction. The
tapes, dating between 1953 and 1971, are
rumoured to contain material by Dylan,
Cash, Roy Orbison, Tammy Wynette,
Charlie Rich and other artists. Sony Music
file a lawsuit preventing the tapes being
released, claiming they belong to them.

20 April
Rosemont Horizon, Chicago, Illinois.

21 April
Toronto, Ontario.

24 April
The Highwaymen tour winds up with a
show at the Cyclone Stadium, Ames, Iowa.

4 May
Memorial Building, Hibbing, Minnesota.

5 May
Two shows at the Auditorium, Thunder
Bay, Ontario.

6 May
Arena, Ft. Frances, Ontario.

7 May
Civic Center, St. Cloud, Minnesota.

8 May
Mayo Civic Center, Rochester, Minnesota.

10-14 May
Taping for the TV series *Dr Quinn-
Medicine Woman*.

15 May
San Bernardino, California.

17-18 May
Further taping for *Dr Quinn-Medicine
Woman*.

23 May
The Highwaymen play a concert in New
York's Central Park as part of the *Country
Takes Manhattan Extravaganza*.

31 May-5 June
Following the collapse of the *Cash Country*
project in 1992, Cash opens at the Wayne
Newton Theatre in Branson, Missouri for
the first of a series of concerts that will run
through to the end of the year. There is one
show a night during the week with two
shows on the Saturday.

7-12 June
Wayne Newton Theatre, Branson,
Missouri.

14-16 June
Wayne Newton Theatre, Branson, Missouri.

June
Rock/rap mastermind Rick Rubin signs Cash to his Los Angeles based label Def-American following his release from Mercury Records. He will join a roster that includes the Red Hot Chili Peppers, Black Crowes, Slayer and the Jayhawks. In a press statement issued after the signing Rubin said "To work with Johnny Cash will be an honour, I have respected him for years, both as a performer and as a songwriter." Both Cash and Rubin refuse to comment on any new musical direction until they're in the studio working on the new album.

June-July
A series of recording sessions in Rick Rubin's living room in Los Angeles results in over 70 tracks, mainly acoustic, being recorded. Many of the songs are recorded more than once. They include material from Cash's career as well as songs by other artists.

4 July
Cash sings three songs at *A Capitol Fourth* in Washington.

6-10 July
Wayne Newton Theatre, Branson, Missouri.

8 July
Cash's brother Roy Cash passes away.

12 July
Hilton, San Antonio, Texas.

21 July
Atlanta Symphony, Atlanta, Georgia.

24 July
Hunter Mt, New York.

25 July
Webster, Massachusetts.

27 July
Elkhart County Fairgrounds, Goshen, Indiana.

28 July
Rock County Fair, Janesville, Wisconsin.

30 July
Chicago, Illinois.

31 July
Norfolk, Nevada.

2 August
Fair, Victorville, California.

3 August
California Mid-State Fair, Paso Robles, California.

4 August
Stanislaus County Fair, Turlock, California.

6 August
Memorial Field, Sandpoint, Idaho.

7 August
Seattle, Washington.

8 August
Alpenrose Dairy, Portland, Oregon.

11 August
Nevada County Fair, Grass Valley, California.

12-13 August
Mountain Winery, Saratoga, California.

26 August
Lake County Fair, Painesville, Ohio.

27 August
Meadville, Pennsylvania.

28 August
Little Nashville, Indiana.

10-11 September
Foxwoods High Stakes Bingo & Casino, Ledyard, Connecticut.

13-18 September
Wayne Newton Theatre, Branson, Missouri.

20-25 September
Wayne Newton Theatre, Branson, Missouri.

29 September
Willie Nelson is inducted into the Country Music Hall Of fame at the CMA Awards.

October-December
Sessions are split between Rubin's home and Cash's Cedar Hill Refuge in Hendersonville, Tennessee, with over fifty tracks laid down. Again many songs are recorded more than once.

5 October
Johnny Cash performs "Don't Take Your

Guns To Town" on the *David Letterman Show*.

14 October
Farmer's Fair, Perris, California.

15 October
Kelsbyville, California.

16 October
County Fair, San Rafael, California.

17 October
University of Arizona, Tucson, Arizona.

23 October
Rahway, New Jersey.

24 October
Middletown, New York.

26 October
Sandusky, Ohio.

27 October
Greensburg, Pennsylvania.

4-6 November
Wayne Newton Theatre, Branson, Missouri.

10 November
The Highwaymen In Central Park is broadcast on The Nashville Network. The show was taped back in May.

11-13 November
Wayne Newton Theatre, Branson, Missouri.

18-20 November
Wayne Newton Theatre, Branson, Missouri.

13 November
Johnny Cash makes his second guest appearance in the series *Dr Quinn, Medicine Woman* in an episode called *Saving Souls*. It is about an overbearing faith healer, played by June-Carter-Cash,

who clashes with Dr Mike over treatment for the deteriorating health of Kid Cole (Johnny Cash) who has tuberculosis.

25-27 November
Wayne Newton Theatre, Branson, Missouri.

December
Viper Room, Los Angeles, California
In the audience for this show were Sean Penn, Juliette Lewis and members of both the Red Hot Chili Peppers and the Butthole Surfers. Live recordings of "Thirteen" and "The Man Who Couldn't Cry" taken from this show will appear on the *American Recordings* album.

5 December
Cash performs "Don't Take Your Guns To Town" on the *David Letterman Show*.

11 December
Ocean City, Maryland.

13 December
Indiana, Pensylvannia.

14 December
Rochester, New York.

15 December
Landmark Theatre, Syracuse, New York.

17 December
Mendel Center, Benton Harbor, Michigan. Scheduled appearances in Mt. Clemens, Michigan (18) and Merriliville, Indiana (19) are both cancelled.

1994-2001

"I've always wanted to do an album that was Johnny Cash alone — that's the concept. This is what I've always wanted to do, and I was able to do it with Rick. I think I'm more proud of it than anything I've ever done in my life. This is me. Whatever I've got to offer as an artist, it's here."

Johnny Cash on his *American Recordings* Album 1994

1994

Early 1994

Wanted Man (Mercury 314-522-709-2) released. This was a best-of package covering the albums released during Cash's brief spell with Mercury Records.

Tracks: "The Night Hank Williams Came To Town", "Let Him Roll", "My Ship Will Sail", "That Old Wheel", "Ballad Of A Teenage Queen", "Beans For Breakfast", "Wanted Man", "The Greatest Cowboy Of Them All", "Goin' By The Book", "I'll Go Somewhere And Sing My Songs Again".

The sleeve of this release also advertised, as soon available, a video entitled *Wanted Man* that would contain music videos of "Goin' By The Book", "Let Him Roll" and "Sixteen Tons" as well as featuring live footage. The video never appeared and no reason was given for its cancellation.

12 January
Punta Gorda, Florida.

13 January
Jacksonville, Florida.

14 January
Van Wezel Hall, Sarasota, Florida.

28-30 January
Tarrant County Convention Center, Fort Worth, Texas.

Johnny Cash performs with the Fort Worth Symphony and a second set with his own band.

13 February
Johnny Cash tours Australia and New Zealand with Kris Kristofferson. The first concert is in Auckland, New Zealand.

15 February
Town Hall, Christchurch, New Zealand.

18 February
Newcastle, New South Wales.

19 February
Brisbane, Queensland.

22-23 February
Melbourne, Victoria.

24 February
Adelaide, South Australia.

26 February
Canberra

27 February
Sydney, New South Wales.

2-3 March
Entertainment Centre, Perth, Western Australia.

17 March
Austin Convention Center and EMO's, Austin, Texas.

Johnny Cash delivers the keynote speech at the South by Southwest conference. At 10.30am he is introduced by co-directors Roland Swenson and Louis Meyers and opens with "Delia's Gone" a track from his forthcoming album *American Recordings*. "I've always known that when I had to make a speech it would be good if I had my guitar handy to fall back on" he joked. During his speech he also performs "Tennessee Stud", "Drive On" and "The Man Who Couldn't Cry". Before he left the stage, Austin City mayor Max Nofziger proclaimed the day 'Johnny Cash Day' and presented him with the key to the city. In the evening he played a show at EMO's, a grungy, partly open-air club that holds around 500 people. Hundreds of people were turned away. Both the keynote speech and his evening show were filmed and broadcast.

28 March
An appearance on *Music City Tonight* with the Statler Brothers during which he sings "Daddy Sang Bass". He is also interviewd on the show.

13 April
The Fez, New York, New York.
The audience at this invitation-only concert included Kate Moss, Johnny Depp, Rachel Williams and Eric Goode.

16 April
Westbury Music Fair, Nassau, New York.

17 April
Valley Forge Music Theater, Devon, Pennsylvania.

18-21 April
The video for "Delia's Gone", the first single lifted from the forthcoming *American Recordings* album, is taped in Hendersonville. Location scouts from Los Angeles picked Hendersonville as the perfect spot and scenes were filmed off Galatin Road, across from the House of Cash, and also a cabin in Monthaven. Supermodel Kate Moss flew in to appear on the video, which included scenes of Moss tied to a chair and shot through the head while Cash is shown shovelling dirt on her face. In between takes they signed autographs and talked to local residents and members of the crew. The director of the

video Anton Corbijn, who also created the concept of the video to tell the story of the song, said Cash was "very straightforward and nice" and "a delight to work with." Moss was condemned by TV bosses for the video while MTV went one stage further and ordered the scenes to be axed. A spokeswoman for Cash's label was quoted as saying "I guess they have a thing about dead women. We don't quite understand their reaction."

22 April
Columbia, Missouri.

23 April
Kansas City, Missouri.

26 April
Johnny Cash's new album *American Recordings* (American 45520-2) is released Tracks: "Delia's Gone", "Let The Train Blow The Whistle", "The Beast In Me", "Drive On", "Why Me Lord", "Thirteen", "Oh Bury Me Not", "Bird On A Wire", "Tennessee Stud", "Down There By The Train", "Redemption", "Like A Soldier", "The Man Who Couldn't Cry".

The album features originals by Cash along with material from Kris Kristofferson, Tom Waits, Leonard Cohen and Nick Lowe. Two tracks recorded live at the Viper Room back in 1993 are also included. The cover artwork featured Cash with two dogs, one white and one black, which sums up the theme of the album – sin and redemption. It is a stark, serious collection and one which Cash was proud of — "I've always wanted to do an album that was Johnny Cash alone — that's the concept. This is what I've always wanted to do, and I was able to do it with Rick. I think I'm more proud of it than anything I've ever done in my life. This is me. Whatever I've got to offer as an artist, it's here."

The album received rave reviews from the press – "Cash has collected 13 songs that peer into the dark corners of the American soul… A milestone work for this legendary singer." – *Los Angeles Times* (25 April).

"AMERICAN RECORDINGS…the alternative-rock community has been buzzing about it for months." – *Newsweek* (2 May)

"Never has the man in black produced a work of such brilliance as this one." – *Billboard* (7 May)

"He has re-asserted himself as one of the greats of popular music." – *Time* (9 May)

"His voice is the best it has sounded in more than thirty years… Cash has made what is unquestionably one of his best albums." – *Rolling Stone* (19 May)

29 April-1 May
Cash plays two shows each day at Foxwood Casino, Ledyard, Connecticut.

5 May
Neenah, Wisconsin.

6 May
Milwaukee, Wisconsin.

7-8 May
Cash appears at the Macomb Center, Mt. Clemens, Michigan and the Holiday Star Plaza Theatre, Merriliville, Indiana. Both these shows are re-scheduled from December 1993.

26 May-1 June
Shenandoah South Theater, Branson, Missouri.

Early June
Johnny Cash and Marty Stuart appear at the Country Music Radio Awards show broadcast from the Tennessee Performing Arts Center's Johnson Theater. The audience gave him a standing ovation as Stuart presented him with the first CMRA Legend Awards. Accepting the award Cash told the audience "That's all I ever wanted to do, take my guitar and sing. I told my mama when I was a little boy some day I'm going to sing on the radio." He then performed "Drive On" and, accompanied by Marty Stuart and a full band, "I Walk The Line". The show was broadcast to over 200 stations live across the country.

June
It is announced that Cash will appear at Woodstock '94, to be held in Saugerties on 14 August but unfortunately his appearance never materialises due to a problem with the promoters.

June
A show at the Manhattan Center in New York is filmed by VH-1 for broadcast later in the year.

3 June
Davenport, Iowa.

4 June
La Crosse, Wisconsin.

5 June
Hinkley, Minnesota.

10 June
Johnny Cash performs "Delia's Gone" on the David Letterman Show.

19 June
Cash opens his promotional tour of Europe and the UK with a concert at the Country Cavalcade in Karjala, Finland.

20 June
Copenhagen, Denmark.

21 June
Museum Of Modern Art Garden, Stockholm, Sweden.

22 June
Paradiso, Amsterdam, Holland.

23 June
Midtfyns Festival , Ringe, Denmark.

26 June
Glastonbury, England
Johnny Cash is a surprise triumph at the Glastonbury Festival where, despite a sore throat, he gives a performance covering his past glories, along with material from his recent *American Recordings* album. This show is recorded and broadcast, in part, on radio and television in the UK. During his time at Glastonbury, Cash is interviewed by Andy Kershaw and Johnnie Walker and the interviews are broadcast on radio and shown on TV.

29 June
Elysée Montmartre, Paris, France.

30 June
Nightown, Rotterdam, Holland.

2 July
Following the successful Glastonbury appearance Cash plays his only other concert date in the UK with a sold-out show at the Shepherds Bush Empire in London.

5 July
Jazz Festival, Montreux, Switzerland
This show is filmed and broadcast by local television.

6 July
RTL Nacht-Show, Cologne, Germany.

7 July
Tanzbrunnen, Cologne, Germany.

8 July
Circus Krone, Munich, Germany.

9 July
Stadtpark, Hamburg, Germany.

25-30 July
Shenandoah South Theatre, Branson, Missouri.
There are two shows per day for most of the dates in Branson.

1-13 August
Shenandoah South Theatre, Branson, Missouri.

26 August
Bismarck Theatre, Chicago, Illinois.

27 August
Orpheum Theatre, Minneapolis, Minnesota
With The Jayhawks.

28 August
State Theatre, Detroit, Michigan.

30 August
CNE Fair, Toronto, Canada.

1 September
Concert in Tonawanda, New York.

1 September
Johnny Cash performs 'Delia's Gone' on the *David Letterman Show*.

2 September
Latham, New York.

3 September
The Manhattan Concert from June is shown on VH-1. Strikingly shot in black and white, songs include "Folsom Prison Blues", "I Walk The Line", "Ghost Riders In The Sky", "Ring Of Fire" and a selection from his new album.

3 September
Oyster Bay Arboretum, New York.

4 September
Nashville, Tennessee.
Cash appears at the 40th Annual Italian Street Fair backed by the Nashville Symphony Orchestra conducted by Bill Walker. This was Cash's first hometown show in six years. During the show he recited the "Gettysburg Address" and sang "The Night They Drove Old Dixie Down".

9 September
Roxy Theatre, Atlanta, Georgia

11 September
Keswick Theatre, Philadelphia, Pennsylvania.

12 September
Warner Theatre, Washington, DC.

13 September
Cash is interviewed and performs a song on the *Jon Stewart Show*.

14 September
Carnegie Hall, New York, New York
During a show lasting just short of two hours Cash performed 30 songs and was joined on stage by his daughter Rosanne, who joined John on "I Still Miss Someone". "Cash Still Walks The Line With Style" stated the *NY Newsday*.

22-23 September
Cerritos, California.

24 September
Luther Burbank Center, Santa Rosa, California.

26 September
The Fillmore, San Francisco, California.

6-8 October
Shenandoah South Theatre, Branson, Missouri.

10-15 October
Shenandoah South Theatre, Branson, Missouri.

17-22 October
Johnny Cash and June Carter-Cash tape their third guest appearance on *Dr Quinn Medicine Woman*. Cash recreates his role as ex-gunslinger Kid Cole in a story titled *Thanksgiving*. Mike (Jane Seymour) and Sully (Joe Lando) meet newly-weds Kid Cole (Cash) and Sister Ruth (June Carter-Cash) in Denver and ask them to return home for Thanksgiving. Before they arrive home they are victims of an ambush. The show is broadcast on CBS in November. Cash performs the title track during the show.

30 October
Cash appears with Billy Graham in Atlanta, Georgia.

31 October-8 November
The Highwaymen record tracks for their new album at Ocean Way Recording Studios in Hollywood, California with producer Don Was.

10-12 November
Shenandoah South Theatre, Branson, Missouri. During these shows Cash performs several Christmas songs.

14-15 November
Casino, Bay St. Louis, Missouri.

17-19 November
Shenandoah South Theatre, Branson, Missouri. Other scheduled appearances in Branson in November and December are cancelled by mutual agreement.

13 November
Thanksgiving, the 50th episode of *Dr Quinn Medicine Woman*, is broadcast.

December
Outtakes from the *American Recordings* sessions start appearing on bootleg tape and CD.
Tracks: "What On Earth Will You Do", "The Drifter", "I Witnessed A Crime", "Banks Of The Ohio", "The Next Time I'm In Town", "Breakin' Bread", "To Beat The Devil", "Friends In California", "The Caretaker", "The Wonder", "East Virginia Blues", "I'm Just An Old Chunk Of Coal", "Go On Blues", "If I Give My Soul", "Bad News", "All God's Children Ain't Free", "One More Ride".

7 December
Worthington Hotel, Ft. Worth, Texas.

8 December
Frank Erwin Center, Austin, Texas.

10 December
Sagamon State University, Springfield, Illinois.

16 December
Vacation in Montego Bay, Jamaica.

1995

Early 1995
The third Highwayman project *The Road Goes On Forever* (Liberty C2-28091) released.
Tracks: "The Devil's Right Hand", "Live Forever", "Everyone Gets Crazy", "It Is What It Is", "I Do Believe", "The End Of Understanding", "True Love Travels On A Gravel Road", "Death And Hell", "Waiting For A Long Time", "Here Comes That Rainbow Again", "The Road Goes On Forever".

Promotion for the album includes appearances on the *David Letterman Show* and the *Jay Leno Show*.

4-6 January
Franklin Electronics Convention, Las Vegas, Nevada.

7 January
Pantages Theatre, Los Angeles, California.

8 January
Graham Central Station, Phoenix, Arizona.

13 January
328 Performance Center, Nashville, Tennessee.

19 January
Waylon And Friends is taped at TNN Studio A in Nashville, Tennessee. Johnny Cash and June Carter-Cash are guests on the show. As well as songs by Waylon and Jessi Colter, Cash performs "Get Rhythm", "Big River" and "Bird On A Wire". He also appears in conversation with Waylon and together they sing "I Wish I Was Crazy Again".

21 January
Disney World, Orlando, Florida.

22 January
Gusman Center For The Performing Arts, Miami, Florida.

24 January
Ruth Eckert Hall, Clearwater, Florida.

27 January
Kravis Center For The Performing Arts, West Palm Beach, Florida.

28 January
Center For The Performing Arts, Gainsville, Florida.

31 January
Bob Carpenter Center, University of Delaware, Newark, Delaware.

February
Johnny Cash's latest album *American Recordings* wins a Grammy Award in the category 'Best Contemporary Folk Album.'

2 February
Spirit Square Center For The Performing Arts, Charlotte, North Carolina.

3 February
Norfolk, Virginia.

16 February
Twenty-five years after it was first released *The Johnny Cash Show* finally achieves gold status. Also on this day *Johnny Cash Portrait/His Greatest Hits Volume 2* reaches platinum status.

23-25 February
Concerts scheduled at The Nugget, Sparks, Nevada and the Performing Arts Center, Thousand Oaks, California are postponed.

23-24 March
House of Blues, New Orleans, Louisiana.

25 March
Sams Town Casino, Robinsonville, Mississippi.

27 March
GTE Party, Dallas, Texas.

April
Country Music News & Routes, the UK magazine, devotes the front cover and a three-page article to Johnny Cash.

1 April
Alabama Theatre, North Myrtle Beach, South Carolina.

3 April
Turnberry Isle Resort, Aventura, Florida.

5 April
Waylon And Friends is broadcast.

6 April
Memorial Coliseum, University of Kentucky, Lexington, Kentucky.

7 April
Palace Theatre, Louisville, Kentucky.

8 April
Palace Theatre, Columbus, Ohio.

22-23 April
Opryland, Nashville, Tennessee.

HARVEY GOLDSMITH ENTERTAINMENTS
PROUDLY PRESENTS

JOHNNY CASH

PLUS SUPPORT

ROYAL ALBERT HALL

WEDNESDAY 3rd MAY
7.45pm

TICKETS: £17.50 and £15.00 (subject to booking fee)

TICKETS AVAILABLE FROM:
ROYAL ALBERT HALL BOX OFFICE 0171 589 8212 (credit cards accepted)
FIRST CALL 0171 240 7200, TICKETMASTER 0171 344 4444,
STARGREEN 0171 734 8932

COUNTRY 1035

1 May
The Highwaymen appear on the *David Letterman Show* and perform a track from their latest album.

3 May
Royal Albert Hall, London, England
Following this opening night of Cash's UK tour he returns to America due to health problems resulting from recent facial surgery. The remaining dates on the tour - Cork and Dublin in Ireland; Hanover, Germany; The Hague, Holland; Halle and Berlin, Germany; Vienna and Linz, Austria; Munich, Germany and Zurich, Switzerland are all cancelled.

Late-May
The Highwaymen perform *Everyone Gets Crazy* from their new album *The Road Goes On Forever* on the *Jay Leno Show*.

31 May
The Highwaymen undertake a tour of America. The set list for this tour is taken from the following song list: "Highwayman", "It Is What It Is", "Only Daddy That'll Walk The Line", "Folsom Prison Blues", "Me And Bobby McGee", "Blue Eyes Crying In The Rain", "Live Forever", "I've Always Been Crazy", "Ring Of Fire", "Sunday Morning Coming Down", "Help Me Make It Through The Night", "Still Movin' To Me", "Everyone Gets Crazy", "Will The Wolf Survive", "Get Rhythm", "Shipwrecked In The Eighties", "Undo The Wrong", "Wild Ones", "Ain't No Good Chain Gang", "Bird On A Wire", "Here Comes That Rainbow Again", "End To Understanding", "Ghost Riders In The Sky", "Till I Gain Control Again", "Orange Blossom Special", "Between Heaven And Hell", "Night Life", "Good Hearted Woman", "Mamas Don't Let Your Babies Grow Up To Be Cowboys", "Chase The Feeling", "Desperadoes Waiting For A Train", "Always On My Mind", "Big River", " I Do Believe", "Death Or Hell", "Why Me Lord?", "Even Cowgirls Get The Blues"

The tour opens with a show at the Shoreline Amphitheatre, Mountain View, California.

1 June
Reno, Nevada.

3 June
Rio Hotel, Las Vegas, Nevada.

4 June
Universal Amphitheatre, Los Angeles, California.

8 June
Pine Knob, Clarkston, Michigan.

10 June
Patriot Center, Fairfax, Virginia.

11 June
Kings Island, Cincinnati, Ohio.

14 June
John Carter-Cash marries Mary Ann Joska at a ceremony in Hendersonville. Taking a break from touring with the Highwaymen, Cash wears an uncharacteristic white suit for the ceremony. Guests include long-time friend Waylon Jennings.

15 June
Chastain Park, Atlanta, Georgia.

17 June
The Mark, Moline, Illinois.

18 June
Chippawa Valley Court, Cadot, Wisconsin.

22 June
Foxwoods, Ledyard, Connecticut.

23 June
University of Massachussets, Amherst, Massachusetts.

25 June
Paladium, Charlotte, North Carolina.

28 June
Ft. Brie, Ontario.

July
It is announced that the House of Cash Museum and Gift Shop is to close. For many years it had been a popular tourist attraction for visitors to Hendersonville but diminishing numbers forced the closure. There are provisional plans to move the museum to another site.

20-21 July
The Nugget, Sparks, Nevada.

23 July
Frost Amphitheatre, Palo Alta, California.

26 July
Wente Bros Winery, Livermore, California.

27 July
Cash records "Time Of The Preacher" for an upcoming Willie Nelson tribute album titled *Twisted Willie*. The song had originally appeared on Nelson's classic album *Red Headed Stranger*. Appearing with him on the track are Kim Thayil, Nirvana's Kris Novoselic and the drummer from Alice In Chains, Sean Kinney.

28 July
Fifth Avenue Theatre, Seattle, Washington. During the show Cash talks about the previous days recording session.

29 July
Raceway Park, Spokane, Washington.

30 July
Rose Garden Amphitheater, Portland, Oregon.

3 August
Westbury Music Fair, Westbury, New York. Kris Kristofferson appears on this show and the following days concert.

4 August
Valley Forge Music Fair, Devon, Pennsylvania.

5 August
International Society of Poets Convention, Hilton Hotel, Washington.

6 August
Dover, Ohio.

9 August
Michigan Festival, East Lansing, Michigan.

11 August
State Theatre, Easton, Pennsylvania.

12 August
Hunter Mountain Festival, Hunter, New York.

13 August
Harvey Lake Amphitheatre, Harvey Lake, Pennsylvania.

2 September
Cleveland, Ohio.
A crowd of 57,000 watch a 5-hour show to celebrate the opening of the Rock And Roll Hall Of Fame. Among those appearing are Aretha Franklin, Johnny Cash, John Mellencamp and Steve Cropper.

3 September
Johnny Cash performs during Waylon Jennings Day in Littlefield, Texas.

7 September
Replacement dates for the cancelled May tour are undertaken, although there are no shows in England or Ireland. The tour kicks of with a show at the Aladin in Bremen, Germany.

8 September
Eissporthalle, Halle, Germany.

11 September
. Unterfrakenhalle, Aschaffenburg, Germany.

12 September
Stadthalle Germering, Munich, Germany.

13 September
Kongresshaus, Zurich, Switzerland.

15 September
Beethovensaal, Stuttgart, Germany.

17 September
Congresgebouw, The Hague, Holland.

18 September
The Cirkus, Stockholm, Sweden.

19 September
Turkuhall, Turku, Finland.

22 September
Music Hall, Hanover, Germany.

23 September
Grugahalle, Essen, Germany.

25 September
Oberfrankenhalle, Bayreuth, Germany.

26 September
Austria Center, Vienna, Austria.

28-29 September
Tempodrom, Berlin, Germany.

October
Bear Family Records issue *The Man In Black, 1963-1969* (BCD-15588). This was the third in the series covering Cash's career. A 48-booklet accompanied the 6 CD set which included Cash's first Christmas album, his work with June Carter and the complete *Keep On The Sunnyside* album featuring The Carter Family and Cash as a special guest. Among the previously unreleased material were tracks recorded at the 1964 Newport Folk Festival.

14 October
Hamel, Minnesota.

15 October
Wisconsin Dells, Wisconsin.

16 October
The Grand Theatre, Wausau, Wisconsin.

18 October
Vogue, Indianapolis, Indiana.

20-21 October
Trop World, Atlantic City, New Jersey.

29 October
Billy Graham Crusade in Saskatoon, Saskatchewan, Canada.

3 November
The Highwaymen travel to Australia, New Zealand and Asia.

7 November
Mt. Smart Supertop, Auckland, New Zealand.

10-11 November
Entertainment Centre, Brisbane, Queensland.

13-14 November
Entertainment Centre, Sydney, New South Wales.
During their time in Sydney they held a press conference and reflected on life, death, and maturity.

15-16 November
Entertainment Centre, Newcastle, New South Wales.

18-19 November
Flinders Park, Melbourne, Victoria.

21-22 November
Entertainment Centre, Adelaide, South Australia.

24 November
Burswood Centre, Perth, Western Australia.

26 November
Suntek City, Singapore.

28 November
Queen Sirikat National Convention Centre, Bangkok, Thailand.

29 November
The Marty Party is broadcast on The Nashville Network. Johnny Cash is one of Marty Stuarts guests and performs "Doin' My Time" with Marty and "Tennessee Stud" from his new album.

1 December
Private Party at the British Military Base, Hong Kong.

3 December
Honolulu, Hawaii.

8 December
Performing Arts Center, Thousand Oaks, California.

9 December
Hard Rock Cafe, Las Vegas, Nevada.

10 December
Private Party, Houston, Texas.

1996

14 February
Maces Spring, Virginia.
Johnny Cash appears at the Carter Fold in Scott County. He performs his recent recording "Meet Me In Heaven" and, with June Carter-Cash, their Grammy award winning single "Jackson".

22 February
McCallum Center, Palm Desert, California.

23 February
Primadonna Casino Resort, Primadonna, Nevada.

24 February
Rawhide, Scottsdale, Arizona.

25 February
House Of Blues, Los Angeles, California.
After performing a selection of his hits Cash brings Tom Petty And The Heartbreakers on stage.

27 February
Convention Center, South Padre Island, Texas.

29 February
Silver Star Casino, Philadelphia, Mississippi.

1 March
Sam's Town, Robinsonville, Mississippi.

3 March
Fairgrounds, Ft. Pierce, Florida.

7 March
Avalon Ballroom, Boston, Massachusetts.

8-9 March
Ledyard, Connecticut.

26 March
Van Wezel Performing Arts Center, Sarasota, Florida.

30 March
Silver Springs Park, Silver Springs, Florida.

2 April
Philharmonic Center For The Arts, Naples, Florida.

4 April
Broward Performing Arts Center, Ft. Lauderdale, Florida.

11-12 April
Sparks, Nevada.

13 April
Anaheim, California.

14 April
Escondido, California.

21 April
Sams Town Casino, Kansas City, Kansas.

Early–May
An episode of the TV series *Renegade* is broadcast featuring Cash. The episode, *The Road Not Taken*, features Cash as escaped convict Henry Travis who is tracked down by bounty Hunter Reno Raines, played by Lorenzo Lamas. Both wind up in jail and when Reno thinks about suicide Travis gives him a lesson in what life would have been like without him. The shows executive producer, Rick Okie, said "Johnny was terrific."

15 May
930 Club, Washington, DC.
This show and those on the 16/18 and 19

May are billed as 'An Evening With Johnny Cash'.

18 May
Highland Park, Rochester, New York.

19 May
The Strand, Providence, Rhode Island.

21 May
Grand Casino, Biloxi, Mississippi.

25 May
Jubilee Jam, Main Stage, Jackson, Mississippi.

13 June
Cabe Festival Theatre, Little Rock, Arkansas.

14 June
City Stages, Birmingham, Alabama.

16 June
Fischgrund Center For Performing Arts, South Bend, Indiana.

17 June
Cain Park, Cleveland, Ohio.

18 June
Power Center For The Performing Arts, University of Michigan, Ann Arbor, Michigan.

20 June
Minneapolis, Minnesota.

21 June
The Hemmens, Elgin, Illinois.

22 June
Galaxy Theatre, The Dells, Wisconsin.

23 June
Grand Casino, Hinkley, Minnesota.

24 June
Greenway Auditorium, Coleraine, Minnesota.

27-29 June
American Academy of Achievement Convention, Sun Valley, Idaho.

11-12 July
Door Community Auditorium, Fish Creek, Wisconsin.

13 July
Riverfest, Beloit, Wisconsin.

17 July
Fairgrounds, Oakdale, California.

18 July
Radisson Hotel, Sacramento, California.

19 July
Britt Festival, Jacksonville, Oregon.

21 July
Merritt Mountain Music Festival, Merritt, British Columbia.

22 July
Edmonton Coliseum, Edmonton, Alberta.

24 July
Spirit Mountain Casino, Willamina, Oregon.

26 July
The Hilton, Las Vegas, Nevada.

27 July
Fox Theatre, Bakersfield, California.

29 July
House of Blues, Atlanta, Georgia.

31 July
Clare County Fair, Harrison, Michigan.

2 August
Pat Garrett Music Park, Strausstown, Pennsylvania.

3 August
Ohio State Fair, Celeste Center, Columbus, Ohio.

4 August
Ponderosa Park, Salem, Ohio.

21 August
World Mardi Gras, Indianapolis, Indiana.

23 August
Peace Center, Greenville, South Carolina.

26 August
Saratoga Performing Arts Centre, Saratoga Springs, New York.

30 August
Pier 6, Baltimore, Maryland.

31 August
Planting Fields Arboretum, Oyster Bay, New York.

1 September
Meadowbrook, Gilford, New Hampshire.

4 September
Flynn Theatre, Burlington, Vermont.

5 September
Theatre St. Dennis, Montreal, Quebec.

7 September
Irving Plaza, New York.

8 September
Wallingford, Connecticut.
In a rare double bill Johnny Cash and George Jones perform at the Oakdale Music Theatre.

21 September
Civic Center, Mankato, Minnesota.

22 September
Chester Fritz Auditorium, University of North Dakota, Grand Forks, North Dakota.

24 September
Lied Center, Lawrence, Kansas.

25 September
Golden Bullet, Columbia, Missouri.

27 September
Lady Luck Casino, Lula, Mississippi.

October
A cassette-only release of Johnny Cash reading the Lebanese poet Kahil Gibran's *The Prophet* is released by Audio Literature.

5 October
Performing Arts Center, Poway, California.

9 October
Weidner Center, Green Bay, Wisconsin.

11 October
Miller Auditorium, Kalamazoo, Michigan.

13 October
Performing Arts Center, Topeka, Kansas.

14 October
Factory Outlet Mall, Newton, Kansas.

November
Unchained (American 43097-2) released.

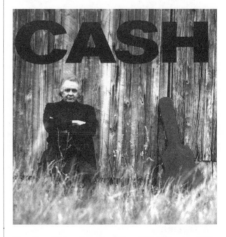

Tracks: "Rowboat", "Sea Of Heartbreak", "Rusty Cage", "The One Rose", "Country Boy", "Memories Are Made Of This", "Spiritual", "Kneeling Drunkard's Plea", "Southern Accents", "Mean Eyed Cat", "Meet Me In Heaven", "I Never Picked Cotton", "Unchained", "I've Been Everywhere".

Unchained demonstrated Cash's willingness to combine the classic with the cutting edge and was full of astonishing surprises. Back in February 1996, and as part of an encore set backed by Tom Petty and The Heartbreakers, Cash had unleashed his version of 'Rusty Cage'. A creative risk that paid off. In fact it was Soundgarden's harrowing 'Rusty Cage' that was one of the standout tracks on the album although at first Cash had his doubts about the song. "When Rick mentioned 'Rusty Cage' to me and I heard it, I didn't think it was for me, although I loved the lyrics" Cash said at the time. "Then he put down an arrangement that he thought I would like, and when I heard it, I really did—the lyrics and music felt so good to me". This willingness to experiment was further demonstrated with the inclusion of Beck's "Rowboat", Tom Petty's "Southern Accents" and the title track written by Jude Johnstone

6 November
Rose Garden Arena, Portland, Maine.

8 November
Auditorium, Santa Cruz, California.

9 November
Fillmore, San Francisco, California.

11-17 November
Filming for *Dr. Quinn, Medicine Woman* takes place at the Paramount Ranch, California.

22 November
Electric Factory, Philadelphia, Pennsylvania.

23 November
Convention Center, Niagara Falls, New York.

26 November
Massey Hall, Toronto, Canada.

26 November
Country Weekly includes an article entitled

'Johnny Cash - the making of his new album' in which he talks about his new album *Unchained*.

7- 8 December
Kennedy Center, Washington, DC.
Along with two-times Oscar winner Jack Lemmon, jazz great Benny Carter, ballerina Maria Tallchief and playwright Edward Albee, Johnny Cash is honoured at the 19th Annual Kennedy Center Awards Ceremony. The ceremony is televised and features a medley of Cash's hits performed by Kris Kristofferson, Emmylou Harris and Lyle Lovett. It was vice- president Al Gore who had recommended Cash for the honour as an artist who examines "the entire range of existence, failure and recovery, entrapment and escape, weakness and strength, loss and redemption, life and death."

9 December
Cash appears on the *Larry King Show* in Washington DC.

10 December
Paramount Theatre, Anderson, Indiana.

11 December
House Of Blues, Chicago, Illinois.

12 December
High School Auditorium, Neenah, Wisconsin.

14 December
Civic Center, Des Moines, Iowa.

16 December
Orchestra Hall, Minneapolis, Minnesota.

1997

1 February
The Most Fatal Disease, the latest episode of *Dr Quinn Medicine Woman* to feature Johnny Cash and June Carter-Cash, is aired. Kid Cole and Sister Ruth stop in

Colorado Springs on their way to San Francisco, bringing with them a group of mail-order brides and the news that Kid Cole and Sister Ruth intend to divorce when they reach California.

14 March
New Mexico State University, Las Cruces, New Mexico.

15 March
Majestic Theatre, Dallas, Texas.

18 March
Taping of the *Tonight TV Show* in Los Angeles, California. Cash performs "Rusty Cage" with Marty Stuart on guitar.

19 March
Private party at LaQuinta Ballroom, Palm Springs, California.

22 March
Private Party at Westin Mission Hills, Palm Springs, California.

26 March
The Cash Family Scrapbook by Cindy Cash is published by Crown Trade Paperbacks in New York. The book contains over 200 family photographs and memorabilia telling the story behind their family life.

29 March
Cindy Cash is at Tower Books in Nashville to sign copies of her book. Both John and June also show up for the signing.

April
The latest issue of the UK magazine *Country Music* people has a feature on Johnny Cash titled *Cash Icon Of Rock*. The same month *Country Music News & Routes*, another UK publication, has Cash as their cover artist with a two-page article written by editor Brian Ahern.

7 April
Palác Kultery, Prague, Czechoslovakia.

8 April
Kulturpalast, Dresden, Germany.

10 April
Philipshalle, Dusseldorf, Germany.

12 April
Konserthaus, Oslo, Norway.

13 April
Grieghallen, Bergen, Norway.

14 April
Cirkus, Stockholm.

16 April
Printemp de Bourges, Bourges, France.

17 April
Zenith, Paris, France.

19 April
Zenith, Munich, Germany.

21 April
Orpheum, Graz, Austria.

22 April
Kurhalle Oberlaa, Vienna, Austria.

25 April
Royal Albert Hall, London, England.

28-29 April
Tempodrom, Berlin, Germany.

30 April
Congresscentrum, Hamburg, Germany.

3 May
Worb, Switzerland.

12 May
Taping *VH-1 Storytellers* with Willie Nelson.

13 May
Following the *Storytellers* taping Cash appears with Willie Nelson at the Westbury Music Fair, Nassau, New York.

15 May
Cash and Willie Nelson appear at the Bob Carpenter Fieldhouse, University Of Delaware, Newark, Delaware.

21 May
Arena, Spokane, Washington.

23-24 May
House Of Blues, Chicago, Illinois.

31 May
House Of Blues, Myrtle Beach, South Carolina.

June
VH-1 Storytellers is broadcast. During the relaxed show Cash and Nelson trade stories and sing many of their greatest hits. Nelson turns in classics like "Crazy", "Night Life", "Always On My Mind" and "Me And Paul" while Cash makes familiar songs like "Worried Man", "Folsom Prison Blues", "I Still Miss Someone" and "Don't Take Your Guns To Town" sound fresh.

13 June
Villa Montalco Centre For The Performing Arts, Saratoga, California.

14 June
Greek Theatre, Los Angeles, California.

17 June
Boulder Theater, Boulder, Colorado.

19 June
Bluegrass Festival, Telluride, Colorado.

21 June
Crystal Grand Music Theatre, The Dells, Wisconsin.

22 June
Porterfield County Festival, Porterfield, Wisconsin.

24-25 June
Big Top Chatauqua, Washburn, Wisconsin.

27-28 June
Shooting Star Casino, Mehnoman, Minnesota.

14-15 July
Christian Bookseller's Convention, Atlanta, Georgia.

18 July
Broitel, Hillstrop, Sweden.

19 July
Slootsruinen, Gotheneburg, Sweden.

20 July
Summer Castle, Oland, Sweden.

23 July
Aalborg Festival, Aalborg, Denmark.

25 July
Lollipop, Stockholm, Sweden.

26 July
Festival, Lorach, Germany.

28 July
Stuttgart, Germany.

30 July
Stadtpark, Hamburg, Germany.

31 July
Koblenz, Germany.

9 August
National Poets Convention, Sheraton Ballroom, Washington, DC.

10 August
Atlanta, Georgia.

14-15 August
Vegas Kawadin Casino, Sault Ste. Marie, Michigan.

September
The September/October issue of *Country Music* is a *25th Anniversary Celebration* and Johnny Cash is featured in the *25*

Questions With... section. Normally 20 Questions, the article is expanded to celebrate the 25th issue. Cash appeared on the cover of the very first issue back in 1972, and his image appeared on the cover a further eight times.

11 September
Harbor Lights, Boston, Massachusetts.

13 September
Meadowbrook, Gilford, New Hampshire.

14 September
Flynn Theatre, Burlington, Vermont.

16 September
Private Party, Ford's Theatre, Washington, DC.

19 September
Mid-South Fair, Memphis, Tennessee.

20 September
University of Illinois Assembly Hall, Champaign, Illinois.

27 September
Nissan Company Picnic, Smyrna, Tennessee.

2 October
University Of New Mexico, Albuquerque, New Mexico.

3-4 October
House Of Blues, Los Angeles, California.

7 October
Fox Theatre, Hanford, California.

9-10 October
The Nugget, Sparks, Nevada.

11 October
Kingsbury Hall, Salt Lake City, Utah.
14 October
Country Weekly prints a six-page article about the forthcoming autobiography.

15 October
CASH: The Autobiography, written with Patrick Carr, is published by Harper SanFrancisco. Cash says – "This book will be my whole story–what I feel, what I love, what's happened, as I remember it. It's time to cut through some of the rumours. If my life has anything to say, I'll say it here."

22 October
Cash tapes an interview with Ralph Emery and talks about his career and the new autobiography. Both Sam Phillips and Tommy Cash make contributions to the show.

23 October
Tennessee Theatre, Knoxville, Tennessee.

25 October
Whiting Hall, Flint, Michigan
During the show he nearly falls over as he tries to pick up a guitar pick. He tells the shocked audience that he is suffering from Parkinson's Disease but adds "It's alright. I refuse to give it some ground in my life."

Following the announcement, headlines appear in many of the national papers in the US and around the world: 'Johnny Cash's brave fight for life', 'Last-ditch battle to save Johnny Cash', 'The moment of truth for battling Cash' and 'Cash's battle against Parkinson's'. Although there is no doubt that it is serious the papers make it sound much worse.

22 October-8 November
A book tour is scheduled to take in the following shops/cities - Davis-Kidd Booksellers (Nashville), Barnes & Noble (New York), Gene's Books (Philadelphia), Borders Bookshop (Chicago), Chapter 11 Bookstore (Atlanta), Barnes & Noble (Dallas), Tattered Cover (Dallas) and Brentano's (Los Angeles). Although he does make some appearances to promote the book on television, health problems force the tour to be cancelled.

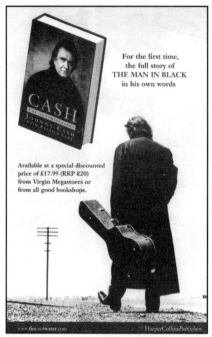

For the first time,
the full story of
THE MAN IN BLACK
in his own words

CASH
THE AUTOBIOGRAPHY
JOHNNY CASH
WITH PATRICK CARR

Available at a special discounted
price of £17.99 (RRP £20)
from Virgin Megastores or
from all good bookshops.

www.fireandwater.com   HarperCollins*Publishers*

27 October

A press release from Cash's management reads "Entertainer Johnny Cash announced today that he has developed Parkinson's Disease. Although Johnny was able to perform his recent concerts, he is cancelling his book promotion tour for 'CASH-The Autobiography' because the Parkinson's Disease has progressed. Johnny and his wife June Carter Cash are sorry to have to postpone their personal appearances but Cash's manager Lou Robin states 'Johnny feels confident that once the Parkinson's is medically stabilized, he can resume his normal work schedule.'"

4 November

Cash's appearance on *On The Record*, hosted by Ralph Emery, is broadcast. On the show he talks about his new autobiography.

5 November

A further press release is issued "Recently, entertainer Johnny Cash entered Baptist Hospital in Nashville for tests to establish proper treatment for Parkinson's Disease. Lou Robin, Cash's manager, stated today that tests have now determined that Johnny has a Parkinson's related illness known as Shy-Drager Syndrome. The treatment for Shy-Drager has begun and Cash looks forward to resuming his concert and work schedule as originally planned in early 1998."

November-December

The remaining concerts for the year are cancelled. Concerts had been booked in the following cities:

Seattle, Washington
Eugene, Oregon
Arcata, California
The Fillmore, San Francisco, California
San Luis Obispo, California
Bakersfield, California
Cheyenne, Wyoming
Denver, Colorado
St. Louis, Missouri
Mystic Lake, Minnesota
Sloan, Iowa
Decorah, Iowa
Chicago, Illinois

20 December

Both John and June fly to Jamaica and on to their Cinnamon Hill home.

Late-December

Country Weekly reports that Cash has had cards arriving at Baptist Hospital, the Grand Ole Opry and the House of Cash and that there were over 1,500 cards when he arrived home. Kelly Hancock, the administrative assistant at the House of Cash, said "He's overwhelmed. It means so much to him."

1998

January

Plans are made to sell various properties in Hendersonville including the House of Cash, previously offices and a museum, railroad depot and several acres of real estate. Cash intends to keep his house overlooking Old Hickory Lake.

19 January

Carl Perkins, who had written "Blue Suede Shoes" and had his material covered by artists including Elvis Presley and The Beatles, died in his hometown of Jackson, Tennessee following a series of strokes. Perkins had toured with Cash in the fifties and became a regular on the Johnny Cash Road Show in the late sixties and early seventies. He also appeared regularly on Cash's ABC-TV Shows. He appeared with Johnny Cash and Jerry Lee Lewis on the *Survivors* and *Class Of '55* albums, released in the eighties.

February

Unchained, Cash's second collaboration with Rick Rubin, takes the honours at the Annual Grammy Awards Ceremony when it wins the 'Best Country Album' category.

15 April

Johnny Cash stunned a VIP gathering when he performed two songs at a ceremony for a local hotel. During the unscheduled performance he sang "The Ballad Of Annie Palmer" and, with his wife June, "Far Side Banks Of Jordan".

May

Following years of rumours about a movie it seems plans are finally being made to film a biopic on the life of Johnny Cash. Jane Seymour's husband, director James Keach is planning a movie after securing the rights to his life story following Cash's appearances in *Dr Quinn, Medicine Woman*. Although nobody has yet been cast in the role, Johnny Depp has shown an interest in playing Cash during the early rock and roll years.

2 June

Helen Carter Jones, the oldest of Mother Maybelle's daughters, passes away at Vanderbilt University Medical Center after a long illness. Born on 12 September 1927 in Maces Springs, Virginia, she worked with the original Carter Family (A. P., Sara and Maybelle) and also with Mother Maybelle and The Carter Sisters, joining the Johnny Cash Show in 1961. Her funeral is held on 5 June in Hendersonville, Tennessee, attended by family and friends including Marty Stuart, Emmylou Harris, Connie Smith and Earl Scruggs.

24 June

Ryman Auditorium, Nashville, Tennessee Johnny Cash joins a surprised Kris Kristofferson on stage to perform "Sunday Morning Coming Down". "He didn't do that at the soundcheck" Kristofferson said, wiping away tears.

August

VH1 Storytellers (American CK-69416) released featuring material by Johnny Cash and Willie Nelson.
Tracks: "Ghost Riders In The Sky", "Worried Man", "Family Bible", "Don't Take Your Guns To Town", "Funny How Time Slips Away", " Flesh And Blood", "Crazy", "Unchained", "Night Life", "Drive On", "Me And Paul", "I Still Miss Someone", "Always On My Mind", "Folsom Prison Blues", "On The Road Again"

2 December

Johnny Cash, along with Brian Wilson and Jeff Barry, is awarded the Songwriters Lifetime Achievement Award from the National Academy of Songwriters. The ceremony is held in Los Angeles.

1999

January/February

In 1991 Johnny Cash received the Grammy Legend Award at the Annual Awards Ceremony and this year he is honoured with the 'Lifetime Achievement Award'. Voted for by the National Trustees, the award is presented to performers who,

during their lifetime, have made creative contributions of outstanding artistic significance to the field of recording.

31 March
The Memphis Chapter – National Academy Of Recording Arts & Sciences, Inc. present the 14th Annual Premier Player Awards. Held at The Pyramid in Memphis, the awards are the Memphis music community's celebration of musical creativity and craftsmanship. Johnny Cash receives The Governors Award presented by James Alexander, Memphis Chapter President. John Carter-Cash received the award on behalf of his father who was unable to attend due to ill health. Following the presentation there is a tribute to Johnny Cash featuring Johnny Rivers, Jack Clement, Charlie Rich Jr., and Keith Sykes.

1 April
Super Hits, a Columbia compilation, is awarded gold status by the RIAA.

6 April
Billed as 'The Music Event Of The Year' the *All-Star Tribute To Johnny Cash* is taped at the Hammerstein Ballroom in Manhattan. The show is introduced by actor Jon Voight and includes appearances by Sheryl Crow, Willie Nelson, June Carter-Cash, Kris Kristofferson, Chris Isaak, Trisha Yearwood, Brooks And Dunn, Lyle Lovett, Mary Chapin-Carpenter, Emmylou Harris, Dave Matthews, Marty Stuart And The Fairfield Four and Wyclef Jean. Although unable to appear live on the show Bob Dylan, Bruce Springsteen and U2 all pay tribute via video performances. John Carter-Cash introduced Willie Nelson while Rosanne Cash, who was due to perform but a severe cold prevented her, introduced Marty Stuart. The Mavericks were the house-band and, although not compulsory, most of the artists dressed in black. The highlight of the show was Cash's appearance, his first in eighteen months. Introduced by Tim Robbins, who read the liner notes to the *Folsom Prison* album, Cash opened with his "Hello, I'm Johnny Cash" introduction to thunderous applause and followed with "Folsom Prison Blues". Also on stage with Cash were regulars Bob Wootton, W. S. Holland, Earl Ball, John Carter-Cash and for the first time in many years, original member of the Tennessee Two, Marshall Grant. After thanking the audience he closed the show with "I Walk The Line", during which he was joined by June-Carter-Cash and the entire cast, before leaving the stage to a

standing ovation.
The running order of the show was as follows:

"Jackson & Orange Blossom Special" (Sheryl Crow & Willie Nelson)
"Guess Things Happen That Way" (Chris Isaaks)
"Get Rhythm" (Chris Isaak)
Introduction of Willie Nelson (John Carter-Cash)
"I Still Miss Someone" (Willie Nelson)
"Ring Of Fire" (June Carter-Cash)
"Train Of Love" (Bob Dylan)
"The Man In Black" (The Mavericks)
"The Ballad Of Ira Hayes" (Kris Kristofferson)
"Sunday Morning Coming Down" (Trisha Yearwood & Kris Kristofferson)
Introduction of Brooks & Dunn (Larry Gatlin)
"Ghost Riders In The Sky" (Brooks & Dunn)
"Tennessee Flat Top Box" (Lyle Lovett)
"Give My Love To Rose" (Bruce Springsteen)
"Flesh And Blood" (Sheryl Crow, Mary Chapin-Carpenter & Emmylou Harris)
Introduction of Wyclef Jean (Kevin Bacon)
"Delia's Gone" (Wyclef Jean)
"Long Black Veil" (Dave Matthews & Emmylou Harris)
Introduction Of Marty Stuart (Rosanne Cash)
"Belshazzah" (Marty Stuart & The Fairfield Four)
"Don't Take Your Guns To Town" (U2)
Liner Notes To *Folsom Prison* (Read By Tim Robbins)
"Folsom Prison Blues" (Johnny Cash)
"I Walk The Line" (Johnny Cash, June Carter & entire cast)

The press have nothing but praise for the show:

"Ring of love for a legend. An all-star cast salutes an ill but thrilled to be singing Johnny Cash." – *New York Newsday*

"Concert pays tribute to Cash" – *Branson Tri-Lakes Daily News*

"Cash's fans pay tribute to legend" – *The Tennessean*

18 April
The All-Star Tribute Show receives its world premiere on TNT.

20 April
June Carter-Cash releases *Press On* (Risk/Small Hairy Dog RSK-4107), her first solo album for several years.
Tracks: "Diamonds In The Rough", "Ring Of Fire", "The Far Side Banks Of Jordan", "Losin' You", "Gatsby's Restaurant", "Wings Of Angels", "The L&N Don't Stop Here Anymore", "Once Before I Die", "I Used To Be Somebody", "Tall Lover Man", "Tiffany Anastasia Lowe", "Meeting In The Air", "Will The Circle Be Unbroken".

Johnny Cash appears on "The Far Side Banks Of Jordan" in a duet with June. Musicians on the album include ex-sons-in-law Marty Stuart and Rodney Crowell, along with Norman Blake and Dave Roe. The album was recorded in late-1998 at the Cash Compound in Hendersonville, Tennessee and co-produced by John Carter-Cash.

May

Another Song To Sing is published by Scarecrow Press, Inc. This fourth book by Cash discographer John L. Smith lists over 2,600 entries detailing composers, producers, session dates and much more. Smith's previous books detailed all Cash's recording sessions in chronological order, while this book lists the titles alphabetically.

15 May

June Carter-Cash celebrates the release of her first new solo album in nearly twenty-five years with an intimate performance before an adoring crowd gathered under a large tent on the lawn of her home in Hendersonville. Also there to join in the celebrations are Johnny Cash and their son John Carter-Cash.

July

The Johnny Cash Franklin Bible Sessions 2-CD set is released. On the CDs Cash narrates nearly 400 of his favourite passages from the King James Version of the Bible. Also available are electronic Bibles that also feature Cash's spoken passages.

1-2 July

The Bottomline, New York

June Carter-Cash plays two concerts at this famous club, one of New York's most popular small venues, with a capacity of around 450. Also on stage with June are John Carter-Cash and Rosie Carter. During the show she performs tracks from her new album *Press On*. There is a surprise appearance by Johnny Cash and together they perform "Far Side Banks Of Jordan", "Jackson" and "Will The Circle Be Unbroken".

29 July

Anita Carter passes away following a long illness. Born Ina Anita Carter on 31 March 1933, she was the youngest of Maybelle and Ezra Carter's three daughters and made her first public singing appearance in 1937. She joined the original Carter Family (A.P. Carter, his wife Sara and Maybelle) and in 1943, when the original Carter Family disbanded, joined her sisters and mother as Mother Maybelle and The Carter Sisters. They joined the Johnny Cash Show in 1961 and were regulars on Cash's TV shows. The funeral is held in Hendersonville on 1 August and Johnny Cash reads the Eulogy, while Emmylou Harris and Connie Smith both pay their respects in song.

August
Cotton Club, Atlanta, Georgia
June Carter-Cash appears at this rock music lounge before a crowd approaching 300. John makes a special appearance and joins June for "Far Side Banks Of Jordan" and "Jackson", returning later for "Will The Circle Be Unbroken".

August
Johnny Cash appears at the Carter Fold 25th anniversary and joins June for "Jackson" and "Far Side Banks Of Jordan". He then sings "Folsom Prison Blues" and "Rollin' In My Sweet Baby's Arms", the latter with Tom T. Hall. The festival is held every year to commemorate the recordings of the Bristol Sessions, the first time A. P. Carter, his wife Sara and Maybelle recorded for the Victor Talking Machine Company.

October
Reports appear in the *National Enquirer* that Cash had been 'rushed to hospital' and is in a 'new battle for life.' Apparently he had a bad fall and gashed his leg and was admitted to Baptist Hospital where he received stitches.

19 October
Sony/Legacy release the remastered and expanded version of *Johnny Cash At Folsom Prison* (Legacy CK65955).

Tracks: "Folsom Prison Blues", "Busted", "Dark As A Dungeon", "I Still Miss Someone", "Cocaine Blues", "25 Minutes To Go", "Orange Blossom Special", "The Long Black Veil", "Send A Picture Of Mother", "The Wall", "Dirty Old Egg-Sucking Dog", "Flushed From The Bathroom Of Your Heart", "Joe Bean", "Jackson", "Give My Love To Rose", "I Got Stripes", "The Legend Of John Henry's Hammer", "Green, Green Grass Of Home", "Greystone Chapel"

This release featured the original handwritten sleeve notes by Cash along with additional personal reflections, notes by Steve Earle and unpublished photos from renowned photographer Jim Marshall. On the original release certain comments made by Cash were 'bleeped' but for this release the show was untouched and included extra dialogue and three previously unreleased tracks from the show.

20 October
Cash is admitted to Baptist Hospital in Nashville suffering from pneumonia, the second time this year. Doctors suspect that medication Cash was taking for Shy-Drager's Syndrome has made him more susceptible to infection. He spends the rest of October in hospital.

2000

January-July
Cash records tracks for his forthcoming album with producer Rick Rubin. Among the tracks recorded are covers of Nick Cave's "The Mercy Seat" and U2's "One".

February
At the 42nd Annual Grammy Awards Ceremony June Carter-Cash's album *Press On* wins the 'Best Traditional Folk Album' category.

23 April
Both Johnny Cash and Bluegrass pioneer Ralph Stanley receive Living Legend medals from the Library of Congress in Washington, DC.

23 May
Love, God, Murder (Legacy 48964) is released. The collection, which spans his entire career, was handpicked by Cash and follows the themes of the compilation. Sleevenotes for the set were provided by June Carter-Cash (*Love*), Bono of U2 (*God*) and Quentin Tarantino (*Murder*) as well as Cash's own recollections. The CDs

are released as individual digipaks and as a special limited edition box-set.

Tracks: Love: "I Walk The Line", "Oh, What A Dream", "All Over Again", "A Little At A Time", "My Old Faded Rose", "Happiness Is You", "Flesh And Blood", "I Tremble For You", "I Feel Better All Over", "'Cause I Love You", "Ballad Of Barbara", "Ring Of Fire", "My Shoes Keep Walking Back To You", "While I've Got It On My Mind", "I Still Miss Someone", "The One Rose (That's Left In My Heart)".

God: "What On Earth (Will You Do For

Heaven's Sake)", "My God Is Real (Yes, God Is Real)", "It Was Jesus", "Why Me Lord", "The Greatest Cowboy Of Them All", "Redemption", "The Great Speckled Bird", " The Old Account", "Swing Low, Sweet Chariot", "When He Comes", "The Kneeling Drunkard's Plea", "Were You There (When They Crucified My Lord)", "Man In White", " Belshazzah", " Oh, Bury Me Not (Introduction: A Cowboy's Prayer)", "Oh Come, Angel Band".

Murder: "Folsom Prison Blues", "Delia's Gone", "Mister Garfield", "Orleans Parish Prison", "When It's Springtime In Alaska (It's Forty Below)", "The Sound Of Laughter", "Cocaine Blues", "Hardin Wouldn't Run", "The Long Black Veil", "Austin Prison", "Joe Bean", "Going To Memphis", "Don't Take Your Guns To Town", "Highway Patrolman", "Jacob Green", "The Wall"

10 June
A standing ovation greets Johnny Cash when he walks on stage at the Carter Fold in Maces Spring, Virginia. With a band that includes John Carter-Cash and Jerry Hensley, Cash performs over a dozen songs before being joined by June Carter-Cash for a handful of spirituals. Even though he took a break from singing he never leaves the stage and joins in for the finale. This is his first appearance in nearly a year and his longest concert since 1997.

1 July
John Carter-Cash marries Laura Lynn Weber.

4 July
Johnny Cash At San Quentin (The Complete 1969 Concert) (Legacy CK66017)) is released on CD. This is the complete and unedited show.
Tracks: "Big River", "I Still Miss Someone", "Wreck Of The Old '97", "I Walk The Line", "Darlin' Companion", "I Don't Know Where I'm Bound", "Starkville City Jail", "San Quentin", "San

Quentin", "Wanted Man", "A Boy Named Sue", "(There'll Be) Peace In The Valley (For Me)", "Folsom Prison Blues", "Ring Of Fire", "He Turned The Water Into Wine", "Daddy Sang Bass", "The Old Account Was Settled Long Ago", "Closing Medley: Folsom Prison Blues–I Walk The Line–Ring Of Fire–The Rebel-Johnny Yuma".

This release featured nine previously unreleased tracks, notes by Marty Stuart, an interview with Merle Haggard (an inmate at Cash's first San Quentin show) and recollections from Lou Robin. As with the reissued *Folsom* album, this contained several previously unseen photos.

21 September
BBC Radio Two in the UK start broadcasting *Country Roads With Johnny Cash*. During this eight-part special, which runs weekly through to November, Cash chooses his favourite music and talks about his career. Among the diverse tracks chosen by Cash are "No Expectations" (The Rolling Stones), "I Won't Back Down" (Tom Petty), "Harper Valley P.T.A" (Jeannie C. Riley), "Hello Darlin'" (Conway Twitty) and "Bye, Bye Love" (The Everly Brothers).

13 October
The Highwaymen qualifies for a Platinum Award from the Record Industry Association of America, while *His Greatest Hits, Volume 2* is certified Gold.

17 October
Johnny Cash's new album *American III: Solitary Man* (Columbia 5009862) is released on both CD and limited edition vinyl.
Tracks: "I Won't Back Down", "Solitary Man", "Lucky Ole Sun", "One", "Nobody", "I See A Darkness", "The Mercy Seat", "Would You Lay With Me?", "Field Of Diamonds", "Before My Time", "Country Trash", "Mary Of The Wild Moor", "I'm Leavin' Now", "Wayfaring

Stranger"

On this release Cash went back to his past for "Country Trash", "Field Of Diamonds" and "I'm Leaving Now" and raided the Neil Diamond songbook for the title track. But it is when Cash turned to the Nick Cave songbook that the high point of the album is reached, Cash's interpretation of 'The Mercy Seat'. This dark tale about a prisoner's last moments in the electric chair is a chilling masterpiece and is given an excellent reading by Cash and stands as one of the greatest songs he has recorded in a long time.

"...the song is the thing that matters, before I can record, I have to hear it, sing it, and know that I can make it feel like my own, or it won't work. I worked on these songs until it felt like they were my own." – Johnny Cash. This was Cash's third collaboration with Rick Rubin, who said "He has a way of singing a song you know and making it brand new."

October-November

American III: Solitary Man makes its chart debut when it enters the Billboard Top 200 Album Chart at number 88. On the Country charts it debuts at number 11. In the UK the album enters the country charts at number three.

The CD picks up excellent reviews throughout the world:

"...another superior work that could also be a Grammy contender" – *New York Times*.

"Once again the choice is ingenious. Greying at the edges, its tremor more pronounced, his voice is sober, honest, defiant." – *MOJO* (November 2000).

"...stripped down, vivid and pure, emotionally naked stuff from a 68-year old man who just 12 months ago was very seriously ill" – *New York Times*.

October

Articles appear in the press stating that Cash had been misdiagnosed. It appears that both Parkinson's Disease and Shy-Drager Syndrome had been ruled out and that he was suffering from a form of diabetes. "I'm in better health than I have been in a year or two" Cash told *The Tennessean*. He went on to say "My doctor told me in November that if I'd had it, I'd be dead by now."

November

Johnny and June are scheduled to appear with Billy Graham in Jacksonville, Florida but are unable to attend due to ill health.

November

Renaissance Records release *Return To The Promised Land* (RMED00235).
Tracks: "Return To The Promised Land", "When I Look", "Over The Next Hill", "Old Rugged Cross", "I Won't Have To Cross Jordan Alone", "Far Side Banks Of Jordan", "Let Me Help You Carry The Weight", "Lord, Take These Hands", "What On Earth", "Fishers Of Men", "Gospel Ship", "God's Hands", "Like A Soldier", "Soldier Boy", "Hello Out There", "Poor Valley Girl"

The CD features music from the video release of the same name, along with four bonus tracks recorded in 1993 and previously unreleased.

7 November

Sub Pop Records of Seattle, Washington release *Badlands: A Tribute To Bruce Springsteen's Nebraska*. The album features artists inspired and influenced by the original album. In the spirit of the original release, all the artists were asked to record their chosen song using just four tracks. Among the artists and songs were "Atlantic City" performed by Hank Williams III, "Johnny 99" by Los Lobos and Dar Williams version of "Highway Patrolman". The last two were recorded by Cash for his *Johnny 99* album. There were three bonus tracks, recorded at the same time as *Nebraska* but found on later albums, and one of these, "I'm On Fire", is performed by Johnny Cash.

December

A *Columbia Radio Hour Interview* with Tim Robbins is issued by Sony/American (500986 9). Recorded earlier in the year in New York, Cash talks about his early career and his new album.

December

The UK music magazine *MOJO* publish a list of their favourite albums of the year 2000. On a list that includes albums by Madonna, Radiohead, Oasis and Primal Scream the number one spot is taken by Johnny Cash with *American III: Solitary Man*. *MOJO* commented "A masterpiece, which easily matches up to anything from Cash's legendary Sun days." A quote from Cash read "To *MOJO* and its readers, you have got me all worked up to a big smile. I really appreciate this honour."

26 December

BBC Radio Two broadcast a *Country Roads* special. This broadcast is a compilation of the earlier shows broadcast in September-November, along with additional seasonal material including "Blue Christmas" by Elvis Presley.

2001

January

Mercury Records plan a new compilation covering Cash's short time with the label. It is planned to include a number of previously unissued tracks on the release.

Early February

Cash is admitted to Baptist Hospital in Nashville, where he is diagnosed as suffering from pneumonia.

Early February

It is reported in *Variety* that Columbia Pictures have signed a deal with James Mangold to co-write and direct a movie, provisionally titled *Cash*. The script will be co-written with Gill Dennis and the film produced by Cathy Conrad's Konrad Pictures, in association with James Keach's Catfish Productions. No decision has been made on who will play the lead role, although singer/songwriter Mark Collie has campaigned hard for the role. Keach was quoted as saying the film will be the story of "every man who has descended into hell and found redemption," and in Cash's case it came "in the love of a woman, in his music and in the love of his fans."

13 February

Sugar Hill Records release Rodney Crowell's latest album *The Houston Kid*, which features the track *I Walk The Line (Revisited)* on which Cash appears.

21 February

At the 43rd Annual Grammy Awards ceremony held in Los Angeles, Johnny Cash is nominated for and wins his 10th Grammy in the category 'Best Male Country Vocal Performance' for *Solitary Man*. He was also nominated for 'Best Contemporary Folk Album' but was beaten by Emmylou Harris' album *Red Dirt Girl*. Cash, recently released from hospital, does not attend the ceremony.

June

Plans are made to honour Johnny Cash's 70th birthday in 2002. A tribute is to be held during the first London Music Festival, to be held at Wembley Arena in London. Artists from all genres of music are expected to perform. "It's going to be a who's who", said Trisha Walker, one of the organisers of the event. She went on to say "This man is a hero to so many people". There are plans to film the event for release at a later date. Although it is uncertain if Cash will appear, he said "I want to thank the folks presenting the London Music Festival for choosing to honour me and my music. This will be one of the highlights of my career".

29 June

Cash makes a surprise appearance at the Carter Fold in Virginia. With him is his wife June and daughter Rosanne. He performs a couple of songs during the show.

5 July

Johnny Cash and June Carter-Cash attend the funeral of country guitar legend Chet Atkins.

DISCOGRAPHY

The following discography covers the singles and albums released in the United States and covered in the main body of this book. Many of these albums have been reissued on compact disc and add to this the hundreds of greatest hits packages and compilations and you start to see the volume of Johnny Cash material available worldwide. To compile a complete worldwide discography is far beyond the scope of this book and for a more thorough reference work I would, again, refer you to the books of John L. Smith.

1955
Hey Porter/Cry, Cry, Cry

Folsom Prison Blues/So Doggone Lonesome

1956
I Walk The Line/Get Rhythm

Train Of Love/ There You Go

Home Of The Blues/Give My Love To Rose

1957
Next In Line/Don't Make Me Go

Ballad Of A Teenage Queen/Big River

With His Hot And Blue Guitar

1958
Guess Things Happen That Way/Come In Stranger

The Ways Of A Woman In Love/You're The Nearest Thing To Heaven

All Over Again/What Do I Care

It's Just About Time/I Just Thought You'd Like To Know

Don't Take Your Guns To Town/I Still Miss Someone

The Fabulous Johnny Cash
Songs That Made Him Famous

1959
Luther Played The Boogie/Thanks A Lot

You Dreamer You/Frankie's Man Johnny

Katy Too/I Forgot To Remember To Forget

I Got Stripes/Five Feet High And Rising

You Tell Me/Goodbye, Little Darlin

Little Drummer Boy/I'll Remember You

Bandana/Wabash Blues

Straight A's In Love/I Love You Because

Hymns By Johnny Cash

Songs Of Our Soil

Greatest Johnny Cash

1960
Don't Take Your Guns To Town/Five Feet High And Rising

Seasons Of My Heart/Smiling Bill McCall

Second Honeymoon/Honky Tonk Girl

Story Of A Broken Heart/Down The Street To 301

Loading Coal/Goin' To Memphis

Mean Eyed Cat/Port Of Lonely Hearts

Oh, Lonesome Me/Life Goes On

Locomotive Man/Girl In Saskatoon

Ride This Train

Now, There Was A Song!

1961
Blues For Two/Jeri And Nina's Melody
Forty Shades Of Green/The Rebel-Johnny Yuma

Sugartime/My Treasure

1962
Tall Man/Tennessee Flat-Top Box

The Big Battle/When I've Learned

Blue Train/Born To Lose

In The Jailhouse Now/A Little At A Time

Bonanza/Pick A Bale O' Cotton

Peace In The Valley/Were You There
(When They Crucified My Lord)

Busted/Send A Picture Of Mother

Hymns From The Heart

Sound Of Johnny Cash

All Aboard The Blue Train

1963
Ring Of Fire/I'd Still Be There

The Matador/Still In Town

Blood, Sweat And Tears

Ring Of Fire

The Christmas Spirit

1964
Understand Your Man/Dark As A Dungeon

Fair And Tender Ladies/Keep On The
Sunnyside

The Ballad Of Ira Hayes/Bad News

The Wreck Of The Old '97/Hammers And
Nails

It Ain't Me Babe/Time And Time Again

I Walk the Line

Bitter Tears

Original Sun Sound

1965
Orange Blossom Special/All God's
Children Ain't Free

I Just Don't Like This Kind Of
Living/Rock Island Line

Ring Of Fire/It Ain't Me Babe

Understand Your Man/It Ain't Me Babe

Mister Garfield/The Streets Of Laredo

The Sons Of Katie Elder/A Certain Kinda
Hurtin'

Cattle Call/Bill's Theme

I Walk The Line/Orange Blossom Special

Happy To Be With You/Pickin' Time

Orange Blossom Special

Ballads Of The True West

1966
The One On The Right Is On The
Left/Cotton Pickin' Hands

Everybody Loves A Nut/Austin Prison

Boa Constrictor/Bottom Of A Mountain

You Beat All I Ever Saw/Put The Sugar To
Bed

Mean As Hell

Everybody Loves A Nut

Happiness Is You

1967
The One On The Right Is On The
Left/Boa Constrictor

Jackson/Pack Up Your Sorrows

Long Legged Guitar Pickin' Man/You'll
Be Alright

Outside Lookin' In/Spanish Harlem

The Wind Changes/Red Velvet

Rosanna's Going Wild/Roll Call

Jackson/Long Legged Guitar Pickin' Man

From Sea To Shining Sea

Greatest Hits

*Carryin' On With Johnny Cash And June
Carter*

1968
Folsom Prison Blues/The Folk Singer

Daddy Sang Bass/He Turned The Water
Into Wine

Johnny Cash At Folsom Prison

1969
Folsom Prison Blues/Daddy Sang Bass

A Boy Named Sue/San Quentin

Blistered/See Ruby Fall

If I Were A Carpenter/ 'Cause I Love You

San Quentin/A Boy Named Sue

The Holy Land

Johnny Cash At San Quentin

1970
What Is Truth/Sing A Travelling Song

If I Were A Carpenter/What Is Truth

See Ruby Fall/Blistered
Flesh And Blood/This Side Of The Law

Hello, I'm Johnny Cash

The Johnny Cash Show

Little Fauss And Big Halsy

I Walk The Line

1971
Man In Black/Little Bit Of Yesterday

Singing In Vietnam Talking Blues/You've
Got A New Light Shining

A Song To Mama/One More Summer In
Virginia

No Need To Worry/I'll Be Loving You

Papa Was A Good Man/I Promise You

The Sound Behind Johnny Cash

Man In Black

1972
A Thing Called Love//Daddy

Kate/The Miracle Man

If I Had A Hammer/I Got A Boy And His
Name Is John

Oney/Country Trash

The World Needs A Melody/A Bird With
Broken Wings Can't Fly

Any Old Wind That Blows/Kentucky
Straight

Help Me Make It Through The Night/The
Lovin' Gift

A Thing Called Love

America

Johnny Cash Family Christmas

1973
Children/The Last Supper

Praise The Lord And Pass The Soup/The Ballad Of Barbara

Allegheny/We're For Love

Pick The Wildwood Flower/Diamonds In The Rough

That Christmasy Feeling/Christmas As I Knew It

Any Old Wind That Blows

The Gospel Road

Sunday Morning Coming Down

Johnny Cash And His Woman

1974
Orleans Parish Prison/Jacob Green

Ragged Old Flag/Don't Go Near The Water

The Junkie And The Juicehead/Crystal Chandeliers And Burgundy

Don't Take Your Guns To Town/Father And Daughter

The Lady Came From Baltimore/ Lonesome To The Bone

Children's Album

Ragged Old Flag

Junkie And The Juicehead (Minus Me)

Johnny Cash Pa Osteraker

1975
My Old Kentucky Home/Hard Times Comin'

Look At Them Beans/All Around Cowboy

Texas '47/I Hardly Ever Sing Beer Drinking Songs

Precious Memories

John R. Cash

Look At Them Beans

Destination Victoria Station

1976
Strawberry Cake/I Got Stripes

One Piece At A Time/Go On Blues

Sold Out Of Flagpoles/Mountain Lady

It's All Over/Riding On The Cottonbelt

Old Time Feeling/Far Side Banks Of Jordan

Strawberry Cake

One Piece At A Time

1977
Last Gunfighter Ballad/City Jail

Lady/Hit The Road And Go

After The Ball/Calilou

The Last Gunfighter Ballad

The Rambler

1978
I Would Like To See You Again/Lately

There Ain't No Good Chain Gang/I Wish I Was Crazy Again

Gone Girl/I'm Alright Now

It'll Be Her/It Comes And Goes

I Will Rock And Roll With You/A Song For The Life

Unissued Johnny Cash

I Would Like To See You Again

Gone Girl

1979
Ghost Riders In The Sky/I'm Gonna Sit On The Porch And Pick On My Old Guitar

I'll Say It's True/Cocaine Blues

Johnny And June

Tall Man

Silver

A Believer Sings The Truth

Johnny Cash Sings With B.C. Goodpasture Christian School

1980
Wings In The Morning/What On Earth Would You Do (For Heavens Sake)

Bull Rider/Lonesome To The Bone

Song Of The Patriot/She's A Goer

Cold Lonesome Morning/The Cowboy Who Started The Fight

Death Of Me/One More Shot

The Last Time/Rockabilly Blues

Rockabilly Blues

Classic Christmas

The Legend Of Jesse James

1981
Without Love/It Ain't Nothing New, Babe

The Baron/I Will Dance With You

Mobile Bay/The Hard Way
Chattanooga City Limit Sign/Reverend Mr. Black

Mr. Garfield/I'm A One Woman Man

The Baron

1982
Georgia On A Fast Train/Sing A Song

Fair Weather Friends/Ain't Gonna Hobo No More

The Survivors

Adventures Of Johnny Cash

1983
We Must Believe In Magic/I'll Cross Over Jordan Some Day

I'm Ragged But I'm Right/Brand New Dance

Johnny 99/New Cut Road

Koncert V Praze (In Prague Live)

Johnny 99

1984
That's The Truth/Joshua Gone Barbados

Chicken In Black/The Battle Of Nashville

1985
Three Bells/They Killed Him

Crazy Old Soldier/It Ain't Gonna Worry My Mind

Highwayman/The Human Condition

I Will Dance With You/Too Bad For Love

Desperadoes Waiting For A Train/The Twentieth Century Is Almost Over
Highwayman

Rainbow

1986
I'm Leaving Now/Easy Street

Even Cowgirls Get The Blues/American By Birth

Class Of '55/We Remember The King

Rock And Roll (Fais Do Do)/Birth Of
Rock And Roll

Ballad Of Forty Dollars/Field Of
Diamonds

Rock And Roll (Fais Do Do)/ Sixteen
Candles

Better Class Of Loser/Take The Long Way
Home

The Man In White/The Man In White

Heroes

Class Of '55

Believe In Him

1987
The Night Hank Williams Came To
Town/I'd Rather Have You

Let Him Roll/My Ship Will Sail

W. Lee O'Daniel (And The Light Crust
Dough Boys)/Letters From Home

Johnny Cash Is Coming To Town

1988
Get Rhythm/Cry, Cry, Cry

That Old Wheel/Tennessee Flat Top Box

Classic Cash

Water From The Wells Of Home

1989
Ballad Of A Teenage Queen/Get Rhythm

Ragged Old Flag/I'm Leaving Now
The Last Of The Drifters/Water From The
Wells Of Home

1990
Cats In The Cradle/I Love You, Love You

Silver Stallion/American Remains

Farmers Almanac/I Shall Be Free

Born And Raised In Black And
White/Texas (Columbia 38-73381)

Goin' By The Book/Beans For Breakfast

Highwayman II

Boom Chicka Boom

1991
The Mystery Of Life:/I'm An Easy Rider

The Mystery Of Life

1994
Wanted Man

American Recordings

1995
The Road Goes On Forever

1996
Unchained

1998
VH1 Storytellers

1999
Press On

Johnny Cash At Folsom Prison

2000
Love, God, Murder

Johnny Cash At San Quentin

American III: Solitary Man

Return To The Promised Land

Mail Order

All Helter Skelter, Firefly and SAF titles are available by mail order from the world famous Helter Skelter bookshop.

You can either phone or fax your order to Helter Skelter on the following numbers:

Telephone: +44 (0)20 7836 1151 or Fax: +44 (0)20 7240 9880
Office hours: Mon-Fri 10:00am – 7:00pm,
Sat: 10:00am – 6:00pm, Sun: closed.

Postage prices per book worldwide are as follows:

UK & Channel Islands	£1.50
Europe & Eire (air)	£2.95
USA, Canada (air)	£7.50
Australasia, Far East (air)	£9.00
Overseas (surface)	£2.50

You can also write enclosing a cheque, International Money Order, or registered cash. Please include postage. DO NOT send cash. DO NOT send foreign currency, or cheques drawn on an overseas bank. Send to:

Helter Skelter Bookshop,
4 Denmark Street, London, WC2H 8LL, United Kingdom.
If you are in London come and visit us, and browse the titles in person!!

Email: helter@skelter.demon.co.uk
Website: http://www.skelter.demon.co.uk